D1253587

OUTCOME UNCERTAIN

SCIENCE AND THE POLITICAL PROCESS

OUTCOME
UNCERTAIN

SCIENCE AND THE
POLITICAL PROCESS

BY MARY E. AMES

WITHDRAWN

COMMUNICATIONS PRESS, INC.
WASHINGTON, D.C.

782952

Published by Communications Press, Inc.

Copyright © 1978 by Mary E. Ames

All rights reserved. For information, address Communications Press, Inc. 1346 Connecticut Avenue, N.W., Washington, D.C. 20036

Printed in the United States of America

Library of Congress Catalog Card Number 77-81692

International Standard Book Number 0-89461-028-7

To John

CONTENTS

Author's Note / ix

I. Science and National Policy:
A Retrospective View / 1
The Manhattan Project / Nuclear Weapons Policy and the Cold
War / Genetics, Fallout, and the Origins of Public Interest
Science / Technology, Space, and National Priorities / The
Apollo Program / Epilogue

II. The Case of the U.S. SST:
Disenchantment with Technology / 49
"The Forces He Released in This World . . ." / The Motive
Forces: Profits and Politics / Equal and Opposite Forces:
The Power of the People / Epilogue

III. The Case of the North Anna Nuclear Power Plant:
Public Risk and Public Relations / 83
Site Geology: Ignoring the Obvious / The First Construction
License Hearing / Opponents Organize for the Second
Construction License Hearing / The Show Cause Hearing /
Continuing Problems at North Anna: The Show Must Go On /
Epilogue

IV. The Case of the Saccharin Studies:
Public Protection and Individual Choice / 113
"Safe" Food Additives and Health / The Controversy over
Saccharin / Changing Attitudes: FDA and the Public / Epilogue

V. The Case of Recombinant DNA:
Braving the New World of Bio-technology / 135
Debut of the Recombinant DNA Technique / NIH Research
Guidelines / Ethical Debate / Michigan Regents and the DNA
Decision / "O, You Citizens of Boston": The Cambridge City
Council Decision / Washington Reacts: Introduction of Federal
Legislation / Epilogue

VI. Science and Human Progress:
Summary and Prospectus / 165
Government Organization: Who Decides and How? / Science
and the Political Process: Some New Approaches / Epilogue

Notes and References / 207

Index / 221

AUTHOR'S NOTE

This book was conceived late in 1976 during a conversation with Arthur Kantrowitz, engineering physicist and chairman of the board of Avco Everett, a private research laboratory.

I had undertaken to write a description of a procedure called the "science court" which Dr. Kantrowitz was advocating as a means for providing unbiased technical information to policy makers. While discussing with him his long-standing concern with the problem of how scientific and technical information is used, abused or ignored in decision making, I found his assessment of that problem accurate, but I was concerned that the "science court" idea would meet only part of the larger problem. My feelings were that many social issues which will arise in the future from current developments in the sciences will not be amenable to resolution through improvements in the quality of technical information available to government officials. Worse, by concentrating on technical solutions, policy makers may overlook other perfectly good ways to cope with national crises.

The problems of science policy making are wide reaching. Scientific developments bring with them questions of economics, equity and justice, and individual, national and even international repercussions. To have value for the future, exploration of science policy issues would likewise have to be broader than a study of technical advice giving. Though I have not, in the end, emerged as an advocate of Dr. Kantrowitz' "science court" idea, I am grateful for his long and energetic pursuit of it. By focusing their light on one spot in the path ahead, he and others like him have better illuminated the whole terrain for those who follow.

I owe a debt of gratitude to a number of other persons who have helped shape this book. William "Tom" Thomas, Judge Howard Markey, June Allen, Anthony Nero, Susan Wright, Donald Kennedy, Hans Bethe, Allan Mazur, and Gretchen Kolsrud saved me from errors and omissions by reading parts of the manuscript and making suggestions for improving it. Dozens of others with expert knowledge took time for interviews and conversations; most are cited in the text. I also imposed on a few who are not scientific experts but are expert at the trade of providing technical information to citizens. I should like particularly to acknowledge the help of Bill Carrier and John Kopeck of the Nuclear Regulatory

Commission and Jennie C. Peterson of the Food and Drug Administration, all of whom are helping to make government more accessible and responsive to the public.

Finally, I would like to thank several people without whom this book would never have been written: Jim Coldsmith who tricked me into the writing business ten years ago, Pete Schlabach who kept me in it, and Virginia and Bob Ames who encouraged it all along; Robin and Fred Clarke, Alice and Rodger Digilio, Jean and C. J. Reid, John Kerschbaum and Mary Alexander, Edith and Gerard Ascher, Barb Schwinn and Beth Price, all of whom are as grateful to know the book is finished as I was to know I had their support during the writing.

Mary E. Ames
Kill Devil Hills, N.C.
April   1978

I.

Science and National Policy: A Retrospective View

Americans emerged in the 1970s from a long, tragic war in Southeast Asia wondering whether their government was living up to its democratic ideals at home and abroad. It was a time, perhaps unmatched since the turn of the century, when people questioned whether the federal government was really acting in their best interests. One factor especially underlay the tension between the government and the governed: the growth, both in size and complexity, of the government-supported, business-dominated American technological enterprise.

Scientists sensed the public disenchantment with technology and recognized the division in their own ranks over certain government policies as a symptom of emerging social concerns. In 1972, the National Academy of Sciences proposed an overhaul of the advisory committee system on which government agencies depend for much of their technical advice. While studying what reforms might be appropriate, the Academy discovered that, of the twenty-four hundred government advisory committees, fifteen hundred were scientific. Of all expert advisors to the government, about fifteen thousand—more than three-fifths—were scientists or engineers. [1]

How did this intimate relationship develop between government officials and scientists? How did the government get so involved in the business of science and technology?

Before World War II, government tended to stay aloof from science and technology. National policy favored commerce and was, therefore, often sympathetic to developments in transportation and industry. But the government generally did not underwrite research and development efforts, nor did it, except under extreme public pressure, regulate industry on the grounds of public health and welfare. Only in exceptional cases—usually meaning war—did the government turn to the sciences and engineering professions for technical know-how.

Possibly the first example of government-sponsored technological innovation in America was David Bushnell's little one-man, crank-propelled submarine, the *Turtle,* in which Sergeant Ezra Lee attacked a British warship in New York Harbor in 1776. In subsequent wars, the War and Navy Departments sponsored many other projects, but no consistent government research and development program emerged.

When the Army drew up specifications for the first military aircraft in 1907, full rights to build and sell the plane went to the successful bidder, but by the end of World War II, this was no longer the practice. Industries involved in aircraft and weapons development during the war, and long afterward, cooperated with the military services to keep the work secret, and the government took title to the products that were developed with public funds.

The first union of the U.S. government with the agricultural sciences came about in 1862 under the Morrill Act, which required each state to set aside public land for colleges of "agriculture and the mechanic arts." Passage of this landmark legislation had been held up for several years, so strong was sentiment against the federal government exercising power over the states in education.

The federal government got into the business of regulating the food industry with equal reluctance. Only an extraordinary combination of efforts convinced the Congress that legislation was needed to protect people against adulterated foods. A reformist public mood, on which Theodore Roosevelt and others based their political careers, created a receptive audience for the so-called muckraking journalists: Lincoln Steffens, Tom Lawson, Ida Tarbell, and others. Price fixing and other financial practices of the meat packing industry were exposed by Ray Stannard Baker, and when Upton Sinclair published in a socialist magazine his fictionalized account of the conditions in the Chicago stockyards, the public outcry forced the government to act.

Sinclair meant his work, published in 1906 as *The Jungle,* to bring reforms for the workingman. What resulted, instead, were the first government standards of quality for meat. As Sinclair commented, "I aimed at the public's heart, and by accident I hit it in the stomach."

Another factor behind government regulatory action was the work of Harvey Wiley, who served as chief of the Bureau of Chemistry of the U.S. Department of Agriculture from 1883 to 1912. Wiley was a fighter who took his campaign against impure foods and unsafe drugs to the public, finding little sympathy in the halls of Congress or the corporate board rooms. Newspaper editors, especially William Allen White of the crusading Kansas newspaper, the *Emporia Gazette,* took up the cause. In 1902, Wiley dramatized the health effects of food chemical additives by establishing the "poison squad," a group of twelve healthy young men on whom he carefully tested the effects of food preservatives, common to the American diet. The evidence Wiley amassed and the public support for this "watchdog of the kitchen" finally overcame the recalcitrant politicians. The Pure Food and Drug Act was signed into law on June 30, 1906.

President Roosevelt and Secretary of Agriculture James Wilson, however, actually tried to slow Wiley's zealous attempts to enforce the new law. They succeeded for a while by establishing review boards and appointing to them scientists whose views differed from Wiley's on the safety of specific food additives (including, interestingly enough, saccharin, which the President regularly used for weight control).

The origins of government involvement in medical research came with expanding demands on the Marine Hospital Service in 1887. That year a research laboratory was established at the Marine Hospital on Staten Island. In 1891, the laboratory was moved to Washington, D.C., and eleven years later was given an advisory board and responsibility for all biomedical work done by government researchers. In 1930, the laboratory was renamed the National Institute of Health, and seven years later Congress added the National Cancer Institute and authorized the first research grants. Not until the Public Health Service Act of 1944, however, did the Congress give the NIH general legislative authority to conduct research. From then on, and particularly in the early 1960s, the federal contribution to medical research grew enormously.

The first official recognition that the federal government might benefit from scientific advice came during the Civil War. In March of 1863, the Congress passed a bill appointing fifty scientists and engineers to a National Academy of Sciences and charged them to "investigate, examine, experiment and report upon any subject of science or art . . . whenever called upon by any department of the Government." The legislation was clearly stimulated by the needs of war. Thirteen of those appointed to the Academy were military men. No scientists from the Confederate states were appointed unless they were serving the Union cause. From its inception, the Academy was not as independent from the government as the great institutions of science in Europe, but part of its mandate was to promote the sciences, apart from the government's interest in them. Today it would be hard to name a field in which Academy members labor that the federal government has not sown with seed money.

"God forbid," quipped Woodrow Wilson half a century later, "that in a democratic society we should resign the task and give the government over to experts." Wilson modified his view somewhat, according to an oft-quoted story, when it became apparent that the country was going to enter World War I. Thomas Alva Edison, sixty-eight years old and at the height of a brilliant career, was chosen to chair a board of experts to advise the Navy. The choice was widely acclaimed because of the scientific brainpower that Edison was expected to assemble. Edison, though a master of applied science, did not see a connection between basic science and the needs of the government. He appointed to the board a lone physicist, observing, "We might have one mathematical fellow in case we have to calculate something out."

When the American Chemical Society offered the services of its members in 1916, Secretary of War Newton D. Baker cordially declined the help, saying he had looked into the situation and found that the War Department already had a chemist on the staff.

In England at the same time, the British government sought to persuade physicist Ernest Rutherford to lend his talents to the war. Rutherford refused to leave his independent work for the armed services because, he said, his experiments—on the "artificial disintegration of the atom"—were likely to lead to a discovery that would be more important than the war itself.

Rutherford was right. By the time his successors achieved a controlled and sustained disintegration of the uranium atom in 1942, researchers were no longer able to stay aloof from government, nor government to ignore science.

• THE MANHATTAN PROJECT

The researches of Rutherford and others in Europe and the U.S. over the next two decades slowly brought the prospect of a totally new explosive of incomparably greater power than existing chemical explosives. Experiments with uranium fission in Berlin in 1938 led physicists in several countries quickly to the conclusion that the fission reaction had the potential to release great quantities of energy, all at once or slowly, depending on how the reaction was physically controlled and on the atomic properties of the uranium used.

Among the scientists who came to this conclusion were a handful of recent European emigrés to the U.S. Some of these sought to organize a voluntary moratorium on publication of new experimental results lest they help Hitler to develop a bomb. Others cautiously sounded out the U.S. Navy. Finally, two of them suggested to Albert Einstein, who had been in the U.S. for several years and enjoyed a unique reputation, that he undertake to alert President Franklin D. Roosevelt to the momentous possibility that the Nazis could develop such a weapon.

Einstein wrote a letter to Roosevelt, in July of 1939, recommending that the government assist atomic research and implying that Nazi Germany might be at work on a bomb. [2] This hand-delivered letter is the historic starting point of what came to be known as the Manhattan Project. Its initial impact, however, was slight. The President appointed an advisory committee: two military men, one civilian, an no scientists. Eight months later, $6,000 was transferred from the Army and Navy to Columbia University to buy materials for the research going on there.

The German onslaught on the Low Countries and France in 1940 stimulated a frenzy of defense-related activity in the U.S. government. Roosevelt's designation of Carnegie Institute President Vannevar Bush as director of the Office of Scientific Research and Development was a relatively insignificant event except to the physicists who were all, now, voluntarily censoring their work. The atomic researchers got $140,000 more from the government in the summer of 1940, but not until the fall of 1941 was enough progress made to convince Roosevelt that nuclear fission deserved the attention of a high-level policy committee. The committee finally chosen included Bush, Vice-President Henry A. Wallace, Chief of Staff George C. Marshall, Secretary of War Henry L. Stimson, and James B. Conant, a respected chemist and president of Harvard University. On December 6, 1941, Bush signed a report recommending a top-secret, crash program for the development of the bomb.

Never before had the government committed itself to such a massive research and development program. Never before had research scientists called on the government to undertake such a program nor had science administrators been called on to help formulate government policy. A new partnership between science and government had been formed.

By this time, a group of physicists working under the general direction of E.O. Lawrence at the University of California, Berkeley, had established that uranium undergoes a reaction that eventually produces fissionable plutonium.

Through contracts between the universities involved and the U.S. Army, the federal government set up research programs at Berkeley under Lawrence, at the University of Iowa under Frank Spedding, and at Columbia under Harold Urey and John Dunning. The bulk of the Columbia research group was moved to the University of Chicago under the supervision of Arthur Compton. There, on the afternoon of December 2, 1942, Italian emigré Enrico Fermi directed the final steps of a remarkable experiment: the first controlled atomic chain reaction took place.

With that breakthrough, federal money poured forth in an

abundance never before dreamed of by scientists or politicians. All work proceeded under the tightest security, but untrammeled by budget considerations. Bomb materials were produced (at Oak Ridge, Tennessee, and Hanford, Washington) and assembled at a remote site in Los Alamos, New Mexico. By the summer of 1945, two types of bombs, uranium-235 and plutonium, were ready.

The Decision To Use The Bomb In War

The uranium-235 bomb required no testing. The plutonium bomb did, not because the theory behind it needed verification but because the mechanics of it were uncertain. Its testing, at Alamogordo, New Mexico, on July 16, 1945, was a strange and unique event. Its success was not only the "justification of the several years of intensive effort of tens of thousands of people" as Brigadier General Thomas F. Farrell said in a belated War Department news release. Much more was at stake. Now that Germany was defeated, the sole value of the bomb was to exact surrender from Japan. A "dud," it was thought, would be disastrous. When the test bomb detonated properly, its creators breathed a sigh of relief in their shelter miles away from ground zero. "There was a feeling that no matter what else might happen, we now had the means to insure the war's speedy conclusion and save thousands of American lives," the War Department release said. "As to the future, there had been brought into being something big and something new . . . It was a great new force to be used for good or for evil. There was a feeling in that shelter that those concerned with its nativity should dedicate their lives to the mission that it would always be used for good and never for evil."

Those concerned with the "nativity" of the bomb, however, had little time to debate whether its use would be good or evil, and no one but each other with whom to discuss the moral implications. There was a driving assumption that, if the bomb could actually be developed, it would be used in the war. What remained to be decided, as this fateful assumption went unchallenged, was only the question of timing and targets.

"The policy adopted and steadily pursued by President Roosevelt and his advisors was a simple one," War Secretary Stimson said in his own careful account, published a year and a half after Hiroshima. [3] "It was to spare no effort in securing the earliest possible successful development of an atomic weapon. The reasons for this policy were equally simple. The original experimental achievement of atomic fission had occured in Germany in 1938, and it was known that the

Germans had continued their experiments. In 1941 and 1942 they were believed to be ahead of us, and it was vital that they should not be the first to bring atomic weapons into the field of battle . . . At no time, from 1941 to 1945, did I ever hear it suggested by the President, or by any other responsible member of the government, that atomic energy should not be used in the war."

Secretary Stimson's account fully explains the motivation behind the bomb project up until May 7, 1945, the date of Germany's surrender. But many of the scientists, including some who had brought atomic fission to Roosevelt's attention in the first place, felt that the German surrender removed the reason for using the bomb in the war.

On June 11, 1945, seven nuclear scientists expressed this view in a report over the signature of physicist James Franck. [4] These scientists were among a group at the University of Chicago who had finished their work on the bomb project in 1944 and, realizing the possible use that could be made of the bomb, had formed the Committee on the Scientific and Political Implications [sic]. They knew that a new high-level committee, with the concurrence of its scientific advisors, had recently recommended to President Harry Truman a surprise A-bomb attack on a populated Japanese military installation.

The high-level committee was known as the Interim Committee, because its purpose was to advise Truman on the bomb from the time he assumed the Presidency April 12, 1945, until the war was over. In addition to Stimson and four other government officials, the Interim Committee included scientists Bush and Conant from Roosevelt's original advisory committee, and Karl T. Compton, president of the Massachusetts Institute of Technology. The committee had a special panel of advisors who had actually worked on the bomb project: Arthur Compton, Enrico Fermi, E.O. Lawrence and J. Robert Oppenheimer, director of the Los Alamos laboratory.

"Nuclear bombs cannot possibly remain a 'secret weapon' at the exclusive disposal of this country for more than a few years," the Franck report stated. "The scientific facts on which their construction is based are well known to scientists of other countries. Unless an effective international control of nuclear explosives is instituted, a race for nuclear armaments is certain to ensue following the first revelation of our possession of nuclear weapons to the world. In the war to which such an armaments race is likely to lead, the United States, with its agglomeration of population and industry in comparatively few metropolitan districts, will be at a disadvantage compared to nations whose population and industry are scattered over large areas.

"We believe that these considerations make the use of nuclear bombs for an early unannounced attack against Japan inadvisable. The compelling reason for creating this weapon with such speed was our fear that Germany had the technical skill necessary to develop such a weapon and that the German Government had no moral restraints regarding its use."

The Franck report recommended that the U.S. either demonstrate the bomb to the whole world, after which public opinion could be brought to bear on the decision to use the bomb against Japan, or that the country forgo use of the bomb altogether.

The four-man scientific panel was moved enough by this plea from colleagues that they made note of it in a report to the Interim Committee five days later on June 16, 1945. The report of these official science advisors, however, evaluated the proposal for public demonstration of the bomb only in the sense of whether a demonstration could be devised that would cause Japan to surrender. Their conclusion was negative: "We can propose no technical demonstration *likely to bring an end to the war* [emphasis added]; we see no acceptable alternative to direct military use."

Secretary Stimson later placed great emphasis on this finding by the scientific panel in seeking after the war to justify use of the bombs, when international control of nuclear weapons became such a difficult problem. But in June 1945, the Interim Committee needed little convincing. Truman needed even less. The opinion of the Interim Committee and the concurrence of the scientific panel—that the bomb would be effective in making Japan surrender unconditionally—was enough to convince him. On July 2, Truman's military advisors told him that the alternative to using the new weapon would be a full scale invasion of Japan that would last more than a year and cost a million lives. The strategy was to warn the Premier of Japan of the Allies' resolve to fight to the finish and then back up the threat with the few bombs that were ready. Truman was relatively uninterested in the postwar implications of having used the bomb in a surprise attack.

"Let there be no mistake about it," Truman wrote in his memoirs, "I regarded the bomb as a military weapon and never had any doubt that it should be used . . . The atomic bomb was no 'great decision' . . . not any decision that you had to worry about . . ."

Conclusions

Recent critics, who think Truman's decision was short-sighted, often look for deeper motives than his expressed goal of ending the war and saving American lives. A few speculate that Roosevelt, more mindful of postwar international relations, would have made a different decision. [5] One of the mysteries that leaves room for much second-guessing is why Roosevelt neglected to include Truman, as he had Vice-President Wallace, in the tight circle of bomb project advisors when Truman assumed the Vice-Presidency in January 1945. Did Roosevelt, contrary to Stimson's account, not expect the bomb to be developed in time to be used in the war? Did he simply expect that he would be alive to make the decision when the time came? Or did he never really think an atomic bomb would be developed?

It was known, several weeks before the bombs were dropped, that Japan had been trying to negotiate a surrender, using the Soviet government as mediator. Japan's major condition was that the Emperor not be deposed. Secretary Stimson's account says the problem was that the U.S. wanted an unconditional surrender and Japan would not accept that. The surrender actually negotiated, however, was not unconditional, and permitted Japanese retention of the Emperor, a fact which leaves room for further speculation.

Whether Roosevelt would have used the bomb against Japan and whether Truman had ulterior motives, for example, reducing Russia's role in the surrender, are questions beyond the scope of this book. What is important here is that the advice available to the new President and the momentum behind the Manhattan Project made military use of the bomb a foregone conclusion, not a decision whose consequences were meticulously weighed.

To summarize the factors:

1) *Truman had no opinions to consider except those of the Interim Committee and its scientific panel.* The secrecy of the project precluded all public debate on the use of the weapon. Truman was privy to no opinions, from Roosevelt or any one else, that use of the bomb would have extraordinary implications beyond the rapid surrender of Japan. He was briefed by Stimson on the project soon after assuming office, but nothing in that briefing gave him reason to believe the bomb was not intended for use in the war all along. Never had a government refrained from introducing a new weapon on moral or humanitarian grounds.

2) *The scientific panel was limited in its advice giving to the narrow, technical aspects of a question that had very wide political and social dimensions.* When the larger questions, raised by the advent of atomic power in

the world, did surface, the scientists faithfully pointed out their incompetence in these subjects. The scientific panel report of June 16, 1945, for example, the one that mentioned the views of the Franck Report signers, was full of such disclaimers.

3) *The technical judgments that the scientists rendered necessarily conformed with the objectives of the political and military leaders they were to advise.* Limited to technical considerations, a decision not to use the bomb would only have been possible had the science advisors thought the bomb would be a dud or not effective enough to be likely to make Japan surrender.

4) *Those project scientists who were thought most qualified to advise were those most deeply involved in the project.* In light of their devotion to the goal of building a bomb and in light of the expense of the project, it would have been difficult for the four members of the scientific panel to recommend at the last moment against the use of the bomb.

5) *Even if the view of the dissenting scientists,* as expressed in the Franck Report, *had been so compelling that the four official science advisors* had gone beyond the technical questions and *had recommended against use of the bomb, the President and the Secretary of War could have ignored their advice.* For all practical purposes, the use of the bomb was assured the moment the Alamogordo test succeeded on July 16. The successful test confirmed for military leaders what they had depended on the scientists to tell them about the likely impact of the bomb, physical and political. The opinions of the scientists were not necessary *after* the test explosion, and a recommendation against use of the bomb then would certainly have been ignored. The earlier, positive recommendation of the scientists, however, was extremely useful for justifying use of the bomb to the American people after the fact, as Secretary Stimson's emphasis on it in his later account amply illustrates.

Thus scientists had initiated a vast technological project, requiring intense collaboration between government and science, but they had not been able to secure for themselves or other citizens any real control over the purposes to which their work would be put.

• NUCLEAR WEAPONS POLICY AND THE COLD WAR

The Attempt at Arms Control

When the bombs exploded over Hiroshima and Nagasaki, killing more than one hundred thousand Japanese people, the surrender of Japan followed as rapidly as American military leaders had hoped it would. The American people were delighted. It is true that many

Americans were horrified at the spectacle of the A-bombs' devastation: that they had wiped out two cities, women and children included, and that the U.S. had used such a weapon without giving any warning. But, in the weeks immediately following surrender, other thoughts dominated. The war was over. An invasion of mainland Japan and high casualties on both sides had been prevented. And the United States had emerged very powerful in world affairs.

Because the bomb had been developed under such a cloak of secrecy, the popular notion was that its successful construction was due to a specific secret, like a special formula or blueprint, that only the U.S. possessed. High officials knew differently, but the pronouncements of less informed politicians indicate that they believed or wanted to reinforce the notion that America had a monopoly on the A-bomb.

Hundreds of American physicists, however, even graduate students who had worked in project laboratories during the war, knew that the physicists of other countries could develop the bomb just as American physicists had. And they suspected that other, even more devastating weapons could also be developed by manipulating atomic processes.

The explosion of the bomb meant two things to these scientists.[6] First, the only real secret about the bomb—that it had been successfully developed—was out of the bag. Second, high officials, even revered scientists, had apparently overlooked the terrible precedent they set by using the bomb in warfare. Many bomb project physicists had already concluded that an international agreement would be needed to prevent the surprise use of atomic weapons, once other countries developed them. Some feared that the U.S. had already jeopardized such an agreement by using the bomb in a surprise attack. Now the physicists were free to translate their ideas into political action.

The atomic scientists initiated a tremendous lobbying movement to insure, first, that civilians, rather than the military, would henceforward control atomic energy in the U.S. and, second, that atomic weapons would eventually be brought under international control. Even those scientists who had advised using the bomb against the Japanese saw the need to renounce it, now that the war was over. J. Robert Oppenheimer, director of the Los Alamos laboratory, was soon at the forefront of the movement. Stimson, nearing retirement, and Bush, who had been kept by Truman as director of the Office of Scientific Research and Development, soon also supported the notion of international control of atomic weapons. On November 15, 1945, Britain and the United States officially committed themselves to this idea and called upon the United Nations to establish a commission which would promote peaceful uses of atomic energy and eliminate atomic weapons from the world.

President Truman assigned the task of developing the details of U.S. nuclear weapons policy to Under Secretary of State Dean Acheson. Acheson appointed David Lilienthal to chair a high-level advisory panel. On this panel sat Oppenheimer and through him were funneled the policy views of the atomic scientists.

The plan drawn up by this committee proposed formation of an International Atomic Development Authority which was to have complete control over research, development, and the application of atomic energy to peaceful purposes. The Authority would have a monopoly on fissionable materials and production plants. Fabrication of nuclear weapons would be strictly forbidden and any attempts would be reported immediately to the nations of the world.

In the plan, Oppenheimer explained in a public lecture,[7] the State Department advisors tried to make the best of two gloomy facts. "The first of these facts," he explained, "is that the science, the technology, the industrial development involved in the so-called beneficial uses of atomic energy appear to be inextricably intertwined with those involved in atomic weapons." The same raw materials, the same knowledge, and basically the same industrial processes that would be used for producing electrical power or for doing research were those used for making a bomb.

The second gloomy fact was that there existed no organization or method in the world "for making effective a prohibition against the national development of atomic armaments."

To Oppenheimer, the second problem was at the heart of the matter. Atomic weapons existed. They would be used in any major war in the future unless an effective means could be found for prohibiting their development.

The fact that the good and bad uses of atomic energy were "inextricably intertwined," Oppenheimer reasoned, would not be a handicap if it could be used somehow to make arms control effective. If an international authority could be established to promote the peaceful uses of atomic energy, it could provide the means for prohibiting atomic weapons for aggressive purposes. Seen this way, the close interrelation between military and peaceful uses "ceases to be a difficulty and becomes a help," Oppenheimer said.

In 1946, Oppenheimer's argument was a very tenuous one. No

one had begun to produce electricity from atomic fission. It was just an idea. Even if it could be done, no one knew if it could be done economically. But to guarantee peace, in the view of Oppenheimer and other scientists, a peaceful use of atomic energy *had* to be developed. The International Atomic Development Authority "would not be possible if there were nothing of value to do with atomic energy."

The Baruch Plan, as the Lilienthal Committee proposal was later named (after U.S. negotiator Bernard M. Baruch), would have established the International Atomic Development Authority, with power to monitor arms development, and to set and enforce national quotas on atomic weapons. Under the plan, America would have shared its nuclear know-how with nations that agreed not to make weapons. The Soviet Union, however, wanted the scientific information to be shared first, and then a method for assuring weapons control to be negotiated. The Soviet negotiators were unhappy with the proposed weapons quota system which would preclude the Soviet Union from ever having the quantity of nuclear weapons that the U.S. and Great Britain possessed.

The irreconcilable differences between the Soviet and U.S. positions in the negotiations were caused by conflicting national objectives, borne of insecurity: the Soviet Union felt especially vulnerable, after the war, because of its relative lack of industrialization compared with the European powers. The U.S.S.R. wanted to take advantage of time, and the low risk of U.S. aggression, to develop an atomic weapons program. The U.S. wanted to take advantage of its temporary lead in atomic weapons to create an international mechanism for guaranteeing against a surprise nuclear attack on the U.S.

To the majority of Americans who still considered the bomb an exclusive U.S. secret, the terms of the Baruch Plan—sharing nuclear technology with all nations, regardless of ideological differences— seemed more than generous. To the Soviet Union, however, the plan represented an unnecessary restriction of national sovereignty. To the atomic scientists, the plan was pure logic. It was the "logic of facts," said physicist Eugene Rabinowich in the *Bulletin of the Atomic Scientists,* a periodical he had founded to publicize the views of the physicists, that had converted the drafters of the Baruch Plan to the belief that international control of atomic research and development was the first and necessary step in preventing nuclear war.

The failure of the Soviet Union to follow the logic of their solution to the problem of nuclear war convinced most atomic scientists that the Soviet government was not interested in preventing such war.

By September 17, 1947, when he gave a lecture[8] to military and foreign service officers at the State Department, Oppenheimer said he was still convinced of the correctness of the logic behind the Baruch Plan, but that he had given up on seeing it adopted. "That is because the proposed pattern of control," he said, "stands in a very gross conflict to the present patterns of state power in Russia. The ideological underpinning of that power, namely the belief in the inevitability of conflict between Russia and the capitalist world, would be repudiated by a cooperation as intense or as intimate as is required by our proposals for the control of atomic energy . . . It does not seem to me likely that we have found inducements, or cajolery, or threats which together are adequate to make them take this great plunge."

There was a group of scientists, most notable among whom was chemist Linus Pauling, who believed that the atomic weapon, itself—not the difference in ideology between the Soviet Union and capitalist nations—had become the leading cause of insecurity among nations. This group believed that man's good sense would prevail and atomic weapons would be outlawed, if only people understood what a threat they posed to human survival.

The politically active physicists, however, believed that the Soviet Union was more or less intent on expansion into Western Europe and that Russia would have to be contained militarily. This belief, brought on by failure of the Baruch Plan, created a dilemma for the physicists. It meant that the United States would have to pursue a nuclear arms policy that was internally inconsistent, a policy that had several contradictory objectives.

These objectives, according to Oppenheimer, were international control (the original objective), technical superiority (leadership in the arms race), and strength in defense (good systems for warning, mobilization and retaliation).

"The things you would do to achieve [these goals]," Oppenheimer told his State Department audience, "are not always consistent. And the problem arises of finding a balance that is at all times reasonable and does not sell out any one of these three objectives."

Finding that reasonable balance was a difficult task for scientists who had to advise policy makers about nuclear armament in the coming years. Their intimate knowledge of nuclear weapons, their sense of responsibility for how the world would use nuclear power, and the stifled flow of public information about the weapons themselves placed the physicists in the uncomfortable position of being the exclusive source of advice on matters of high national policy previously alien to them.

Summary. The arms control problem was anticipated before the atomic bomb was ever used. Two solutions were discussed early in the high councils of government: 1) Keeping wraps on the information that led to the development of the bomb; and 2) creating an agency for international control.

The atomic scientists knew that the first solution was futile because other countries would eventually develop the bomb. The second solution seemed feasible, if positive uses of atomic power could be developed.

Out of this logic arose a government policy to promote the peaceful uses of atomic energy but no agency, at this stage, for international control of atomic weapons.

Nothing in their training had prepared the scientists for the failure of their "logical" solution to the arms control problem. The failure of the Soviet Union to agree to the terms of the Baruch Plan led the science advisors to distrust Soviet intentions more, probably, than was warranted. This distrust, in turn, led to a policy of superiority in strategic weapons that could not be reversed even in the face of later Soviet proposals to outlaw nuclear weapons.

Public ignorance about the nature of the atom bomb, especially that it would not long be an exclusive U.S. secret, set the stage for support of a hard-line strategic weapons policy and general panic when the Soviets did develop the bomb.

After the failure of the Baruch Plan, the views of the atomic scientists on weapons policy began to diverge and the scientists never regained their post-war unanimity.[9] Their advice differed based on how they defined the problem: to eliminate the insecurity among nations caused by atomic weapons; to prevent the use of atomic weapons; or to have the capability to win a nuclear war. The advice of the physicists was still indispensable to policy makers, but it was no longer unanimous. How, then, would government officials make decisions about nuclear weapons?

The Decision to Develop the H-bomb

During World War II, work had been proceeding in the Los Alamos laboratory's theoretical division on the potential for energy to be released by atomic fusion. Fusion, the process by which the sun releases its energy, had been theoretically demonstrated in the mid-thirties by physicist Hans Bethe at Cornell University. In the process

Bethe described, two protons combine to form a heavy isotope of hydrogen, called deuterium. A great deal of energy is released during the reaction, but it is much slower (about a trillion trillion times slower, according to Bethe) than the reaction between deuterium and tritium that was later to be used in the H-bomb. Fusion reactions require very high temperature to get started. Such a high temperature was not contemplated on the earth until the advent of nuclear fission.

There is a story, recounted by Edward Teller many years afterward, that Enrico Fermi asked him in early 1942, "Now that we have a good prospect of developing an atomic bomb, couldn't such an explosion be used to start something similar to the reactions in the sun?"

After the war, research on fusion reactions resumed at Los Alamos, but the staff was a small remnant of the war-time group. Most had returned to campus and were busy advising the government. The ultimate goal was to ignite an indefinitely large mass of hydrogen fuel, using a small fission bomb as the fuse. This hydrogen bomb could theoretically produce an explosion a thousand times as large as the war-time atom bombs. By 1949, the prospects for achieving fusion were bright enough to lure Teller and others back to Los Alamos.

Oppenheimer's stature and influence, meanwhile, were growing through his participation in numerous White House, Defense, and State Department advisory activities. Perhaps of greatest importance was his position as chairman of the General Advisory Committee to the Atomic Energy Commission (AEC), the civilian group set up soon after the war to administer weapons policy and promote the peaceful development of atomic power. The commission chairman was David Lilienthal, head of the group that had drafted the Baruch Plan. With Oppenheimer on the General Advisory Committee were, among others, Conant, former member of Truman's Interim Committee and still president of Harvard University; Lee DuBridge, president of the California Institute of Technology; Fermi at Chicago; I.I. Rabi, chairman of the physics department at Columbia; and Glenn Seaborg, professor of chemistry at Berkeley and co-discoverer of plutonium.

This group recommended, and the AEC adopted during this period, the weapons policy that Oppenheimer had been advocating publicly. This policy was based on the opinion that national defense should not rest solely on strategic air power, that is, dropping nuclear weapons from bombers, but that the U.S. should be prepared to wage all kinds of warfare and should have a variety of weapons available to meet whatever circumstances might develop. The AEC science advisors felt the threat of nuclear attack from the Soviet Union was not imminent. In addition, they felt that using industry to make arms might jeopardize the peaceful development of atomic energy on which international peace would ultimately rest.

American public opinion, however, and the official military view was that bigger weapons and strategic air power would be necessary to answer the Soviet threat. This policy required the strictest internal security measures to insure that new atomic "secrets" would not get into communist hands. And it meant permanently sacrificing the free exchange of information which, before the war, had been basic to both science and democracy.

The willingness of the American people to make this sacrifice was heightened when, on August 29, 1949, the Soviet Union exploded an atomic bomb in Siberia.

The immediate reaction of the Atomic Energy Commission was to beef up research on thermonuclear weapons. Promoting development of the hydrogen bomb as the proper response to the Soviet explosion was a group that included both scientists and non-scientists—Teller at Los Alamos, E.O. Lawrence, Luis Alvarez and William Latimer at Berkeley, Senator Brian McMahon of the Joint Committee on Atomic Energy and his chief of staff, and Lewis Strauss of the AEC.

Chemist Harold Urey made a plea in the *Bulletin of the Atomic Scientists* for those physicists who, because they knew the bomb was not a secret and because they called for restraint in the development of atomic weapons, were coming under suspicion: "We scientists not only failed to convince Congress and the public," Urey noted, "of the soundness of our prediction that the Russians would have the bomb in about five years after we had it, but, because we told disagreeable truths, we have even been accused of [being] impractical dreamers or plain traitors."[10]

Oppenheimer called a meeting of the General Advisory Committee on October 29 in response to an AEC request for their views on development of the super bomb and other activities. The committee sought the views of Hans Bethe, who had run the theoretical division at Los Alamos during the war when preliminary work was being done on the fusion bomb. Bethe was highly regarded and he was considered less biased on the question of H-bomb development than other physicists—such as Teller who had established the theory behind the H-bomb. Bethe was opposed to its development. Robert Serber also spoke at the GAC meeting to promote a project of Lawrence and Alvarez to build a hydrogen fuel reactor, but personally he, too, doubted the wisdom of the H-bomb.

The GAC's report from that meeting (not fully declassified until 1974 and even then with a few bits of technical information deleted) recommended that the Atomic Energy Commission step up the production of fissionable material and increase the availability of atomic weapons for tactical use, as opposed to strategic use as in a full-scale nuclear war. But the report recommended *against* the high-priority development of the super bomb.[11]

The GAC's technical arguments were that no experiment existed, short of exploding a bomb, to determine whether the theory behind the hydrogen bomb was correct. Basic research, from this point on, would involve actual detonations unless advances in theoretical calculations could be made. The GAC recommended more theoretical work. Bomb development, the scientists predicted, would take about five years and would have a fifty-fifty chance of succeeding. The GAC also pointed out that, from a military point of view, the bomb could not be used with any sort of discrimination on military targets, unlimited as it would be in destructive power.

But the compelling arguments were not technical. In two attachments to the report, the GAC members explained their differing rationale for opposing the hydrogen bomb. "In determining not to proceed to develop the super bomb," said the majority, including Oppenheimer, "we see a unique opportunity of providing by example some limitations on the totality of war and thus of limiting the fear and arousing the hopes of mankind . . . To the argument that the Russians may succeed in developing this weapon, we would reply that our undertaking it will not prove a deterrent to them . . ."

The minority group, which consisted of Fermi and Rabi, also said development of the super bomb would be "wrong on fundamental ethical principles." They believed, however, that all nations should renounce its development at the same time the U.S. did.

Both factions of the GAC were opposed to the H-bomb and both said the U.S. stockpile of atomic bombs was sufficient to retaliate against agressive use of a super bomb by an enemy.

The committee was unanimous on one other point, which is the legacy that these scientists left for following generations of policy makers:

"The Committee recommends that enough be declassified about the super bomb so that a public statement of policy can be made at this time . . . It should explain that the weapon cannot be explored without developing it and proof-firing it. In one form or another, the statement should express our desire not to make this development. It should explain the scale and general nature of the destruction which its use would entail. It should make clear that there are no known or foreseen nonmilitary applications of this development."

A month after the GAC issued its report, news leaked out that the Atomic Energy Commission had a program underway on the H-bomb. Despite the fact that the GAC had recommended against beefing up the program and even though a three-two majority on the AEC concurred, pressure was put on President Truman not to adopt a policy that meant the U.S. would deliberately lose the arms race. It was still not completely clear to the general public, because of the limitations on what scientists could talk about, that Soviet scientists could do what American scientists could do. But because the Russians had the A-bomb, the public thinking went, our scientists had better come up with something more powerful.

Truman appointed a committee which included the AEC Chairman Lilienthal, Secretary of Defense Louis Johnson, and Secretary of State Dean Acheson. Lilienthal was the only opponent among the three of a crash program for the super bomb and, on January 31, 1950, Truman announced his decision in favor of H-bomb development. Truman gave only a nod, but the AEC took it like a command.

"There is grave danger for us," said Oppenheimer when it became clear the AEC was proceeding with a crash program, "in that these decisions have been taken on the basis of facts held secret. This is not because the men who must contribute to the decisions, or must make them, are lacking in wisdom; it is because wisdom itself cannot flourish, nor even truth be determined, without the give and take of debate or criticism. The relevant facts could be of little help to an enemy; yet they are indispensable for an understanding of questions of policy."[12]

Summary. In the hysterically anti-communist mood of the early 1950s, encouraged by Senator Joseph McCarthy's political witch-hunting, Oppenheimer's views were very unpopular. Klaus Fuchs, a British scientist at Los Alamos during the war, had recently been exposed as a Soviet spy and McCarthy played on people's fears that there might be other spies in responsible government jobs. It did not help Oppenheimer that Lilienthal gave up his chairmanship of the AEC and thus permitted a shift in the majority away from the views of the General Advisory Committee. Nor did it help Oppenheimer's reputation as a technical advisor when, the following year, Edward

Teller and Stanislaw Ulam achieved a technical breakthrough which made the GAC's five-year estimate for development of the super bomb seem intentionally pessimistic. Despite pressure from friends and foes alike, Oppenheimer stayed on as GAC chairman for two more years.

Then in 1954, following allegations that Oppenheimer was a communist sympathizer, the AEC stripped him of his security clearance. In retrospect, the action against Oppenheimer is filled with ironies. Some of the ironies were apparent even before the hearing board rendered its judgment. The dissenter on the board, Ward Evans, thought it ironic that Oppenheimer, the man who had successfully brought the U.S. through the most sensitive project in history and who had been cleared by the AEC in 1947, despite official knowledge that he held left wing political views, was now being challenged.[13] The invasion of South Korea, four years earlier, had demonstrated the truth of Oppenheimer's contention that communist aggression could not be contained by development of big scale strategic weapons. But that insightful prediction was overlooked in the atmosphere of paranoia that existed in 1954.

At the moment Oppenheimer was having his security clearance removed, the United States Congress was incorporating his major premise on the peaceful uses of atomic energy into its 1954 amendments to the Atomic Energy Act. From that point on, the AEC and the increasingly powerful Joint Committee on Atomic Energy became active promoters of the atomic energy industry, a role they were to succeed in despite opposition from the Congressional appropriations committees and the Eisenhower Administration.[14]

Within ten years, Oppenheimer was a national hero. In 1963, he was chosen by President John F. Kennedy to receive the Fermi Award, the highest award the U.S. government bestows in physics. But the recognition did not come until a year after Edward Teller was given the same award.

Conclusions

Decisions about the development of nuclear weapons were made in secret. When science advisors began to sense the responsibility of being surrogates for the public in these matters, rather than mere technical advisors, their advice began to conflict. But already the complicated series of events and changes, brought on by the use of the atom bomb, were underway. And policy makers were more influenced by these than by the conflicting views of their science advisors.

One of these inexorable changes was the nuclear arms race with the Soviet Union. Another was the growth of the nuclear power industry. In 1946, the AEC undertook a research and development program in atomic power production unparalleled in its scope and expense by any other domestic energy program before or since. A whole new industry grew up in this country and abroad after amendments to the Atomic Energy Act in 1954 and 1958 allowed private use of nuclear materials in this country and encouraged the sharing of nuclear energy technology with American allies. An International Atomic Energy Agency was eventually established to discourage the hostile use of nuclear weapons much as the proposed International Atomic Development Authority was intended to. Today, however, trade in atomic materials is so extensive and the technology has evolved in such a manner that it is now a matter of public debate whether government promotion of atomic energy has increased or reduced the potential for nuclear war.

The view today that technological developments do not always, on balance, prove beneficial to mankind, has its origins in the government-supported development of the atom bomb and subsequent attempts to keep atomic energy a peaceful enterprise. It is clear, in retrospect, that undesirable uses of technology cannot be controlled by those who bring the technology into the world. The need is clearer, now, to anticipate the drawbacks of a technology which is developed for a particular purpose and to weigh the drawbacks before a technology is in use. Government promotion of basic research leads to applications which in turn bring a complicated series of events and changes that are not easily reversed once the drawbacks become obvious. The technology develops a constituency. People, nations, become dependent on it for various reasons which usually have to do with the immediate benefits. Long-term effects of relying on the technology tend to be ignored.

Before a particular technology is developed, however, its long-term advantages and disadvantages can be weighed. This process of weighing the benefits and risks requires wide public discussion, because different groups of people perceive the benefits and risks differently, depending on what they know about the technology itself, and what their hopes and fears are for the future of mankind.

Today, these ideas about science and social goals—ideas that were first clearly stated by the physicists who spoke out against use of the atom bomb and those who opposed development of the H-bomb—have taken hold in the public mind. But they did not take hold until a new group of scientists—geneticists—took the responsibility to inform the public about some drawbacks of the hydrogen bomb that were being overlooked.

● GENETICS, FALLOUT, AND THE ORIGINS OF PUBLIC INTEREST SCIENCE

Operation Castle

The Atomic Bomb Casualty Commission, set up in 1946 to determine the genetic effects of the Hiroshima and Nagasaki explosions, failed to turn up any definitive proof that the A-bombs had caused genetic damage. To any geneticist worthy of the title, this came as no surprise. Though the commission delayed for years publishing its findings, the passing time was but a second on the clock of genetic change. Geneticists knew that the kind of proof the commission was looking for would not show up for perhaps hundreds of years. Even without this kind of evidence before them, geneticists knew that atomic radiation was, like certain chemical agents and even excessive heat, a cause of changes in human genes. And these altered genes, or mutant genes, were suspected of being harmful about ninety-nine per cent of the time.

About the time the casualty commission was letting it be known they had failed to find any genetic effects from the A-bombs, the Atomic Energy Commission was embarking on a series of thermonuclear bomb tests known as Operation Castle. Much progress had been made in the design of H-bombs since the first experimental explosion on November 1, 1952. Six variations of the super bomb were to be tested during the operation. The first bomb, Bravo, was made with lithium deuteride, a solid salt-like substance, instead of the bulkier liquid deuterium, the familiar heavy isotope of hydrogen.

The test took place on March 1, 1954, on Bikini Atoll, a secluded spot in the South Pacific. From the point of view of the size of the blast, the Bravo test was very successful. It delivered fifteen megatons of explosive force—the equivalent of fifteen million tons of TNT and more than a thousand times the size of the Hiroshima bomb. Its mushrooming cloud carried radioactive material into the stratosphere.

From the point of view of world opinion, however, the Bravo test was a disaster. Not that people were so perturbed by its size. After all, a 10-megaton bomb had been tested a year and a half earlier. The problem was that scientists and military officials in charge of the Bravo test either underestimated the distance the radioactive fallout would go or just failed to notice a little tuna trawler working the waters ninety-five or a hundred miles from the test site. Within two weeks, the whole world knew about the *Lucky Dragon* and the twenty-three unlucky Japanese fishermen aboard. Stories about the ashes that covered their boat, the strange sickness, the loss of hair, and the eventual death of one of the fishermen spread across the globe. In the United States, the news was met with a considerable sense of guilt and recollection of the wartime bombing. When fish contaminated with radioactivity reached the Japanese market, a panic seized Japan and the pressure of world opinion was brought to bear on Washington.

President Eisenhower and AEC Chairman Lewis Strauss held a press conference in which Strauss said the radioactivity from the test would decrease rapidly. But the results of studies by Japanese scientists on the residual levels of radioactivity were published in the open literature throughout 1954 and the news was not as good as Strauss had made it out to be. The lingering radiation appeared to be the result of uranium-238 intentionally added to the bomb to increase the blast and the fallout.

This information had a dual effect on American scientists who were interested in the biological effects of radiation. First, the AEC was apparently withholding important information about the dangers of its latest weapons. Second, concerns over the lasting genetic effects of fallout—even particles carried hundreds of miles by wind and waves—were confirmed.

Radioactive fallout would pose no threat to future generations if, as Strauss had indicated, the level of radioactivity quickly returned to the normal "background level" (the amount people are subjected to naturally from the sun and the earth) and it would pose no threat if, as scientists had assumed prior to 1950, a relatively large dose of radiation were required to cause genetic mutations, if, in other words, the genes could tolerate radiation until a certain threshold was exceeded.

By 1955, however, the "threshold" theory was being seriously challenged and now it appeared that even a slight increase in the background level of radioactivity was a danger. This meant that the U.S. weapons program had a new dimension. It was placing a genetic burden on future generations, regardless of their nationality or their political views, a burden that would have to be carried by Americans and Russians alike.

The Scientists Go Public

The American scientists decided it was time to spread the word to the American public. Ralph Lapp, a physicist concerned with the effects of fallout, made a particular effort to publicize the potential harm of nuclear testing and the lack of candor of public officials about it.

Scientific American which had been established (in its modern form) in the wake of World War II, published an account by world-famous geneticist Hermann J. Muller on the genetic effects of radiation.[15]

Muller's personal view was that the recent series of bomb tests had been justified on grounds of national defense "despite the future sacrifices that they inexorably bring in their train." Muller took the opportunity to blast the medical profession for its liberal use of X-rays in diagnostic and therapeutic procedures and to warn against the increasing use of organic chemicals and other non-radioactive agents of genetic mutation. He also called on persons likely to have a large number of mutant genes from radiation exposure to voluntarily refrain from having children. All of these warnings, in time, would register in the public consciousness. But, for the moment, Muller's explanation of the genetic effects of radiation, nuclear war, and bomb testing had its impact on U.S. weapons policy.

What Muller explained was this: Every cell in the human body contains thousands of units of hereditary material, or genes. The genes are subject to "rare chemical accidents," called gene mutations. A gene altered in this way naturally carries on the mutant characteristic when it replicates itself for cell division or when it is passed on to offspring.

It is this ability of genes to be altered, according to genetic theory, that accounts for evolution, the infinitely slow process that allows living organisms to improve their chances to survive and reproduce. For a mutation may give a plant or animal an advantage, a new characteristic that happens to coincide perfectly with some change in the environment. The descendants who inherit the advantageous trait multiply more than the rest of the population, until the mutant trait becomes the normal trait.

But this is rare. Much more often—maybe ninety-nine per cent of the time—a mutation has a harmful effect, one that causes some disruption or change in normal body function. Individuals who receive the same mutant gene from both parents are likely to show symptoms of their "genetic disease" or may even die prematurely.

Because of the risk of premature death for individuals who receive the double mutant gene, Muller said, the harmful trait is likely to persist only about forty generations before it is eliminated from the population.

From the work of other geneticists, including those doing mutation studies at the federal government laboratories at Oak Ridge, Tennessee, Muller calculated that each person would have about eight mutant genes among his ten thousand. (Geneticists now estimate the total number of genes to be much higher.)

Muller said that a single dose of radiation, sufficient to double the spontaneous mutation rate, would cause just one mutation in every five individuals. The effects would not appear very clearly in the first generation after exposure. One child in two hundred, he calculated, might show the effects, hardly noticeable in a population that already carried eight mutant genes per individual. But after forty generations, with each generation receiving a similar dose of radiation, the accumulted mutations would have increased to sixteen per individual and the detrimental effects would be noticeable indeed.

Such a persistent condition of radiation exposure, Muller pointed out, would be especially harmful to humans because the low rate of reproduction means normal genes replace mutants at a slow pace and because modern medical practice enables mutant genes to persist far beyond their normal expectancy. "Under these circumstances," Muller said, "a long-continued doubling of the mutation frequency might eventually mean, if the situation persisted, total extinction of the population."

A full-scale war, in which fifteen hundred bombs might be used, he said, would produce radiation greater than the amount necessary to double the spontaneous mutation rate. Muller speculated that the human race could ultimately revive after a single nuclear war, but that human genetic change would be so great as not to be "permissible" under any standards.

As to the effect of the H-bomb test explosions, Muller said, a British scientist estimated that the tests of the preceding year (five large explosions) had doubled the background radiation in regions remote from the blasts, including the U.S.

At the time Muller's article was written, the view had become accepted that any increase in radiation would cause a proportional increase in spontaneous mutations. Thus the background radiation, which was thought to be responsible for five per cent of the spontaneous mutations in man, would now be responsible for twice as many, or ten per cent. Muller calculated that this doubling of background radiation would increase the accumulation of mutant genes by only "a few tenths of one per cent"—practically nothing compared with the doubling of spontaneous mutations he had described earlier as a result of nuclear war. But the overall effect of the article on the non-geneticists, it is safe to say, was that radiation exposure can be extremely damaging to genes and that the U.S. bomb tests had doubled the radiation exposure of everyone in the world.

Disagreement among scientists on weapons policy led to apparent disagreement among them on the genetic effects of fallout. Actually, there was very little disagreement on the facts. Edward Teller and Albert Latter wrote a book called *Our Nuclear Future* in 1958 describing the situation in these terms: One-tenth of spontaneous mutations are caused by radiation and the series of nuclear tests increased the amount of radiation *to which reproductive cells are exposed* by only one per cent. "The atomic tests," the writers said, "are therefore increasing the number of mutations by only about 0.1% (one-tenth of one per cent).[16]

The figures arrived at by Muller and those presented by Teller and Latter for the genetic effects of the bomb testing are very close to agreement, but their interpretation for laymen left sharply differing impressions. The emotional issue of genetic mutation was seized upon by scientists who saw in it the opportunity to appeal for an end to the arms race.

Public Reaction and the Change in Weapons Policy

On January 15, 1958, chemist Linus Pauling, who had emerged as an advocate of complete nuclear disarmament in the mid-forties, presented U.N. Secretary-General Dag Hammarskjold the petition of 9,235 scientists from around the world for an international agreement to stop the testing of nuclear bombs as a first step toward general disarmament.

"Each added amount of radiation," the petition said, "causes damage to the health of human beings all over the world and causes damage to the pool of human germ plasm [that is, the genes of the reproductive cells] such as to lead to an increase in the number of seriously defective children that will be born in future generations."[17]

The petition enjoyed considerable support from U.S. scientists, including many, like Muller himself, who all along had felt the bomb testing was justified on grounds of national defense. Several factors influenced them. Though the Soviet Union had developed and tested its own H-bomb in 1955, the Russians were now taking the lead in calling for disarmament and an end to the tests. The two superpowers (and Britain, which also had tested a hydrogen bomb) had obvious common interests. First, they wanted to avoid the expense of larger bomb arsenals, and prevent the spread of nuclear weapons to other countries. Second, they were under increasing popular pressure to stop the contamination of the atmosphere.

Pauling had recently gathered some damning biological evidence against the H-bomb. Strontium-90 and particularly cesium-137, both radioactive isotopes, had been thought to be main agents of mutation in fallout. Radioactivity from cesium-137 was known to diminish by half in just thirty years and again by half in another thirty years, thus its residual effect would be very slight after a few generations. But Pauling, simultaneously with some Soviet scientists, determined that another radioactive isotope, carbon-14, was formed following a nuclear explosion.

Calculations showed that exposure of human sex cells to radiation from carbon-14 was greater than their exposure to radiation from cesium-137. In addition to that, the researchers said, the radioactivity of carbon-14 does not diminish by half until after 5,600 years—long enough to expose hundreds of generations.

For a time, proponents of the H-bomb had argued that the fusion reaction produces less radioactive fallout and, therefore, is cleaner than the fission reaction in an A-bomb. Their arguments were hard to refute as long as the isotopes of strontium and cesium were the only ones under study. The discovery that carbon-14 is produced by every kind of nuclear reaction, fission or fusion, and that it poses a greater hazard to heredity than the other radioactive isotopes, did away with the "clean bomb" argument altogether.

The risks of nuclear fallout could no longer be denied, but they could still be debated and weighed against the benefits, as various people perceived them, of nuclear testing. The debate, of course, was a political one and unlike the discussion among scientists about use of the A-bomb and development of the H-bomb, it occurred in public. It was a debate between scientists who, on the one hand, felt weapons superiority was necessary to prevent war and those who, on the other, felt a test ban would lead to disarmament and disarmament to peace.

With Pauling's petition to the U.N., the public debate between the two factions became heated. Teller and Latter countered the petition with an article that was published in *Life* magazine a month later on February 10, 1958. The two physicists challenged Pauling's motives and argued that the biological hazards of radiation were slight: "It seems probable that the real root of the opposition to further tests—and not only among the petition-signers—is not so much the fear of fallout as it is this desire for disarmament and for peace."

Teller and Latter said that the desire for peace was admirable but that the belief that a nuclear test ban would lead to peace was not well founded. They said the Soviet government could not be trusted to uphold the ban, an opinion which, they knew, many Americans shared. But the two scientists knew also that the fallout issue had turned public opinion against the tests. They therefore sought, with facts and figures, to demonstrate how insignificant were the hazards of fallout.

"To see fallout radiation in proper perspective," they argued, "it should be compared not only with other kinds of radiation but also with other dangers to health. Some estimates are, for example, that being 10% overweight seems to reduce a person's life expectancy by 1.5 years [and] that the lifelong habit of smoking one package of cigarets a day cuts it by seven years . . . On this statistical scale the reduction in life expectancy from worldwide fallout at present levels totals less than two days. Or, to put it another way, the worldwide fallout is as dangerous to human health as being one ounce overweight, or smoking one cigaret every two months."

The debate was even aired on television, with Teller and Pauling face to face. The public debates upset many scientists who felt that scientific facts were being distorted by both sides for political purposes, and that the image of the objective scientist was being sullied.

To the average person who was not concerned about scientific verification, Teller's arguments were less convincing than Pauling's. Man-made radiation was a scary, new thing in the world. What people feared was that radiation could cause serious chronic illness in future generations or even premature death. Teller's comparisons with familiar health risks that have no effect on genes failed to reassure.

In addition, the public debate brought attention to the theory that small amounts of radiation could increase a person's chance of getting bone cancer or leukemia. And it confirmed for mothers that their children were taking the brunt of the testing because strontium-90 and radioactive iodine in the milk supply finds its way into the bones of growing children. Small organizations grew up in St. Louis, New York, and elsewhere to monitor radioactivity and its effect on children. Leaders of these groups, notably biologist Barry Commoner and social anthropologist Margaret Mead, later formed the broader-based Scientists' Institute for Public Information as many other environmental issues came to public attention. But the genetic effect of fallout was the issue that originally created the demand for the public interest scientist.

Conclusions

The cancer-causing effect of low-dosage radiation and its effect on the genetic make-up of future generations are still unsettled questions. The debate over them runs hot or cold, depending on the question of national policy at hand. If the future of nuclear power generating plants, for example, is at issue, the pro-nuclear scientists will rise to explain that the dangers are minor or avoidable and the anti-nuclear scientists will argue that the dangers may be more serious than we think. As a practical matter, the AEC established standards for how much radioactive material may escape from power plants into the air and water. But controversy still revolves around the question of whether these "acceptable" levels are really safe or just expedient, and nuclear equipment manufacturers have demonstrated that they could eliminate ninety-nine per cent of the allowable emissions, if they had to.

The profound shift in public opinion that followed the debate over the biological hazards of H-bomb testing created an eager new audience for scientists other than the official audience they had been advising in secret. People began to depend on academic biologists just as government officials had come to rely on academic physicists. The demand was for a new set of science advisors who considered themselves more responsible to the people than to the government—a distinction that became important as people began to learn more and to challenge government policies with the information they now had available.

Meanwhile, by 1958, the scientists in influential government advisory positions had already abandoned former, long-defended positions on nuclear weapons policy. With the Soviet development of the H-bomb in 1955, the concept of technical superiority in strategic weapons was out the window. The school of scientists, including Teller and Latter, who advocated technical superiority shifted to a position reminiscent of the old arms control philosophy, argued for so many years by Oppenheimer. They backed a buildup of new, sophisticated tactical weapons, delivered by guided missiles. At the same time, the old arms control advocates, now represented in matters of high policy by Hans Bethe, adopted a position favoring nuclear disarmament—a view that had been dormant for the ten years since the failure of the Baruch Plan.

This time the group with the softer line won the day. Had they developed that much political savvy in the eight years since losing the argument over the development of the H-bomb? Probably not. It is much more likely that President Dwight Eisenhower had become concerned with the expense of the arms race, that the U.S. and Soviet Union were both concerned about what country would next possess nuclear weapons, and that people over the world were registering their opposition to radioactive contamination of human genes.

By August 22, 1958, when he proposed that the nuclear powers negotiate a treaty for the permanent suspension of nuclear testing, Eisenhower simply felt that he had sufficient support from scientists and from the public to counteract those politicians, industrialists, and military officials who were pressing for further development of nuclear weapons. Partly to balance their advice in scientific matters, especially the fledgling U.S. space program, and partly to give greater prestige to U.S. science, Eisenhower had already appointed a White House science advisor, MIT President James Killian, and had put a full committee of scientists under him. Now the President even refrained from telling the Congressional Joint Committee on Atomic Energy of his intention to call for a test ban treaty until the day before he announced it publicly.

Besides that, the launching of the Soviet satellite Sputnik I, ten months before, had shifted military thinking from new weapons to new delivery systems for weapons—from bigger bombs to bigger boosters.

● TECHNOLOGY, SPACE, AND NATIONAL PRIORITIES

Origins of the U.S. Space Program

When the Soviet Union launched the first artificial earth satellite on October 4, 1957, Americans—from officials in Washington to the man in the street—were taken by surprise.

The White House had announced on July 29, 1955, that the United States intended to launch a satellite to celebrate the International Geophysical Year (1957-58). The project was proceeding under auspices of the Navy, but without priority. Some of the people involved, like Werner Von Braun, developer of the German V-2 rocket and now an employee of the U.S. Army, wanted the program speeded up and thought it should take advantage of the progress in Army ballistic missiles. But the orders came from the top, and Eisenhower did not want the military and the scientific rocket programs mixed.

Officials and certainly the ordinary person, if he thought about the subject at all in 1955, assumed that American space technology was more advanced than Russian, especially because that had been the case in the arms race. This was a bad assumption to make because it overlooked two important realities: U.S. preoccupation with nuclear weapons development and the history of Russian work in astronautics.[18]

That history goes back to K. E. Tsiolkovski, who is the Russian counterpart of America's space pioneer James Goddard, but who preceded Goddard by several decades. Tsiolkovski had both the technical skills and the imagination necessary to stimulate future generations of scientists. "The earth," he said, "is the cradle of the mind, but one cannot live forever in a cradle." Tsiolkovski's followers were compelled by his view that space travel was inevitable and in 1929 they established a scientific group which conducted a systematic program of research and development in rocketry.

Though little technical information reached the United States on Soviet progress in astronautics, scientists of the world could infer that important technical advances had been made when a Russian spokesman told the World Peace Council in Vienna, November 27, 1953, that "it is feasible to send a stratoplane to the moon, to create an artificial satellite of the earth . . ."

In late 1956, Soviet scientists began to open up at professional meetings, revealing the advanced state of their rocket testing program and their research on the effects of sub-orbital flights on live animals. By the summer of 1957, the Soviet press carried announcements of an imminent satellite launching.

Americans did not believe it until they saw it. But they *did* see it and seeing it brought a sense of awe and even admiration for the Soviet scientists who had accomplished such a project. Radio and television broadcasters announced the time of evening the little silver ball would be visible in their broadcasting area. If the night were clear, families gathered at the local ball park or in the street to watch Sputnik.

The October 1957 launching of Sputnik and Sputnik II a month later had caught official Washington by surprise. Sputnik itself was not a threat to American security, but U.S. officials knew the Russians had used military Intercontinental Ballistic Missiles (ICBM's) to place the capsules in orbit. The sole test firing of the Air Force's Atlas ICBM had been, by contrast, an embarrassing failure. Secretary of State John Foster Dulles, architect of the policy of massive nuclear retaliation against Soviet aggression, publicly refused to acknowledge the importance of Sputnik. He announced that the U.S. was interested in space for peaceful purposes only, but he also called for an amendment to the Atomic Energy Act to allow the U.S. to share its nuclear technology with allies.

Four days after Sputnik II, Eisenhower shifted the Navy's Vanguard missile program to top priority in the Department of Defense. That same day he appointed MIT President Killian as his special assistant for science and technology and moved to the White House the science advisory committee which had been serving the Office of Defense Mobilization since the Korean War, redesignating it the President's Science Advisory Committee (PSAC). It was this group of science advisors who eventually were to provide Eisenhower an alternative to military advice on nuclear bomb testing. In the emerging political dispute over who would run the space program, the science advisors now aligned themselves with the President, the Bureau of the Budget, and the U.S. House of Representatives in an effort to put space missile development in civilian hands.

On the other side of the issue in the early months of 1958 were the military interests, particularly the Army, and the U.S. Senate, led by a Democrat from Texas, Lyndon B. Johnson. Up to this point, missile development had been competitively pursued by the three military services. Johnson and his older colleague from Texas, Sam Rayburn, decided there were political points to be won by criticizing the Administration's performance in missile and space technology programs. While Presidential Assistant Sherman Adams proclaimed that the U.S. space program was intended to "serve science" rather than to score points "in an outer space basketball game," the Democrats said the Administration was misleading the pulic about the importance of Sputnik and called for a full-scale inquiry into U.S. defense missile capability. Senators Stuart Symington, Henry Jackson, Mike Mansfield, Hubert Humphrey, and Estes Kefauver, among others critical of Eisenhower's tight-fisted defense budgeting, called Sputnik a "devastating blow to the prestige of the United States as a leader in the scientific and technological world."

Like the rest of the Administration, officials in the Department of defense played down Sputnik. Within DOD, however, the Navy's Vanguard missile program was reevaluated and the responsibility for launching a satellite was shifted to the Army, which had an active Intermediate Range Ballistic Missile program under Von Braun. In the nose of a modified Army rocket, the Jupiter C, the U.S. launched its first satellite, Explorer I, on January 3, 1958. "If we put our mind to it," said Secretary of State John Foster Dulles, "we can do almost anything that can be done."

Domestic Interests in Space

The President.   Taking advantage of the boost in morale that accompanied the successful U.S. space shot, Eisenhower pressed his effort to assure that the future of the space program would be in civilian hands.

On February 4, 1958, the President ordered Killian to draw up a schedule for achieving scientific goals in space and an organizational chart for the kind of agency that could best direct space research and exploration. Killian appointed a committee under the direction of Edward Purcell, a member of the science advisory committee.

Meanwhile, Vice-President Richard M. Nixon was dispatched to one of the Army's major ballistic missile contractors, the Jet Propulsion Laboratory in Pasadena, California, to explain why the exploration of space should be a civilian activity. Military needs, Nixon said, would put unnecessary restrictions on scientific investigation and might suggest that the U.S. was interested in space for other than peaceful purposes.

The Science Advisors.   In late March of 1958, Eisenhower announced that he was about to send legislation to Capitol Hill that would provide for a civilian-controlled space program. The same day he released the Purcell committee's report, "An Introduction to Outer Space." The report was based on the premise that the space program should proceed for four reasons: scientific inquiry, the "urge of man to explore and discover," national prestige, and defense. Among these, the committee said, the scientific questions come first. The Purcell committee thought it would be logical to establish the national space program under an organization like the National Advisory Committee on Astronautics, an independent body that had been established way back in 1915. The Bureau of the Budget liked the idea because of its economy. Besides, NACA chairman, World War II Air Force General James H. Doolittle, with the help of H. Guyford Stever, associate dean of engineering at MIT, was already pushing for a role in the space program for the committee. NACA's view was that the need was now apparent for a national research and development program "leading to manned satellites, lunar and interplanetary flight."

Most scientists whose opinions were sought stated a distinct preference for civilian rather than military control of the space program, but not all of them endorsed a program as ambitious as NACA's, particularly on the need for manned space flight. Early on, the civilian scientists had backed a joint proposal of the American Rocket Society and the Satellite Research Panel of the National Academy of Sciences for what was called a National Space Establishment. The NSE was similar to the Administration's eventual proposal with respect to its independence from the military. What is striking about the NSE proposal is how the scientists viewed the goals of the space program. Research in space, the architects of the NSE proposal said, would be an "endless frontier" improving life on earth by providing mankind with meteorological, medical and commercial advances. These scientists were pushing a space program based on the new technical applications that would ultimately arise. Manned space flight was not an immediate objective of their program. It could not, they said, "be very clearly justified on purely rational grounds."

The deans of science advice-giving, Edward Teller and Vannevar Bush, stressed, in testimony before the Senate Armed Services subcommittee, that all areas of scientific activity in the U.S. needed improvement, not just the space effort. Many scientists, even those who had joined the space bandwagon to assure civilian control, agreed that space research should not be the number one priority in the national research effort.

The Congress.   The space program, however, had political appeal. Lyndon Johnson, in particular, recognized that Americans were excited by the idea of venturing into space and felt threatened by the possibility that the Soviet Union might make some sort of prior claim there. Johnson advocated a space program, civilian and military, big enough to give all the competing interests a piece of the action. He called for a United Nations agreement to insure the peaceful exploration of space, and said that U.S. dominion in space would, meanwhile, help insure peace on earth.

Addressing the Democratic party caucus two days before the President's State of the Union Message, he identified American superiority in space as the major task before Congress and outlined a program to achieve it. In addition to the immediate scientific effort in space, he proposed far-reaching programs in aid to education, basic research, and advanced military research and development.

The Senate passed a resolution on February 6, 1958, creating a Special Committee on Space and Astronautics to frame appropriate legislation. Johnson was elected chairman. The House of Representatives responded by forming its own select committee and putting House Majority Leader John McCormack, who had geographical ties with Killian and MIT, in charge. Then the Congressional leadership waited for the Administration's proposed legislation.

The Department of Defense. Secretary of Defense Neil H. McElroy, meanwhile, had been trying to get the space activities of the military services better coordinated. He established the Advanced Research Projects Agency to "pull under a single manager" the poorly coordinated anti-missile, satellite, and ballistic missile technology programs. McElroy envisioned a space program in which a civilian agency would plan a space mission and the Department of Defense would execute it.

The Congress did not like the organizational change in the Defense Department because it put another layer of bureaucracy between the leglislators and the military services. The Navy favored a centralized space agency, but was not concerned whether it was inside or outside of the Defense Department. The Army welcomed the new agency within Defense because Army officials saw the bureaucratic shift as an opportunity to extend their influence over the military space program. The Air Force had just expanded its Atlas, Titan and Thor intercontinental ballistic missile programs and was opposed to the change.

The Air Force, in fact, argued persuasively during the Congressional inquiry into the missile program that its ballistic missile program was so sound that no new space agency was needed, inside or outside of the Defense Department. Said General Bernard A. Schriever, commander of the Air Force ballistic missile division, "Our present studies have shown that by using our presently existing rocket engines and missiles, we can provide both at the earliest date and at the greatest economy, not only unmanned reconnaissance of the moon, but also a basic vehicle for manned space flight."[19]

Schriever testified that by the 1960s the Titan booster could be lifting payloads greater than a ton and a half into orbit—could be used for manned flights—and the Atlas could be adapted to make soft lunar landings. On this point, General Schriever was supported by the Air Force's own civilian science advisors.

When Eisenhower submitted his civilian-controlled program to the Congress, however, the military services quickly glossed over their differences of opinion and pushed for control of space programs in a central agency of the Defense Department.

Eisenhower sent the Administration bill to Congress on April 2, 1958. Hearings began April 15 in the House and May 6 in the Senate. Defense officials were particularly opposed to a section of the bill requiring that space activities be directed by a civilian agency "except insofar as such activities may be peculiar to or primarily associated with weapons systems or military operations, in which case the agency may act in cooperation with or on behalf of the DOD." Defense saw this provision as a severe reduction of its mission in space. Undersecretary of Defense Donald Quarles and others argued that the civilian space agency should be responsible for only those activities which fall clearly outside military research and development.[20] In this they were supported by Army and Navy spokesmen. The Air Force, however, had begun to consider the civilian space agency less of a threat to its missile programs than a military-dominated agency. A civilian agency might, in fact, increase Air Force involvement in space. Thus Air Force spokesmen reversed their previous position and strongly endorsed the civilian agency. They warned, however, that it should take care not to impinge on military programs.

NASA and the Congressional Compromise

The two houses of Congress split on the issue. McCormack and the House committee, though seeing no reason to exclude the Defense Department from conducting basic research in space or performing its military function there, if necessary, preferred civilian control. The House committee thought it especially important that the space agency director have a firm hand over policy decisions and liked the Administration bill's approach.

The Senate space committee, with its heavy representation from the Armed Services Committee, and influenced by Johnson's desire for military domination of outer space, was opposed to major parts of the Administration bill. The Senators did not want Defense to be dependent on policy decisions made by a civilian bureaucracy when matters of national security might be at stake. If, for example, the DOD should decide it would be militarily desirable to put a man into space, said a Defense spokesman, it should not have to justify its decision to "this civilian agency." The Senate committee's proposed solution to the problem was to create a high-level board which would establish national space policy and mete out project assignments according to their military or civilian nature. The high-level board would have more Defense Department representation than the agency envisioned in the Administration bill but would still have a civilian majority.

On May 12, 1958, the Administration amended the section of its own bill which had provoked the most resistance. The amendment said clearly that Defense would be responsible for space activities in which weapons systems or military operations were concerned, rather than, as previously, that the civilian agency would cooperate with or act on behalf of the DOD in space. The Army was still unhappy with the wording and pushed for a stronger Defense Department role in space missions.

On May 24, the House committee reported out a bill even stronger in its guarantees of civilian control of space than the amended Administration bill. The bill cleared the House unanimously, an indication of the importance the congressmen attached to the space program in general.

Nine days later the Senate committee reported out a bill much stronger than the amended Administration bill in its guarantees of Defense responsibility in space. The Senate, too, unanimously passed its bill, including a provision for a high-level policy board to assure that military as well as civilian interests in space were protected.

For the next couple of weeks, attempts to reach a compromise failed. Then Johnson contacted the President directly and persuaded him to go along with the Senate position on the policy board. Eisenhower agreed, certain that the program would be in civilian hands and eager to get the legislation enacted. This deadlock broken, arrangements were made for a Senate-House conference to hammer out a bill agreeable to both sides. The conference committee met July 15 and Senator Johnson presided.

The final version of the bill provided for space activities to be directed by a civilian agency except where weapons development, military operations, or national defense was concerned, in which case the Department of Defense would direct the activities. These explicitly included research and development activities in the interests of defense as well as defense missions in space. The new high-level policy board was named the National Aeronautics and Space Council. It included the President, the secretaries of State and Defense, the chairman of the Atomic Energy Commission, the administrator of NASA, one other undesignated government official, and up to three private citizens appointed by the President.

Conclusions

The space program provided for in the National Aeronautics and

Space Act of 1958 was no typical program of scientific research and development. Its scope so exceeded the requirements of science—as envisioned by the scientists who advocated the exploitation of space for the benefits it could bring to mankind—that it was not really a scientific program at all.

The importance of the space program for national defense was clearly established in the Act, despite the fact that the National Aeronautics and Space Administration (NASA) was not to be controlled by the Defense Department. The importance of the space program for maintaining national prestige was also established by placing policy direction in the hands of the highest officials of government.

Of the four reasons for space exploration, outlined in the Purcell committee's report, "An Introduction to Outer Space", the one this committee of scientists thought most important, "scientific observation and experiment," was relegated to last place during the legislative battle. The U.S. Senate, under the energetic leadership of Lyndon Johnson, had managed to broaden the space program far beyond the interests of science.

In November, Eisenhower sent Johnson to the United Nations to present a U.S. resolution urging that the exploration of outer space be undertaken for peaceful purposes and be a cooperative international effort. "Men who have worked together to reach the stars are not likely to descend together into the depths of war," the resolution said. It belied Johnson's own thoughts of U.S. domination in space and the goals of the new space program. By the following September, the House Select Committee on Astronautics and Space Exploration had become so convinced of the importance of space for national defense that it reported on the matter in no uncertain terms:

"It cannot be overemphasized that the survival of the free world—indeed, all the world—is caught up in the stakes. Outer space is fast becoming the heart and soul of advanced military science. It constitutes at once the threat and the defense of man's existence on earth."

The House committee had argued during the year that the U.S. was behind the Soviet Union in the technology of astronautics. Who was ahead in the space race was the subject of much dispute and political rhetoric. Just as the committee was meeting to adopt its report, the news broke that the Russian rocket Lunik II had hit the moon. Lunik II was the first successful moon probe and the committee took the event as vindication of all the views in its report.

The possibility of Russian explorers reaching the moon before Americans was real.

The House committee insisted that yearly budget pressures should not get in the way of the space program. Success in space, the report said, would depend on a long-term effort. The House is the traditional watchdog of the federal budget. Here, from within its ranks, was a plea to loosen the purse strings for the space program. The peaceful applications of space technology, the committee report said, would more than repay the economy within a decade. The expectations for the space program, then, were that it would contribute to national security and pay for itself through the commercial application of space technology.

By this time there was a growing body of opinion, public and Congressional, that reaching the moon might provide the sense of national security that nuclear weapons had failed to provide. Besides, reaching the moon had been an aspiration of mankind for centuries. In a highly competitive world, better the competition be linked to the hopes of mankind than to his ultimate destruction.

Eisenhower believed that American security depended on whether a nuclear test ban treaty could be successfully negotiated, not whether an American would be the first to walk on the moon. This view and the desire to keep the space program a scientific enterprise worked against the kind of massive effort required for NASA to undertake a moon program. In addition, Eisenhower was opposed to big spending, even for purposes of recovering from the economic recession of 1957-58. He preferred to let the economy recover by giving industry a free hand. But there was a growing danger here, too. The alliance formed between government and science during World War II had necessarily enlisted industry in its gigantic research and development efforts. By the end of Eisenhower's first term, government and private spending for research and development was ten times what it had been just before the war, and half of the money was being spent on weapons development.[21]

By the end of his second term, Eisenhower had found the trend so difficult to reverse that he thought it prudent to warn the nation of the dangers he foresaw. "In the councils of government," Eisenhower said in his farewell address, "we must guard against the acquisition of unwarranted influence, whether sought or unsought, by the military industrial complex." He was concerned, he said, that the alliance of the military and industry might become so powerful that "public policy could itself become the captive of a scientific-technological elite" rather than the domain of all the people.

Eisenhower, by the end of his Presidency, was beginning to understand the wisdom of Woodrow Wilson's comment almost fifty years earlier about the dangers of a democratic society resigning the task and giving the government over to experts. But Eisenhower's view was influenced by developments in science and technology that would have been difficult for Wilson to conceive of in 1912. After two years of arduous nuclear test ban negotiations by the "experts," a self-imposed moratorium on nuclear testing, and an unsuccessful summit conference in Paris, Eisenhower began to give up hope for a test ban agreement.

Such was the situation when John F. Kennedy took office in January 1961. Kennedy was committed to ending the nuclear arms race as much, or perhaps even more, than Eisenhower. He even made concessions to the Russian position on nuclear test site inspections, but the Soviets became more demanding with each concession. What was to be done?

● THE APOLLO PROGRAM

John Kennedy came to office with a compulsion to restore confidence in the intellectual and technological capabilities of America and to reduce insecurity in foreign affairs. He had a Congressional majority that was willing to appropriate funds to achieve these aims.

Kennedy thought of science and technology as a vast national resource that could be tapped to do good works and to accomplish national goals. He thought of scientists as objective thinkers with a strong sense of public responsibility. He shied from the military industrial complex, but placed confidence in the scientific-technological elite. These were the sentiments he expressed on April 25, 1961, when he dedicated a new wing of the National Academy of Sciences:

"For those of us who are not expert," Kennedy said, "and yet must be called upon to make decisions which involve the security of our country, which involve the expenditures of hundreds of millions or billions of dollars, we must turn, in the last resort, to objective, disinterested scientists who bring a strong sense of public responsibility and public obligation. So this Academy is most important."[22]

The decision of whether to commit the nation to an all-out effort in space must have been weighing heavily on the President's mind when he made that speech. His modest budget proposals for space activities had reflected the view of those "disinterested" Academy members who feared that a manned moon program would rob other research efforts of vital government funds. Only thirteen days before, however, Yuri Gagarin, the Russian cosmonaut, had electrified the world by becoming the first man in space, while America's own first manned flight into space lay some distance in the future.[23] American inferiority in the size and thrust of rocket engines was a national embarrassment.

Kennedy's special assistant for science was Jerome B. Wiesner. He had been a member of the President's Science Advisory Committee under Eisenhower and had testified in favor of improvements in the Air Force missile program. One of Wiesner's jobs was to keep Kennedy informed of the opinion of his colleagues around the country. In the case of whether to pursue a crash program in space, of the magnitude of the bomb project two decades earlier, the majority of scientists were opposed. Of the minority who favored dedication of massive resources to space, most did so for the prestige they thought it would bring to science and the inspiration to mankind, not because they thought the U.S. had to beat the Russians to the moon. Few favored a manned moon expedition. Philip H. Abelson, editor of *Science,* the journal of the American Association for the Advancement of Science, later took an informal poll of his readers and found that an overwhelming 110 of 113 working scientists who responded thought the government should not undertake it.[24] Kennedy knew the scientists' views.

Pressing the issue from the other side, of course, was Lyndon Johnson, now Vice-President, who had used all his political skill to fashion a space agency that would be capable of achieving American superiority in space. And then there was the Defense Department.

Defense had its back to the wall. Its missile bases were plagued by strikes and cost overruns that the Senate was investigating. And in May 1961 the news broke that the CIA was behind the inglorious Cuban Bay of Pigs invasion. Something had to be done to restore pride at home and to regain prestige abroad. The Pentagon responded by supporting the moon program.

The Decision to Land a Man on the Moon

According to one trustworthy account,[25] the Apollo program was worked out over a "hectic" weekend session in late May attended by a small group of government officials, including Secretary of Defense Robert S. McNamara and NASA Administrator James E. Webb. The

President wanted to make a decision on the program that Monday, so the work went on round the clock. Wiesner was there off and on, according to the account, and he was torn by his loyalty to his colleagues and his loyalty to the President, who was looking to the space program as a graceful way to get himself and the country out of a jam.

On May 25, 1961, Kennedy presented the program in an address to the Congress: "First, I believe that this nation should commit itself to achieving the goal, before this decade is out, of landing a man on the moon and returning him safely to earth. No single space project in this period," Kennedy said, "will be more exciting, or more impressive, or more important for the long range exploration of space; and none will be so difficult or expensive to accomplish."[26]

Kennedy asked for an immediate authorization of $531 million, mainly for research and development of various types of boosters "much larger than any now being developed." And he outlined a program for subsequent years approaching two billion dollars per year, the equivalent of the war-time level of spending on the A-bomb project. By the time Neil Armstrong took that one small step onto the moon in 1969, NASA was spending four billion dollars a year for research and development alone.

Those National Academy scientists whom Kennedy had addressed exactly a month before he announced the Apollo program may have been insulted or amused that he had not turned, as he had promised, to their objective advice on a matter of such financial and technical magnitude. But Kennedy had found no time for the deliberations of scientists.

Thus abruptly, the U.S. was in the outer space ball game. To restore U.S. prestige, a victory would be required. Once the decision was made to send a manned space craft to the moon, only technical considerations were relevant. As in the decision to use the A-bomb, the technical goals were those that would guarantee success in the mission and speed in development.

NASA officials believed that success depended on developing a rocket that could make a direct flight to the moon and back. Their position was that the other option, to use a smaller rocket which could be refueled in earth orbit, would increase the chance of failure. Developing the huge boosters necessary for a direct flight would take time and money, but money was no object.

There was another school of thought, as the following story illustrates. Arthur Kantrowitz was among a dozen scientists whose advice on missile programs was regularly sought during this period by the Air Force. He was (and still is) an engineering physicist and chairman of Avco Everett, a private research laboratory which helped develop the technology for the reentry of ballistic missile nose cones into the earth's atmosphere.

Kantrowitz' recollections are interesting historically for what they tell of the political circumstances and the mood in the months just before the President proposed the manned lunar landing. But his story also illustrates one of the recurring problems in the politics of science—the frustration of the scientist called on to inject what he considers to be clear scientific facts into the murky business of political decision making. It was this experience in frustration that started Kantrowitz thinking about reforms in the advisory process. Here is his story, transcribed from notes taken during a conversation with him in October 1977.

"I was on a committee with a bunch of other scientists—I can't even remember the name of the committee now—but Trevor Gardner, the assistant to the secretary of the Air Force, chaired it and we reported to General Schriever. Our job was to advise the Air Force on the space program. That was in the days when NASA was brand new and it really hadn't been cleared up yet whether the Air Force had responsibility for the program or NASA.

"Anyway, the discussion on the committee centered on two alternatives we felt we had for getting a payload to the moon. We could go with the boosters we already had in production and make the moon launch from an assembly in orbit around the earth. Or we could develop a new booster with enough thrust to take off directly from the earth.

"I was in favor of going with the available technology. There was no doubt it could be done. The boosters were in production. Their production costs were going down. The development cost alone for the earth to moon booster would be very high. And then after all that development, it would be a one shot production. You see, this booster had to have a precise amount of thrust to get to the moon. It couldn't be a thousand pounds over or a thousand pounds under.

"The general feeling on the committee was that we should go with what we already had developed. And this was the feeling among other scientists outside the committee, too. Sometimes I find myself in the minority on these things, but on that occasion I was with the majority. The NASA representative on the committee, though, did not agree.

"The committee produced a report. Twenty-five copies of it were made. They were classified top secret—not even distributed to members of the committee—and locked up in some White House safe. To this day, I imagine, they are still there.

"I found it shocking at the time that the report was classified. It could have been circulated. It didn't contain any secrets. I felt something had to be done to get the message across. So I sat down and worked out the arithmetic to show how much cheaper the earth orbital assembly approach would be. And it came out to be ten times cheaper.

"I sat down with Jerry Wiesner and we went over the arithmetic together for a couple of hours. Wiesner went to Kennedy with it—it would be interesting to see what Jerry says about this now—but he said then that Kennedy's answer was, 'This is none of your damn business.' That set me back on my heels. That's when I knew something was terribly wrong," Kantrowitz said. Then he was silent.

Wiesner admits freely now that political considerations and not scientific ones were behind the decision to go to the moon and the decision to develop a new rocket for the mission. The decision was "totally politically stimulated," Wiesner told a Congressional science advisory group in February of 1977 during an informal discussion of federal funding of research. "I was a bit reluctant about it," he reminisced, "because the challenge was not 'can we do it' [land a man on the moon], but 'what is the fastest, most efficient way.' "

As it turned out, NASA did end up with a space craft rendezvous, but the plan—a lunar orbital rendezvous—was not even conceived until 1962 and, by then, development of the new and more expensive prototype Saturn rocket was already well underway.

Conclusions

The decision to undertake the Apollo program and major decisions about how the manned moon mission should be carried out were marked by disagreement among scientists. It galled many scientists that the huge public expenditure for the Apollo program was being justified on the grounds that it was a scientific program. Warren Weaver, in the May 1963 issue of the *Bulletin of the Atomic Scientists* said the pace of the program was "frantic, costly and disastrous" and that the prestige of science would suffer if people were led to believe that scientific progress came from dramatic thirty-billion-dollar extravaganzas like the manned lunar program. He suggested—a very popular idea among scientists—ways that thirty billion dollars could better be spent on science and said the emphasis of the program on the physical sciences would be detrimental to the biological and medical sciences.

But other scientists, like L.V. Berkner writing in the same issue of the *Bulletin,* felt that the scientific benefits of the space program would justify the huge engineering costs. "The scientific cream of the program," wrote Berkner, "involves less than ten per cent of the total costs, yet it embraces essentially all of those elements from which the ultimate success of the program will be measured."

President Kennedy, no doubt, saw in the space program the opportunity to serve many national purposes: maintaining strength in foreign affairs, increasing capability in defense, raising national morale and purpose, and giving a boost to the economy. According to an account by Wiesner, published in *Science* a week after Kennedy's assassination, the President was convinced that the U.S. should be first in the mastery of space and remained convinced throughout his administration.

Public opinion was on the President's side and he nurtured it with wit and skill during numerous news conferences. The public was better informed about the space program than it had been about weapons development and supported the space effort. Kennedy's zeal and Russian successes in space combined to convince Congress that the technological enterprise in general was worthy of extended high levels of government support. The annual increase in government spending for research and development was more than twelve per cent during the Eisenhower and Kennedy years. After Kennedy, the annual increase dropped to about five per cent.[27]

• EPILOGUE

America was, during the early 1960s, in love with big technology, the kind associated with advancement in space, defense, and atomic energy. These took almost ninety per cent of the public dollars spent on research and development. One per cent went to universities for basic research, the kind of research dearest to most of the highly placed science advisors who were themselves mostly university researchers-turned-administrators. The other nine or ten per cent of research and development money was spent in agriculture, manufacturing, health, and related fields of study.[28]

By the time Neil Armstrong took his walk on the moon, national priorities had shifted. A limited test ban treaty in 1963 and the prospect of success in the space program in subsequent years put the country at ease about the potential for nuclear war. As the reasons for a hard-line policy toward the Soviet Union began to disappear,

Cold War defense policy collapsed and with it public support for science in the cause of national security and prestige. "By improving our technological intelligence capability," Wiesner told a gathering of scientists who supported the Johnson and Humphrey ticket in 1964, "we learned we had vastly overestimated the Soviet military strength and in the process probably misinterpreted their intentions as well."[29] The news that yet another technological breakthrough— this one in intelligence—was responsible for our new friendship with the Russians may have delighted Wiesner's audience. But people were beginning to wonder whether technology had not been as much the cause of Cold War insecurity as it had been the cure. And whether the present security was not due as much to renouncing the nuclear arms race as it was to discovering Soviet military weakness with new sophisticated techniques.

President Johnson read the changing public mood correctly. He wanted to shift national resources to the domestic front, but he was unable because of the country's deepening commitment to the disastrous Vietnam war. Yet his aim is worth noting. His Great Society was to be "a place where man can renew contact with nature . . . a place which honors creation for its own sake and for what it adds to the understanding of the race . . . a place where men are more concerned with the quality of their goods than the quantity . . . where the meaning of our lives matches the marvelous products of our labor." Johnson's ideal society was going to be a place where basic science and craftsmanship flourished. It was not going to be a society run by big technology.

By the time Johnson left office, the pace of government spending for technological research and development *had* slowed and the pace of spending for social programs *had* picked up. The research and development budget reflected a growing interest in environmental research. But about eighty per cent of the funds was still going to defense, space, and atomic energy. Two per cent was spent on basic research at universities and the remaining eighteen per cent was spent for agricultural, manufacturing, health, and environmental research and development. Only six-tenths of one per cent of research money, about ninety million dollars, was spent on the urban improvement and poverty programs of the Great Society.[30]

The society Johnson described, with its love of art, quality, and nature, was based on an astute observation of social changes about to take place. By Johnson's election in November of 1964, the reaction was beginning to set in against rapid technological change and its step-children: unplanned growth, consumption, waste, damage to the natural environment, economic vulnerability, and inflation.

But the Johnson Administration did not try to stop—in fact supported—many of the technical development programs initiated earlier. Big technology behaved as an object, set in motion during World War II and accelerated by the post-Sputnik programs of John Kennedy. There were twenty-five years of gathering inertia behind it. To slow it would take a movement nearly equal in force and opposite in purpose. Big technology was encouraged by scientists and lawyers, bureaucrats and congressmen, economists and consumers. The movement to slow it down would need scientists and lawyers, bureaucrats and congressmen, economists and consumers who saw the world differently. And most of all, the movement would need one really good issue.

In 1970, such an issue appeared, so to speak, out of the clear blue sky.

II.

The Case of the U.S. SST: Disenchantment with Technology

- **"THE FORCES HE RELEASED IN THIS WORLD . . . "**

Theodore Sorenson said in his biography of John F. Kennedy that generations would remember the President for "the forces he released in this world." The drive of people to use technology to free themselves from physical and psychological limitations was one of the forces Kennedy helped to release. He did it with the space program and everyone over thirty years old remembers the part he played. He provided a release for our technical impulse through other government programs which we undertook almost without questioning their ultimate value, or even our immediate goals. One of these was a program to develop a U.S. supersonic transport plane.

Origins of the U.S. SST Program

On a summer day in the shadow of the Rocky Mountains, President Kennedy announced the first government venture in civilian aircraft development to—of all people—the 1963 graduating class of the Air Force Academy. "It is my judgment," he told the graduates and the assembled Air Force brass, "that this government should immediately commence a new program in partnership with private industry to develop at the earliest practical date the prototype of a commercially successful supersonic transport superior to that being built in any other country in the world . . ." [1]

The British and French governments already had a cooperative supersonic transport program underway and the Soviet Union was developing its own SST. In the back rooms of the Federal Aviation Agency and NASA, the idea of commercial supersonic transport had been receiving official attention for several years. Likewise in the basic research divisions of the nation's aircraft manufacturers, the design problems of supersonic transports had been under study for years. As a commercial venture, however, the SST was a poor risk. In the committee rooms of Congress, talk of the SST evoked one of two reactions: do it now for national security reasons regardless of the cost, or wait and let private industry develop it when the economic conditions were more favorable.

Kennedy tried to steer a course down the middle, between the faction that saw the foreign competition as a threat and the faction that would not support the SST unless its commercial merit could be demonstrated. To win the support of the latter group, the program would proceed as a private venture and, to reassure the security-minded group, the government would put up most of the capital for development. The guardians of national security in the Congress and in the Air Force were still smarting from a cutback in the Defense Department's B-70 bomber program and were lamenting the end of manned weapons systems. For them Kennedy had this comment during his Air Force Academy speech. Some people, the President said, claim "that Air Force officers of the future will be nothing more than 'silent silo sitters,' but nothing could be further from the truth." Civilian aviation, he continued, has long been "both the beneficiary and the benefactor of military aviation."

In reality, advances in military aircraft had regularly, up to this point, led to the development of commercial planes. In 1960, Science and Astronautics Committee members and Armed Services Committee members in the Senate, Lyndon Johnson chief among them, had argued for the B-70 program on grounds that it was essential to a future SST program. By 1963, no one had found a way to adapt the B-70 design for commercial use. Could the President be suggesting that the tables might be turned, with development of a commercial SST somehow leading to future manned military transport aircraft?

This notion was surely in the back of Vice President Johnson's mind as he chaired a cabinet-level committee on the SST in the early months of 1963 and reported its conclusions to the President five days before the Air Force Academy speech. By the day of the speech, however, the major reason for a government-supported SST was economic: to maintain the country's lead in commercial aircraft sales. Poorly documented assertions about the commercial potential of an SST, made in the interest of justifying the B-70, took on new importance. American air carriers were in financial trouble from overextending their resources on the last generation of passenger jets, for which the manufacturers had not recouped their development costs, either. If industry was to take on a new project, it had to be commercially viable, for both the manufacturer and the airlines. The alternatives for the airlines were to buy the British-French Concorde or risk losing passengers. The day before Kennedy's speech, the president of Pan American World Airways announced that his company was taking options on six Concordes, so that Pan Am could stay competitive with BOAC and Air France.

Economics of the U.S. SST: 1960-63

The first estimate of the cost of developing an SST that got serious Congressional attention came during the 1960 hearings of an investigating subcommittee of the House Committee on Science and Astronautics. Chairman Overton Brooks (D-La.) asked for an estimate from Ira H. Abbott, director of NASA's Office of Advanced Research Programs. The research director demurred and joked about how the cost would exceed the estimate, however high, but he suggested a figure of one billion dollars. [2] It stuck.

The estimate came to be thought of as the outside limit the following year when the FAA queried airframe and engine builders and was told that the most elaborate development program could be done for about seven hundred million dollars. [3] The manufacturers also told the FAA that direct operating costs of the SST would be the same as or slightly higher than the costs of operating subsonic jet transports.

Independent economic analyses of the SST program were not as optimistic as cost estimates that rolled off the tongues of government and industry officials who favored the program for subjective reasons. Rand Corporation economists, in a 1962 report contracted by the FAA, said that SST development would cost at least two billion dollars, twice the ball park estimate that NASA's Abbott had given the House investigating subcommittee in 1960. The FAA was not satisfied with the Rand analysis and cancelled the company's contract for further work. [4] The FAA supplied the Rand data to the Stanford Research Institute (SRI) and asked for a separate analysis.

About two months after Kennedy's announcement of the program, SRI sent the FAA its final report. " . . . There is no direct economic justification for an SST program," the report said. "On the basis of presently available technical and preliminary design information, the most economic SST will not be as economic an aircraft to operate as the present long range subsonic jet." The SRI report made it clear that the only economic justification for U.S. SST would be so that the U.S. could stay competitive in aircraft sales. The price to be paid for achieving this goal, the report said, would be "extensive underwriting of ownership costs and/or fare surcharges on some route segments."

The SRI economists estimated that U.S. manufacturers could sell 115 SSTs to foreign carriers if the planes were considerably faster than the Concorde, had a better flying range, and were available within three years after the Concorde. The plane would cost $1.3 billion to develop, would probably require operating subsidies, and would bring $3.6 billion in foreign money to America. A plane with the same speed as the Concorde but better flying range, the report said, would cost $1 billion to develop and would bring in $1.4 billion in foreign exchange. [5]

The FAA did not publicize these findings; the distribution of the report was restricted. The Congress was left to believe some earlier testimony of FAA Director Elwood R. Quesada that "operating costs would be generally in line with those for current subsonic jet transports." [6]

President Kennedy knew that the economics of the SST were uncertain when he presented the program to the Congress on June 14, 1963. He had decided, however, that it would be worth putting up a certain amount of government money just to stay in the game, to see if "the flexibility and ingenuity of private enterprise," as he put it, could meet the competition from abroad.

Kennedy outlined a program for the Congress in which the federal government would pay three-quarters of the development cost of the SST and industry one-quarter. He estimated that the total program would cost one billion dollars and promised that, whatever the cost, the government share would not exceed $750 million. The government would be paid back with royalties from the sale and use of SSTs. And there would be no government subsidies to the manufacturers or the airlines after the plane was developed. The first SST would take off in 1969, about the same time the first American would walk on the moon.

The President asked the Congress for a modest sixty million dollars that year for the government's share of SST design work. Immediately the request met with some opposition. But the opposition was centered around one issue: Whether the program was justified on the grounds of its contribution to national prestige.

The nation's prestige, said Senator J. William Fulbright (D-Ark.), would not suffer if someone other than America this time were to build "a bigger—and more expensive—mousetrap." Fulbright said he failed to see how three-quarters of a billion dollars in government subsidy to airplane builders would square with the concept of free enterprise.

Fulbright's view was shared by some very liberal and some very conservative members of Congress. But the vast majority believed there was also a direct correlation between a nation's investment in technology and its economic well being. Conventional wisdom in 1963 was that technological development pays for itself directly, through jobs, profits, and a favorable shift in the international balance of payments, and indirectly through a phenomenon known in Washington as "technology fall-out"—unforseen applications of new techniques.

Jerome Wiesner, Kennedy's science advisor, knew he could get a sympathetic hearing for the SST program if he talked generally about the payoffs of technology. "I believe we will all agree," he said to the aviation subcommittee of the Senate Committee on Commerce in October 1963, "that the economic progress and security of the nation are closely tied to its level of scientific and technological development. It is our objective to increase our competence, in depth and breadth, as we proceed into the future, and we should not willingly allow our scientific or technological capability to deteriorate in any significant technical areas.

"Even if we were not faced with imminent international competition," Wiesner said, "I believe that the development of a commercial supersonic transport is a step that we would wish to take sooner or later in a logical advance of our long-distance transport capability." [7]

Wiesner's and similar arguments won the day. The sixty million dollars was finally appropriated in November 1963, just days after Kennedy's assassination. Despite the objection of Congressional opponents of the SST, the action came before the Administration worked out a plan for marshalling the financial resources of government, industry, and the lending institutions in a way that would be likely to meet the goal of developing a commercially successful airplane. Kennedy had appointed Eugene R. Black of the Chase Manhattan Bank as a special advisor on the financial aspects of the program in August. Black spent four months talking with executive officers of major air-frame and engine manufacturing companies and with his colleagues in the money-lending business. He made his recommendations to President Johnson on December 19.

Black's report [8] heartily endorsed the SST program but recommended that the government assume more of the financial risk while giving industry considerable leeway over the design of the prototype plane. The banking executive said, among other things:

- that the government share for producing a prototype airplane should be ninety per cent of the successful bid and industry's share, ten per cent;

- that the U.S. SST should be a superior alternative to the planned Concorde, especially as regarded speed, and that the exact design should be determined during development by the manufacturers in consultation with the airlines.

Black's report also pointed out that commercial success would depend on two things: 1) how economically the SST could be operated under actual airline conditions, and 2) what restrictions would have to be imposed on SST operation because of the compression wave, or sonic boom, that results at supersonic speeds. "Unless solutions to these important unknowns are found," Black said, "the entire program could fail to become commercially feasible, regardless of all other considerations."

Despite the cautious tone of the Black report, the FAA was eager to get on with the design phase of the project. The deadline for preliminary design proposals from industry was only a month away. Tacitly, government was counting on industry to come up with the technical breakthroughs necessary to meet some very optimistic performance objectives. And industry was likewise counting on government to yield where necessary on cost and technical specifications in order to develop a plane, more advanced than the Concorde, that the airlines of the world would want to purchase.

Design of the U.S. SST: 1960-63

The staff of NASA's Langley Research Center had, indeed, done preliminary design studies of the SST in anticipation of the House investigating subcommittee hearings. It was those studies which FAA Director Quesada had cited when he testified in 1960 that SST operating costs would be in line with the costs of subsonic jet transports.

What Quesada failed to point out was that the NASA staff had concluded "that the cruise part of the flight can now be achieved with efficiencies comparable to those of present jet transport aircraft" but that planes designed to fly efficiently at supersonic speeds "have serious limitations in the off-design areas, specifically: take-off, climbout, inflight emergencies, and holding."

The NASA staff was convinced that the subsonic part of the flight could be as efficient as the cruise part if the plane could be designed to change the position of its wings during the flight and if some fundamental improvements could be made in engine design. [9]

The basic technical problem that had to be solved if the SST were to be commercially successful had to do with the payload that could be carried. Each plane had to be able to carry enough passengers to make its operation profitable. The great advantage of the SST in the profit picture was its speed. A faster plane could make more trips in a given period of time, and the enthusiasts at the FAA frequently emphasized this point. What they deemphasized was that speed would have no commercial value if, to attain it, the design of the plane could not accommodate enough passengers to make a well-booked flight profitable. In other words, the airline executives knew they could not make up with extra trips what they lost on each trip.

When NASA did its technical studies in 1960, the staff was talking about an SST that would cruise at Mach 3 (three times the speed of sound, or 1,980 mph) and carry 100 passengers between New York and Paris in two and a half hours. The plane would weigh 375,000 pounds. More than half the take-off weight would be fuel and only about five per cent would be passengers and cargo.

To illustrate the technical problems involved, the NASA staff postulated what would happen if such a plane had simply to change its hold altitude from 35,000 feet to 5,000 feet. A maneuver like this for which the SST would not be well suited, NASA said, "requires an increase in fuel reserve of one ton, which effectively eliminates approximately twelve passengers if this weight is taken out of the payload."

When the FAA talked with the manufacturers the following year, the consensus was that a 400,000 pound SST could be designed to travel at Mach 3 and carry 120 passengers. The companies were nearly unanimous in their belief that the best design would include a large, triangular (delta) wing and a small, stabilizing wing known as a canard, located near the front of the plane. The government request for design proposals and bids from manufacturers in August 1963 specified simply that the plane had to better the Concorde's Mach 2.2 cruise speed and carry 125-160 passengers (30,000 to 40,000 pounds) a distance of 4,000 miles.

Already, the FAA, under Kennedy-appointee Najeeb E. Halaby, was putting a premium on both the payload and flying range of an airplane that was no more than a concept and whose development costs could only be guessed at. Because the commercial objectives were high, so were the expectations of the airlines. Two days before the Senate avaition subcommittee hearings in October 1963, Trans World Airlines ordered six of the non-existent U.S. aircraft, not from the manufacturer—there was no manufacturer yet—but from the FAA. Pan American, upstaged by TWA and concerned lest its earlier announced plan to buy Concordes would be unfavorably construed, placed an order for fifteen planes. The apparent interest of the airlines brightened the aircraft industry's view of getting involved in a crash government program.

At this time, there had been no technical progress to justify hopes for an SST that could outperform the Concorde in speed *and* payload. The technical problems were dutifully mentioned by administration spokesmen. Wiesner, for example, told the aviation subcommittee about the problem of the SST's small payload to gross weight ratio and the operating inefficiencies that would result from flying a supersonic plane at subsonic speeds. But Administration officials also stressed that the necessary technical improvements could be made, and this was encouragement enough for that group of influential congressmen who believed, as Wiesner put it, that the country "should not willingly allow our scientific or technological capability to deteriorate."

Eugene Black, the Chase Manhattan executive, thought that a technically superior SST could be developed and that it might even be a commercial success in competition with the Concorde. But he thought the FAA was handling the program, like other crash development programs, without the prudence that commercial development projects require. And he feared that the results might be a colossal failure unless the government gave the manufacturers free rein in determining what design trade-offs would have to be made in order to come up with a plane that could be operated profitably.

Airport Noise and the Sonic Boom: 1960-63

The sonic boom is a noise created by a compression wave that occurs along the path of an airplane traveling faster than sound. An airplane produces an especially intense boom when it accelerates from subsonic to supersonic speed. But the compression wave is produced all during supersonic flight and reaches the ground with varying intensity, or overpressure as it is called. A wave that exerts just two pounds more per square foot than air pressure (2,116 pounds per square foot) can produce a very loud cracking sound, like a whip, and a sonic boom of three pounds overpressure can shatter glass.

The sonic boom is one of the intractable problems of supersonic flight. The NASA staff noted this in their 1960 studies of the SST and decided that the solution would be to restrict planes to subsonic speeds until they reached high altitudes. "The noise problem of the sonic boom requires subsonic operation in climbout until high altitudes are obtained," the NASA staff reported.

General Quesada, the FAA director, mentioned NASA's solution when he testified before the receptive House investigating subcommittee, in 1960, but he told the congressmen there was a difference of opinion on whether high altitude would "meet the sonic boom problem effectively." Some respected aeronautical engineers, the most outspoken of whom was Sweden's Bo Lundberg, did not agree that altitude would necessarily mitigate the boom. Unlike the other problems of supersonic flight, no technical improvements had been postulated that would significantly reduce or do away with the boom. Generally, the only way to keep the boom small was to keep the plane and especially the protruding wing area small. That, however, would mean an unacceptably small payload.

Engine noise, the technicians thought, was a different story. Increased power requirements of the SST, Quesada testified, would not have to mean increased noise. The burden of his testimony, in general, was that an SST could and should be designed to meet existing environmental standards, including noise and pollution limits, and airport requirements, including airplane weight and runway length limitations. "If it is made clear from the outset that the next generation of aircraft must be compatible with the flying environment," he said, "there is no reason why we cannot enjoy the benefits of further aviation progress without suffering any offsetting penalties."

The FAA said in its 1961 report, "United States Development of a Commercial Supersonic Transport Aircraft," that the sonic boom was the primary operational problem facing the SST. By that, the FAA did not mean the sonic boom was the problem SST designers would be expected to concentrate on. They meant it was the problem least likely to be solved. And the report acknowledged that up-to-date information suggested that the intensity of the boom might not be acceptable even if supersonic flight was restricted to high altitudes. The FAA theorized that people would tolerate a boom of two pounds overpressure, but no more, and decided to verify the theory by having NASA and the Air Force conduct some actual test flights.

The FAA report barely acknowledged the problem of engine noise. A new engine had to be designed to meet the thrust requirements of the SST. The FAA expected that noise limitations could be an integral part of the design work, that technology would provide the solution.

When the performance objectives came out in the FAA's August 1963 request for proposals, it became apparent what the government was expecting. The plane designers had to be sure the boom intensity would not exceed two pounds per square foot during acceleration and one and a half pounds during supersonic cruise. And the SST engines had to be at least as quiet during approach and take-off as those of subsonic jets.

- ## THE MOTIVE FORCES: PROFITS AND POLITICS

Back to the Drawing Boards: 1964-68

In January of 1964, three airframe and three engine manufacturers responded to the FAA's request for preliminary design proposals. The FAA had announced publicly that if a combination of plane and engine designs were proposed that would meet the performance criteria, the government would proceed with that "winning combination." If not, the FAA's Halaby had said, the government would choose two airframe and two engine manufacturers who would continue design work until one combination emerged as superior. This combination would be given the go-ahead early in 1965 and the competing manufacturers would drop out of the picture.

Though the airlines saw some merit in this procedure—it could result in a more economical plane and, meanwhile, they could be amortizing their debt on the subsonic jets—industry was lukewarm. Somebody was going to lose millions of dollars in the competition and, worse, the design schedule and other corporate decisions would be subject to political demands and pressures quite different from those ordinarily imposed by the market. If the manufacturers' return on investment had been more promising at this early stage or if the program goals had been better defined, the first round design effort might have been more enthusiastic.

Lockheed proposed the fastest and theoretically the safest SST design. It would fly at Mach 3 and carry 218 passengers. Its "double delta" wing configuration was chosen after years of experimental work that had convinced Lockheed of its safety and efficiency at slow speeds. But the flying range of this craft was limited by its speed and payload characteristics.

Boeing proposed a design that would fly at Mach 2.7 and carry 150 people. It was based on a "swing wing" design—the wing could be swept back during supersonic flight—that the company had developed while competing unsuccessfully for a contract on a military supersonic plane. The design was radically different from that of the Concorde and from what most manufacturers considered practical. The plane's modest passenger carrying capacity and technical complexity were drawbacks, but the concept was right in line with NASA's thinking.

North American, designer of the B-70 prototype bomber which had encountered such political controversy, proposed an SST designed for Mach 2.65 and a capacity of 187 passengers. North

American's design featured a fixed delta wing with a stabilizing wing up front, much like the B-70 design.

The three engine manufacturers—Pratt & Whitney, Curtis-Wright, and General Electric—proposed various turbojet and turbofan engine designs with nothing superior enough about any of them to promise both quiet and fuel-efficient operation.

A team of government and airline specialists, called the Supersonic Transport Evaluation Group, gathered to review the designs. By May 1964, they had concluded, much to Halaby's dismay but to the surprise of no one in the industry, that none of the engine/airframe combinations would meet the FAA's objectives for both payload and range. The designs gave absolutely no assurance of meeting the sonic boom limitations chosen arbitrarily by the FAA, nor the overriding, general requirement that the SST would be profitable in commercial operation.

The hard fact that the British and French governments had faced when they decided to underwrite the Concorde in 1962 was that the operating costs of a supersonic transport were certain to exceed those of its subsonic counterpart regardless of design. The Europeans did not base their program on expectation of commercial success. The FAA did, for political reasons. The prospect of a program that would eventually pay its own way would appeal to congressmen who were generally opposed to extravagant federal spending; thus the FAA maintained the fiction that the SST could be designed for economic operation.

When the design proposals came in and none met the FAA requirements, the whole program might have foundered on the rocky shore of reality had other forces not kept it on course. Industry had already invested much of its own money in SST research and design studies. One of the companies stood to make a handsome profit from the sale of a plane that compared favorably with the Concorde, regardless of operating economics. It also looked as if the airlines were going to have to buy Concordes, regardless of their operating costs, if a superior American plane were not produced. That, or lose first-class fare passengers to their European competitors.

The airline representatives on the evaluation team decided the prudent course would be to have the government let contracts for further development of at least two different airframes and engines. This squared with Halaby's fall-back plan and it was all right with the manufacturers if the government contracts were big enough to demonstrate the federal commitment to the project. Though this delay in the original program would cause him some bad publicity in an election year, President Johnson had favored SST development from the start, had urged Kennedy's cabinet to report favorably on it, and wanted to see the program through. He preferred stretching out the program to scrapping it altogether. On April 1, 1964, he appointed a special Presidential Advisory Committee on the Supersonic Transport and put Defense Secretary Robert S. McNamara in charge of it.

On June 1, 1964, the FAA awarded six-month design contracts to Boeing and Lockheed and to General Electric and Pratt & Whitney. By the time the contracts had expired and the government had tested dozens of variations on the original designs in NASA's wind tunnels, however, there still was no clearly superior design.

Out from under the political pressure for accountability that comes at election time, Johnson found it expedient to extend the design contracts and let the companies continue to compete. On July 1, 1965, on the recommendation of the McNamara committee and with the President's concurrence, the FAA awarded eighteen-month contracts to the four companies to proceed with detailed design work and the testing of component parts. The objects of this final competition, according to public pronouncements from the FAA, was to design an SST that would be safe and reliable for passengers, that would have the potential for profitable operation, and that could be produced in time to be competitive with the Concorde. In reality, the pressure to pick a design that would be superior to the Concorde in speed, range and payload and a company that the airlines would have confidence in overrode all the other considerations that the FAA had emphasized in Congressional testimony and public statements since the inception of the program. If these other considerations—engine noise, sonic boom, development and operating economics, safety, and reliability—had been more important than gross sales, the clear choice, according to independent economic analyses, would have been an SST designed to be superior to the Concorde only in flying range.

Indecision at the FAA, bred of the lingering hope that SST designers might find a way to meet all of the program objectives, turned to decisiveness only after certain of the standards were abandoned. The FAA turned over its responsibility for evaluating the effects of the sonic boom to the National Academy of Sciences and responsibility for reviewing SST economics to a group at the Department of Commerce. The design choice was as difficult as ever to make in December 1966, but time was running out on the program. The Concorde prototypes were being built. The Congress would not appropriate money indefinitely without seeing results. The government group decided to go, for better or worse, with Boeing's swing wing design.

It was a debatable choice, because, at the last minute, Boeing designers had decided they could not cut down on the weight and size of the wings and engines as much as they had hoped in the interest of increasing the payload and reducing the boom. What they came up with was a very large plane, larger in all respects than the gigantic Lockheed SST. The moveable wings held promise of greater fuel efficiency at supersonic speeds and of reducing the sonic boom, but to get the required payload off the ground, they had to be big. Lockheed had solved that problem with a wing design which had excellent lift characteristics and would assure smooth handling at slow speeds—but at a sacrifice in fuel efficiency and, therefore, in flying range.

Until Boeing went to the large wings and heavy, rear-mounted engines in the summer of 1966, Lockheed's more conservative design was clearly the only one the government reviewers could choose and still believe the thing would fly safely. In Boeing's final design, however, they saw an SST that would fly safely and that just might, because of the theoretical efficiencies of the variable wing, have a commercial advantage over the Lockeed design. In Boeing, the airlines saw a proven builder of commercial aircraft. There was skepticism about the novel design, but there was also confidence that Boeing would make it sound before going into production with it.

Once the design choice was made, it was obvious that previous FAA design requirements, like gross weight limitations and other standards that would make the plane "compatible with the flying environment," no longer applied. The Boeing SST was going to weigh 675,000 pounds—almost twice the original specification—and it was not clear whether there was an airport big enough to handle it.

The same sort of sacrifice of the original program goals occurred in the choice of engine design, because engine designers faced the same basic problem that airframe designers did: What was efficient at supersonic speeds was not efficient at subsonic speeds and vice versa. Supersonic flight called for a turbojet design and subsonic, a turbofan. Pratt & Whitney went with the turbofan, because it could be modified to produce extra thrust without a noisy feature of the turbojet called afterburning. General Electric went with the turbojet, partly because of the flight time logged with GE turbojets on military supersonic aircraft. In spite of the potential noise problems of the turbojet afterburners and in spite of tests that showed superior thrust from the relatively lighter-weight engine that Pratt & Whitney had, so far, developed, the FAA went with the turbojet design. Experience with the engine and confidence in GE were big factors. Noise and weight—originally integral parts of the design problem—were not the major considerations in the choice.

On April 29, 1967, the President authorized the Department of Transportation to sign an eighteen-month contract with Boeing to produce two identical prototype SSTs. Within ten months, it had become clear that the company was having serious trouble with its swing wing design. In February 1968, Boeing asked for a delay in the construction, and a little less than a year later, admitted failure. Abandoning the swing-wing concept altogether, Boeing submitted a proposal to the FAA for a new fixed-wing design.

Politics and Congressional Financing: 1964-68

At the beginning of the design competition in the spring of 1964, with $91 million already spent on the SST program, President Johnson began drumming up Congressional support for the more expensive phases of the program. Najeeb Halaby had decided not to stay on as FAA chief, and the Administration had to find a replacement who had the management skills necessary to run an agency which, in addition to other pressing programs, was conducting a huge new experiment in cooperative public and private enterprise.

Secretary of Defense McNamara, whom Johnson had appointed his top SST advisor, recommended retired Air Force General William F. McKee. Since leaving the Air Force, McKee had spent six months in a research management position with NASA and no one questioned his administrative qualifications. The prospect of the general's appointment, however, stirred comments in the press about the militarization of the SST program and debate in the Congress about the militarization of the FAA, an agency which, by law, was to be run by a civilian.

To opponents of the SST, aware that the program originated in the interest of national security and prestige, McKee's appointment was the fulfillment of Eisenhower's prophecy about the dangers of the military-industrial complex. To proponents of the program, McKee's appointment raised the prospect that the program would progress, unhampered, much like a military development program and that the military value of the SST would not be overlooked. It was this Congressional coalition—mainly moderate to conservative

Democrats—that the President nurtured. The Senate confirmed McKee's appointment on June 30, 1965, and the next day President Johnson announced the eighteen-month extension of design contracts that eventually led to the choice of Boeing and General Electric.

To finance this last round of design work, in August of 1965 the Administration proposed a $140 million appropriation for fiscal year 1966. The figure was large enough to keep the program going but not so large that it converted Congressional believers into critics. Many members of Congress simply did not take the time to scrutinize the budget proposal because the war in Vietnam and the space program, among other things, were attracting their attention.

There had been rumors of a Commerce Department report that was very pessimistic about the operating economics of a plane with the speed, range, and carrying capacity FAA was looking for. But no Commerce Department study saw daylight on Capitol Hill. Some objection had also been raised in the Senate when, on August 20, General McKee named another Air Force General, Jewell C. Maxwell, as director of the SST program. The protest was short-lived, however, because nothing in the law prevented FAA subordinates from being military men and Maxwell had an impressive record as chief of Air Force bomber development in the 1950s. The House subcommittee that handled the appropriations of the independent agencies, of which the FAA was one, endorsed the President's budget request and that was good enough for most congressmen. They appropriated the funds.

As budget time came around again in the late summer of 1966, the Congress was looking at a $280 million appropriation—the kind of outlay characteristic of defense and space programs with the highest national priority. Eighty million dollars of it was to finance the last six months of the design competition and the remaining $200 million was to cover the first six months, or one-third, of prototype construction. Anyone could look at the figures and tell that more than $500 million would be spent on the SST by mid-1967 and a minimum of $400 million more would be needed to finished prototype construction, and still no guarantee that the plane would be a commercial success. Anyone in the Congress could look at the figures this way, but few wanted to.

As long as the French and British stuck with their plans to introduce the Concorde into commercial operation, SST proponents had persuasive economic arguments on their side. To stay competitive, U.S. airlines would buy Concordes; American dollars would flow by the billions to Europe and upset the balance of payments. If U.S. airlines ignored the competition and lost passengers to BOAC and Air France, they would probably need government subsidy to stay alive—more, perhaps, than they would need to subsidize an American SST that turned out to be an economic failure. All of these arguments were reinforced by the airlines' rush to place orders. There were deposits, now, for about one hundred planes and the demand gave the non-existent SSTs the appearance of value, though the value was totally unrelated to the ultimate ability of the planes to generate revenue.

The whole economic framework of the SST program, in fact, rested on the assumption that the Concorde would be an economic success. Because the Concorde was designed to carry only 120 passengers, it was evident that the passengers were going to have to pay a hefty premium for the savings in travel time, if the Concorde was to operate economically.

SST critics in Congress began to challenge these basic assumptions when they faced the $280 million SST appropriation in the summer of 1966. "This is more than a quarter-billion dollars," said Representative Clark MacGregor (R-Minn.), "for a project which at best rests upon a speculation—that the Concorde is going to be successful."[10] In the Senate, William Proxmire (D-Wis.) argued that the SST would benefit only the very wealthy "jet set." The overwhelming majority of Americans, he said, though they would spend billions on the plane, would never ride in one.

Those arguments were not powerful enough to kill the big SST outlay at this critical stage in the design competition and on September 6, 1966, the appropriation bill passed. But the program managers knew they had a public relations job in front of them, especially on the economic questions, if they wanted government funding to continue. So the FAA got Boeing to come up with all the necessary figures for FAA economists to review. The agency published an Economic Feasibility Report in April 1967. As it happened, the study was very positive about the return on investment for everyone involved—the manufacturers, the airlines, and the U.S. government—and the report was released just weeks before the President authorized Boeing's prototype construction contract and submitted his fiscal year 1968 SST request for $198 million.

The economic study estimated that growth in long-distance air travel would create a market for a minimum of five hundred SSTs by the year 1990, and perhaps as many as 1,200 planes by then. The minimum figure was twenty-five per cent higher than FAA's own optimistic estimates four years earlier. That figure had been double the estimate of banker Eugene Black and, likewise, twice the market estimate made by the Stanford Research Institute in 1963.

The FAA and Boeing, however, thought recent growth in air travel justified the estimates, even if the sonic boom problems might rule out overland routes and regardless of how profitable the SST would be to operate. If a majority of the Boeing SSTs were sold abroad, the FAA figured, the U.S. would have an overall gain of $32 billion in its balance of payments as against a $6.5 billion loss if U.S. airlines had to buy foreign SSTs. Not only did the FAA analysis assume high sales of U.S. planes, but it credited the U.S. balance of payments ledger for Concordes that American carriers would not have to purchase. The analysis assumed only a small reduction in sales of 747s, as if sales and production of the jumbo jets would not be affected by Boeing's SST program. The FAA's economic analysis did not include any estimate of potential losses in U.S. tourist dollars. Though other government economists thought the U.S. SST would cause a deficit in the tourist trade account, the FAA ruled out of its analysis everything but aircraft sales figures. Thanks to these dubious devices, the FAA figures furnished an impressive justification for the program. The balance of payments argument was one that got political mileage.

For those airlines who did not believe FAA's claim that the SST would be as economical to operate as subsonic jets, General Maxwell, the SST program director, spread the word that SST passengers would be willing to pay a surcharge for the time they saved. The surcharge, he said, could be as much as one and a half times the passenger's hourly earning rate for every hour he saved—so highly did people value their time. The FAA did not survey people to determine whether the figures had any basis in reality or what effect, if any, a fare surcharge would have on ridership. This was simply the agency's way of admitting that a surcharge might be needed and would be officially condoned.

To this positive economic picture was added the promise that, if the program continued, the government would not only recover, but make money on, its investment which was now ninety per cent of contracted SST development costs and seventy-five per cent of overruns. "The taxpayers of this Nation will benefit," President Johnson said in his April 29, 1967, statement. And, he added, there would be intangible benefits. "Jet aircraft have already brought the world closer to us. Commercial supersonic transports—traveling at

1800 miles an hour or even faster—will make South America and Africa next-door neighbors. Asia will be as close to us as Europe is today."[11]

Presidential poesy and the overblown figures from the FAA did not influence Senate SST critics, but it made their case more difficult to argue. Among their ranks, now, was Senator Robert F. Kennedy (D-N.Y.), the late President's brother, who favored postponing the program until the need for it could be more carefully documented. The fight for the $198 million appropriation was led by the two Democratic Senators from Washington State, the home of the Boeing Company, Senator Warren G. Magnuson and Senator Henry "Scoop" Jackson, plus two influential members of the Armed Services and the Space and Aeronautics committee, Senator Stuart Symington (D-Mo.) and Senator A.S. "Mike" Monroney (D-Okla.).

Congress appropriated $142.4 million in October. The figure was $55.6 million less than President Johnson had requested, but it was plenty to keep the program alive, and enough to bring the public expenditure within $100 million of the $750 million ceiling that John Kennedy had promised.

- ## EQUAL AND OPPOSITE FORCES: THE POWER OF THE PEOPLE

From the spring of 1968 to the spring of 1969, there was a lull in SST development. President Johnson was having problems waging a war overseas and keeping peace at home and announced that he would not run for reelection, a decision that heightened election-year tension for many congressmen. They had neither the time nor the desire to debate the merits of the SST program and they appropriated no funds. The Boeing Company, wrestling with the swing-wing problem, was hardly ready for more construction money anyway. The company waited to announce its shift to the fixed-wing design until the elections were over.

Dissent Within the Administration

A month after taking office, President Richard M. Nixon decided he had better have an interdepartmental committee, under Secretary of Transportation John A. Volpe, review the whole SST program. Simultaneously a group of science advisors, chaired by IBM physicist Richard L. Garwin, was reviewing the program under the auspices of the White House Office of Science and Technology.

The Garwin committee, also known as the Supersonic Transport Review Committee, issued a concise report to the President on March 30, 1969, but it was kept so confidential that no one outside the White House knew what it said or even that it had been completed.[12] The next day, the interagency review group sent its report to President Nixon who withheld that, too, from release.

Not until the morning of September 23 did the new President step into the Roosevelt Room of the White House to give reporters the first official news from his Administration about the SST program. "The supersonic transport is going to be built," the President told them. "The question is whether in the years ahead people of the world will be flying in American supersonic transports or in the transports of other nations. And the question is whether the United States, after starting and stopping this program, after stretching it out, finally decides to go ahead . . . I have made the decision," he said, "that we should go ahead."[13]

Nixon hinted that there had been some dissent—"a very spirited debate," he called it—within the Administration, but he refused to discuss the substance of the debate and he kept the interagency report and the Garwin committee report under wraps. His stated reasons for continuing the program were to keep American aircraft manufacturers outselling foreign competitors—four out of every five jet transports in operation were American-made—and "to bring the world closer together."

The President asked the Congress for $96 million for the 1970 budget year. That figure still left the total funding below the promised $750 million limit. To assure program continuity, however, Nixon said he planned to request $566 million more over the next four years.

When the House subcommittee which handled Department of Transportation appropriations held hearings on the SST, the only official documentation they had to consider was the President's message and a new FAA report which updated the 1967 economic feasibility report. The new report made essentially the same point as the earlier one: "The basic conclusion is that the program is not only economically viable but reasonably profitable to all participants over a wide range of assumptions."[14] In the report, however, the FAA revised its uppermost estimate of the market for SSTs downward from 1200 to 800 planes. The estimate of minimum sales remained at 500 planes. A more striking revision was a change in the estimated net foreign revenue from $32 billion to $17.1 billion.[15] Nevertheless, the figure remained sufficiently impressive, and the subcommittee voted out the appropriation bill.

Meantime, Representative Henry Reuss (D-Wis.) was battling the Administration over the release of the report of the SST Ad Hoc Interagency Review Committee, charging that Nixon had violated the federal Freedom of Information Act. Reuss won the fight and, on October 31, 1969, Representative Sidney R. Yates (D-Ill.) had the full report added to the appropriations subcommittee hearing document and printed in the *Congressional Record*. "The report is so unfavorable to the program," Yates said, "that I am amazed that President Nixon approved the request for the SST."[16]

The report was, indeed, pessimistic and was obviously an accurate account of the views of the agency representatives, many of whom appended comments objecting to an earlier attempt to soften its critical tone. The report noted that the program might actually result in a balance of payments deficit, if American tourist dollars spent abroad, and not only aircraft sales, were accounted for.[17] It questioned whether Boeing could finance a plane-building program which would cost twice the company's net worth without sacrificing its other programs, for example, the 747.[18] The report questioned whether the SSTs would actually sell and whether they would be economical to operate. It concluded that the sonic boom and engine noise would not be within acceptable limits. Finally, it suggested that water vapor emissions from SSTs might disturb the chemical composition of the stratosphere.[19]

Negative as it was, the report of the interagency committee sent no shock wave through the House of Representatives. Though for the first time an Administration report challenged every economic assumption on which the program was based and pointed out other potential problems of SST operation, it did not conclusively refute the assumptions. To proponents of the SST, it was only the other side of a debatable issue. Yates and Reuss led the fight against the SST appropriation, but their efforts to reduce the funds ended in defeat, with a two to one margin in favor of the full $96 million budget request.

The SST ran into bumpier weather in the Senate, however, partly because the interagency report legitimized the debate that had long been raging there. The Senators voted to appropriate only $80 million, and a conference committee of the two houses finally compromised at $85 million for fiscal 1970. That made a total of $738.4 million in public funds, or $708 million not counting the money spent on research before fiscal 1964.

Congressional critics of the SST program were bothered by the lack of information provided by executive agency spokesmen during hearings that session and began to suspect that Administration dissenters knew more than they were saying. Lee A. DuBridge, the President's science advisor and a member of the ad hoc interagency committee, for example, was personally opposed to continuing the SST program. He had told the chairman of the interagency group in March 1969, "the government should not be subsidizing a device which has neither commercial attractiveness nor public acceptance."[20] But when President Nixon announced that the program would proceed, DuBridge began to support the decision in his public statements. During the course of Congressional hearings, however, DuBridge mentioned the Garwin committee report which he had been instructed by the President not to release. He staunchly refused to release the report, citing loyalty to the President as his reason, but word of the report's existence was enough for some of the legislators who promptly invited Garwin to testify at the next round of hearings. Meanwhile, the Administration's refusal to face the sonic boom issue was generating popular opposition to the SST program.

Overpressuring the Grass Roots

By the winter of 1969, when the reduced appropriations bill went through, American citizens had gained considerable experience with sonic booms from military aircraft exercises and flights designed to test public tolerance. General Maxwell, the SST program director, said that people would become adjusted to the sound of commercial SSTs booming their way across the country on regularly scheduled flights, as they had become adjusted to the annoyances of other forms of transportation.

The big Boeing plane, however, was going to create a boom even bigger than most FAA and higher-level government officials thought would be tolerated. It would produce at least two pounds overpressure during supersonic cruise and two and a half pounds during acceleration to supersonic speed. There was much evidence to show that the sonic boom would not be accepted, despite a reassuring 1968 report from the National Academy of Sciences that the effects on buildings and other structures would be negligible.[21] The Nixon Administration, therefore, promised to restrict supersonic flight to routes over oceans and unpopulated land masses.

Popular experience with the sonic boom had not been happy. The first test that NASA and the Air Force ever conducted to see what the public reaction would be to a transcontinental supersonic flight was a public relations disaster. The test actually had two purposes: to demonstrate the speed and endurance of the Air Force's B-58 "Hustler" bomber, thus quieting the detractors of manned strategic aircraft, and to evaluate the public reaction to the boom. On the first point, Operation Heat Rise, which took place on March 5, 1962, had been a rip-roaring success. The plane raced all the way from Los Angeles to New York in two hours and 57.2 seconds, at nearly twice the speed of sound, and returned to the West Coast 45 minutes ahead of its New York departure time. The relatively small B-58, however, left in its historic wake shattered windows and upset citizens. Hundreds of claims were filed against the Air Force; the exact number is obscure because the government hastily settled the claims out of court.

Between 1960 and 1964, the Air Force conducted sporadic tests over major U.S. cities, under the guise of Strategic Air Command training sessions. People complained to their representatives in Congress, but often got the official justification in response—that the flights were somehow part of defense preparedness—even after the Air Force admitted its real motives. People who came to realize that the booming was connected with the SST development program and not with the national security were as appalled by the deceit as they had been by the booms.

One of these people was Representative Roman C. Pucinski (D-Ill.), whose Chicago constituents has been subjected to the Air Force tests in the early months of 1963. The same week that the FAA issued its very first requests for SST design proposals from manufacturers, Pucinski introduced a bill to ban any future civilian flights over the U.S. that would produce booms of one and a half pounds overpressure or more. As most legislative measures which anticipate the public mood rather than react to it, this bill died a very early death. It was a signal to SST advocates, however, that the sonic boom was going to be one of the most serious obstacles in their path. Because NASA and FAA officials reported no technical solution in sight, the government redoubled its effort to gather data showing that people could tolerate the boom.

On February 3, 1964, the FAA undertook its first systematic study of public reaction to scheduled booms. In government circles the project was known as Operation Bongo. Publicly, it was known as the Oklahoma City Sonic Boom Study. The government probably could not have picked a more accepting group of people to blast with the sound of progress than these hardy Westerners whose prosperity was bolstered when the FAA moved to town, and one of whose Senators, Mike Monroney, was a devoted SST backer.

At first, there were jokes about the eight daily booms, but little public opposition. As the intensity of the booms was increased to two pounds per square foot overpressure, however, the complaints increased. After about six months and 1,250 booms, the portion of Oklahoma City residents who said they could accept the noise had dropped from ninety per cent to seventy-three per cent. And the wire services spread the news across the country, though the FAA failed to report it, that the booming had cracked dozens of windows in two Oklahoma City skyscrapers.

At the conclusion of the Oklahoma City study, the FAA began to realize that its boom experiments were making people angry without really proving that the preordained boom limit would be acceptable. At this point, the FAA decided to turn the research over to the National Academy of Sciences and to have further tests confined to a row of dummy buildings, standing like a movie set in the New Mexican desert. But it was too late. People who had served as guinea pigs in half a dozen cities had organized to protect themselves from perceived and real damages. By 1967, when most of the five thousand estimated boom damage claims had been settled and appeals had made their tortuous way through the federal courts, confidence in government programs generally was very low, especially ones in which the military was involved.

The FAA tried to counter the opposition in a report called "The supersonic transport; the sonic boom and you." The report echoed the shallow optimism of the economic and technical reports on the SST, but press agentry did not work well on people who had contradictory information available from their own experience. Instead, it made the other pronouncements suspect.

William A. Shurcliff, a Harvard physicist, decided the case against the sonic boom would have to be as carefully documented by citizens as the case for it was being documented by the government, if citizens wanted their views to be taken seriously by policy makers. In March of 1967, Shurcliff and a colleague in the biology department formed a group in Cambridge, Massachusetts, called CLASB (Citizens League Against the Sonic Boom). Within six months he had fifteen hundred donating members, ordinary citizens from all over the country who recalled their bad experiences with the boom. CLASB was also in touch with citizen groups in Europe, intent on preventing overland flights of the Concorde. By 1969, Shurcliff had compiled enough information on the sonic boom to print a handbook for members of CLASB to use when they wrote to their congressmen. The subject was gaining popular recognition, press coverage was increasing, and Shurcliff's book was published commercially in 1970.

Shurcliff can be credited with striking the first grass-roots blow against the SST in Congress, but he was not the only scientist or even the first to protest. Bo Lundberg, director general of the Aeronautical Research Institute of Sweden and a former test pilot, irritated by what he thought were unjustified assumptions of the U.S., British, and French governments that sonic booms would be acceptable, raised the problem at a variety of forums, International Air Transport Association conferences, and U.S. Congressional committee hearings as early as 1960. Though bills were pending in the Congress in early 1967 to let the Secretary of Transportaion determine "acceptable" boom overpressure limits, Lundberg raised so many technical objections to the FAA's evaluation of the Oklahoma City booms, that the legislation never passed.

In 1969, DuBridge, the President's science advisor, recommended to the interagency review group a policy against SST flights over populated areas.[22] But Lundberg and the Shurcliff group at once protested the implication that people in sparsely populated areas should have to tolerate the booms. By 1970, the grass-roots sentiment had made the sonic boom a hot political issue, and the FAA was forced to rule out all but over-water routes. In so doing, they eliminated about a third of the trips on which SST market estimates—though not FAA's high estimates of 1967 and 1969—had originally been based.

The Environmental-Taxpayer Coalition

When the ninety-first Congress reconvened in 1970, all the basic arguments for and against the SST program seemed to be out in the open, but one. Environmental protection groups entered the fight that session, raising a novel and alarming specter: that SST flights might cause dramatic changes in the earth's climate, and, as a result, might even increase the incidence of skin cancer. Their statements were based on the theory that water vapor emissions from a fleet of five hundred SSTs could alter the chemical composition of the stratosphere.

In 1966, the National Academy of Sciences had published a report, "Effects of Supersonic Transport Aircraft on the Stratosphere," in connection with a larger study of weather and climate modification. The report concluded that SST operations would probably have no adverse effect on the climate. But subsequent research on the chemistry of the stratosphere led some investigators to believe that incomplete data might have led the Academy to erroneous conclusions.

One suggestion that stimulated particular interest was that accumulations of water vapor in the stratosphere, greater than the Academy study postulated, might have the effect of reducing the amount of ozone. Ozone, essentially oxygen with an extra atom per molecule, is an indispensable element in the stratosphere because it limits the amount of the sun's ultraviolet rays that strike the earth. Overexposure to ultraviolet radiation was, at the time, generally accepted to be a cause of skin cancer and was also thought to retard the growth of plants.

Through the spring of 1970, Congressional battle lines hardened. President Nixon, realizing that the future of the SST program would depend on support from highly placed Administration officials, moved the program from the FAA to the Office of the Secretary of Transportation and appointed a new director of SST development.

William M. Magruder, the new director, had been the SST technical manager at Lockheed. It was Magruder who had insisted on the large, fixed-wing and aft engine configuration for the Lockheed SST and whose wisdom had been affirmed when Boeing scrapped their swing-wing design. Magruder had also been the world's first pilot to travel faster than the speed of sound in a commercial transport, and was definitely bullish on the SST. On his recommendation, Nixon requested $290 million for the 1971 budget year.

Opponents of the SST also were preparing for a fight on the appropriations bill. A dozen national groups, including environmentalists, labor unions, and conservative taxpayers, formed a Coalition Against the SST and developed a lobbying strategy. CLASB, the sonic boom group, and the labor unions used traditional lobbying techniques—visits to Congressional offices, newspaper ads, and letters from their members.

The Sierra Club and Friends of the Earth took another tack, making an issue of the President's continuing refusal to release the Garwin committee report, the only major review of the program conducted by non-government scientists. Their legal maneuvers failed to get the report released in time for Congressional hearings that year (it was not made public, in fact, until August of 1971), but the effort served to focus attention on Garwin's personal testimony, scheduled for early May of 1970 before Senator Proxmire's subcommittee on economy in government.

Because it was part of the Joint Economic Committee, the subcommittee had members from both houses of Congress. The record of that hearing, therefore, had a potentially wider Congressional audience than the record of other subcommittee hearings. In addition, Garwin, as an IBM scientist, was an especially credible witness: he had no anti-industry bias that might make criticism of the program suspect. And he stated, at the outset of his testimony, that he would honor the President's decision to keep the work of his panel confidential by basing his comments only on reports and documents that were publicly available. Garwin nevertheless made a powerful case against the SST program.

The IBM physicist described how, in the past three years, the characteristics of the prototype SST had been changed, without the knowledge of the Congress, to the point that the plane would produce intolerable airport noise, require longer runways than those of the most modern airports and, probably, require the government to underwrite production costs as well as development costs. To illustrate just how far the SST had evolved beyond the plane Congess had agreed to, Garwin offered this comparison: the SST, he said, would produce as much noise as the simultaneous takeoff of fifty jumbo jets.[23] The Congress had recently enacted legislation to limit subsonic jet noise, expecting the SST to come within the limit or at least very close. The subcommittee members were surprised to learn how far the FAA had strayed from the original intent of the program.

"Regardless of the benefits or lack thereof of the supersonic transport program," Garwin said, "there is a question of the adequacy of the procedure by which the Administration and the Congress decide to proceed with such a program . . . [I believe] there has been less than adequate, and in many cases distorted, information available for this decision process . . ."[24]

Garwin got his point across. Congress was not being told the whole story. He had evidently studied in great detail a series of amended contracts between the FAA and Boeing. And he had come to this conclusion: "I recommend," he said, "the immediate termination of the U.S. government's direct or indirect support of the SST program. When the conditions are ripe for a commercial program which can be accommodated without severe environmental penalties, U.S. industry and finance will rise to the occasion. Government support before that time seems to result in great pressure to continue an uneconomic program, in warping of the environmental protection regulations to suit the machines and not the people, and may well lead to an increase in all air fares if the airlines and passengers are expected to bear some part of the cost of procurement or operation of the SST."[25]

The report of the hearings, published August 17, 1970, showed that a majority of the subcommittee members agreed with Garwin that further subsidy of the SST would be a mistake. They had two major reasons: the dubious commercial prospects for the plane and its environmental drawbacks. Among the stated disadvantages were the sonic boom, airport noise, and the possibility, however remote, that SST exhausts might affect the climate or increase the amount of ultraviolet radiation falling on the earth. The last point was brought to the subcommittee's attention by Russell Train, chairman of the recently established Council on Environmental Quality. Train's testimony was the first from a government official on the subject.

Dissent on the joint subcommittee was based on the belief that the environmental drawbacks either were minor compared with the benefits of the program or could be mitigated. Even if the problems of ozone depletion turned out to be serious, SST proponents argued, other countries would be flying SSTs and the U.S. would be in no position to urge restraint if it had no SSTs in operation—an argument identical to one used by advocates of nuclear weapons development. One of the dissenters on the subcommittee, Representative Clarence J. Brown (R-Ohio), considered the preoccupation with environmental risks a bar to human progress and the spirit of adventure. "If the Joint Economic Committee had been advising Queen Isabella," Brown later told a group of constituents, "you and I would still be sitting in Barcelona wondering whether the world was round."[26]

The House Committee on Appropriations, meanwhile, had approved the full $290 million request in April and the issue was debated on the floor of the House on May 27. The antagonists in this debate were Representative Edward P. Boland (D-Mass.), chairman of the transportation subcommittee, and Representative Yates, the staunch SST critic from Illinois who had attached the unfavorable interagency report to the Appropriations Committee hearing document the previous year.

"To halt the program at this time," argued Boland, "would mean not only the loss of all $708 million appropriated to date . . . but it would also signify a stopping of aviation progress in this country . . . I don't think the world's greatest technological country should attempt to stop such progress." Boland acknowledged the problems of airport noise and the sonic boom and said that federal regulations and design requirements would take care of all the environmental problems. "it has been alleged," Boland said, "that the SST might cause a modification in the world's climate. Such allegations simply are not supported by fact. Even those who make such claims indicate that they are merely speculative . . . "[27]

"I believe the SST," countered Yates the next day, "is a colossal waste of the taxpayers' money. Even if the plane flies successfully—and there is a very serious question as to whether it will—it is doubtful that it will be able to fly into any airport in the United States or to fly out of such airports because of the infernal racket that is created by the noise on takeoff."[28]

Yates reminded his colleagues that the program was going to cost taxpayers twice what had been spent already, twice what had been expected, and several billion dollars more if the government had to finance the production of the plane, too. And, after investing all that money, the government would not even own the plane.

"The Administration says that they will not fly the supersonic planes across the land," Yates said at another point in his speech ". . . I believe if and when the SST comes into being it will be accompanied by the biggest kind of propaganda campaign to woo the American people into accepting [the sonic boom]."[29] After all, Yates said, the program had been going on for seven years and information about its drawbacks was just now coming to light.

The House passed the appropriations bill the day of Yates' speech but the SST money survived by only a fourteen-vote margin—"far narrower," reported *Aviation Week,* "than even the most optimistic opponents of the supersonic transport had been predicting."[30]

Realizing that the vote could go either way in the Senate, the Coalition Against the SST redoubled its lobbying efforts and looked for new ways to bring pressure to bear. The Environmental Defense Fund filed a petition to have the FAA set legal standards for SST airport noise as the agency had for subsonic jet noise. Subsonic jets were restricted to 108 decibels of perceived noise, and the Concorde was being designed to meet that limit. But the FAA was allowing the American SST to exceed it considerably.

The Department of Transportation was required to file an extensive report on the environmental effects of the SST under the terms of the National Environmental Policy Act of 1969. The report was expected to takes months, so officials of the Sierra Club and Friends of the Earth filed suit to halt SST funding until the report was available. At most, the environmental statement would provide some powerful arguments against the SST; at least, the legal maneuver would delay the Senate vote on the appropriations bill.

Senator Jackson, to whose state most of the SST money would flow, was caught in a bind. Though he wanted the project and the jobs for residents of Washington State, he had to honor the spirit of the environmental protection act because its passage had been due, in no small part, to his personal efforts. Backers of the SST thought it could not hurt their cause, anyhow, to wait and see if the opposition would die down.

So the Senate waited, but the environmentalists did not rest. A group of politically savvy young people were working that summer as volunteers in Senator Fulbright's office along with a few Sierra Club members. This group saw, firsthand, the smooth functioning of the pro-SST lobby and read glib assertions in government documents about the economic benefits of the program. Though their own efforts to make legislators aware of the environmental costs of the SST were succeeding, the work would be in vain if the majority of congressmen remained persuaded that the direct economic benefits outweighed these indirect costs. At the urging of Joyce Teitz, coordinator of the Coalition Against the SST, Fulbright's aides solicited statements on the SST from eminent economists around the country.

Even as SST Development Director Magruder sat reciting the litany of economic benefits for the Senate appropriations subcommittee in August, contrary opinions from the nation's foremost economists were arriving in Senator Fulbright's mail. Of the sixteen economists who responded, fifteen flatly disapproved of further government subsidy of the SST and one gave the program a lukewarm endorsement.

Senator Fulbright inserted the statements in the *Congressional Record* on September 15,1970.[31] He was quick to point out that the near unanimity was remarkable among such a diverse group of economic thinkers. Editors all over the country jumped at the opportunity to report that economists Milton Friedman and Walter Heller had agreed on something. "Why," Fulbright asked Proxmire during a rhetorical conversation on the floor of the Senate that day, "has this rather ridiculous program acquired such momentum? . . . It had its origin years ago, I believe, somewhat under the same circumstances as the space program originated, in the idea of competing with the Russians . . . I think it is a sort of childish emotional compulsion that started this thing. But it gets started, and then certain members of the Senate and the Administration and industry become involved and get interested in it and you cannot stop it . . . "[32]

Proxmire had a surprise of his own to spring that day, hoping it would shake up some of his colleagues who still trusted the

Administration to take the environmental issues seriously. The previous Sunday, Proxmire told his colleagues, during a debate with Magruder on the national TV show "Issues and Answers," the SST director had held up a report which he told the viewing audience was the document required to comply with environmental protection laws. In the two days since the show, however, Proxmire's legislative assistant had made some phone calls and determined that the document was, in fact, a draft environmental statement that had been rejected by the Council on Environmental Quality because it was incomplete.[33]

Proxmire's little exposé of public deceit—"SST McCarthyism," he called it—did not win the program any friends among Senators who now questioned its economic justification and who could see the popular support behind the environmental lobby. The Senate vote on the SST appropriation was only a week away and some powerful Senators, like Presidential candidate Edmund Muskie (D-Ma.) were now giving full support to the forces of opposition.

Senator Magnuson counted noses and decided the vote, as scheduled, would surely go against the SST. Through parliamentary maneuvering, he managed to have the vote postponed until after the Congressional break for elections, but still it would be close.

The full Senate acted on the appropriation bill less than three weeks before Christmas. The vote was 52-41 to withhold the SST money. One of the seven missing senators, according to a *Newsweek* story,[34] was SST opponent Senator Mark O. Hatfield (D-Ore.) who found it expedient to be out of town after Senator Magnuson introduced an amendment that would have done away with funds for the Portland airport. Hatfield left town and Magnuson dropped the amendment, but the effort was not enough. No less than eleven such amendments would have been necessary to even up the vote, for rarely is a senator owed a large enough political debt that he can get a colleague to vote contrary to his own predilection on a close issue like the SST.

While the full Senate was voting to cut out the SST money, the Appropriations Committee was bucking up the aerospace industry by restoring aircraft and missile funds to the Senate defense appropriations bill. But a $28 million defense contract was not much of a consolation prize for Boeing. Contractors, subcontractors, the FAA, some of the airlines (which now had made $1 million downpayments on each plane) and the White House had lingering hopes that the SST money would be restored by a House-Senate conference committee. The hopes rose when the conferees agreed to continue to fund the program at a $210 million annual rate, through March 1971. In early February 1971, the chairmen of the boards of Boeing and General Electric met with Nixon aides at the White House and emerged with announcements that the President would help them get the funds restored.[35] An intense lobbying campaign followed under the direction of former Senator Monroney, who had since become president of the National Aeronautic Association. The campaign was so intense a few days before the House was scheduled for a final vote that Minority Leader Gerald Ford told Nixon not to worry.

The lobbying on the other side of the issue, however, was just as intense. Senator Proxmire called a news conference at which he released the statements of twenty-four biologists and chemists warning of ozone depletion and the dramatic rise in skin cancer that could result. The scientists were much more emphatic, now, about the potential for harm. Though computer models of the possible reactions that might take place with extra water vapor in the stratosphere turned up little cause for alarm, a couple of University of California researchers[36] had found evidence that nitrogen oxide emissions, from SSTs and other sources, were much more potent catalysts for the destruction of ozone.

The funding question went to the floor of the House late in March and there, to everyone's surprise, the SST was shot down by eleven votes, a net change of twenty-five votes from the position the House took ten months earlier. The composition of the Congress, of course, had changed. Of fifty-one new members, thirty-three voted against the SST. Eight new Republican congressmen refused to go along with the Administration's position because, they said, their constituents—especially the newly-enfranchised young voters—were writing, urging a vote against the program.

● EPILOGUE

Fortune magazine saw the SST debate as the harbinger of a new era of environmental politics. "A number of Americans," said a January 1971 editorial, "have long been conditioned to assume that government should support and encourage—or, at least, not interfere with—*any* technological advance. The opposite attitude, spreading rapidly in the last three years, is deeply suspicious of new technologies and inclined to assume that the environmental disruption of any advance will outweigh its benefits." The editorial recommended that both of these simplistic attitudes be rejected in favor of "discriminating political judgment that will permit and support certain new technologies . . . and will discourage or repress other technologies," judgment that would take environmental risk into account but not at the cost of stifling technology generally.[37]

It is true that anticipation of the possible adverse effects of the SST on the natural environment was a decisive factor in the 1971 Senate and House votes against the SST. Senator Proxmire attributed final defeat to the ozone depletion issue alone: "It is hard for me to say," he commented at hearings of his economic priorities subcommittee the following year, "but I think the killing blow against the SST last year was the revelation . . . that a large fleet of SSTs could have some effect on the radioactivity on earth, and increase the incidence of skin cancer by depleting the ozone. This is a pretty complicated argument for a lot of people but, as I say, it became one that a number of Senators became aware of, and it may have tilted the balance."[38]

Without popular support and lobbying, however, the environmental arguments would not have been politically convincing. And if the economic promise of the SST were not seriously in doubt, convincing environmental arguments probably would not have tipped the balance. The sonic boom problem was known to everybody before the program began, but the FAA and the Congress could ignore it until citizens organized. The problem of excessive engine noise was a well-kept secret until Garwin exposed it in May 1970, and, even then, the House voted for full funding.

The economic drawbacks of the SST were successfully disguised by the FAA until the statements of the economists came out in the September 15, 1970, *Congressional Record.* Those statements, on the heels of Garwin's testimony, were enough to swing the vote against the SST in the Senate. The ozone depletion problem was still speculative in the spring of 1971 when the House reversed itself. (The precise effects of nitrogen oxides on ozone are still uncertain. Though their potential to catalyze ozone has been experimentally verified since 1971, more recent studies indicate that other gaseous compounds are probably more potent catalysts.[39])

What the public and congressmen began to realize was that, because they lacked information that the FAA had, they could not exercise discriminating judgments about the SST. This stimulated the opposition to dig up facts for themselves. When negative information was found that government officials could have come forward with, it reinforced the distrust of government decision-making, already common among the young. It was this same distrust that had led college students to organize against the war in Vietnam. Their political skills were already sharp, but their influence was increased because now they could vote.

A final, and significant result of the SST fights: in 1972, convinced of its need for independent data on government-supported technical development programs, Congress created an Office of Technology Assessment (OTA).[40] The idea had been discussed for six years in the House Science and Astronautics Committee, but the need for it was insufficiently clear until Congress had been through the experience of having to make a decision without really understanding the technical facts.

The power of the Congress in national affairs had been diminishing since World War II. The executive branch had been growing and the President had assumed powers over the prosecution of war and the spending of government money previously exercised by the Congress. Now the Congress had a chance to regain some of its influence. The OTA would provide an independent source of information for use in evaluating whether technical development programs, pursued by the executive agencies, would meet Congressional goals.

III.

The Case of the North Anna Nuclear Power Plant: Public Risk and Public Relations

Ever since the uses of atomic energy came dramatically into the world, federal government policy has favored development of nuclear technologies—first, to preserve this country's lead in the nuclear arms race and, later, to forestall the use of nuclear weapons by sharing nuclear energy technologies with foreign countries.

Commercial use of nuclear fission for the production of electricity was a by-product of these policies. Fission became an economically competitive way to produce electricity only because of the tremendous government subsidies to developers of fission reactors, arbitrary or non-existent standards for emissions, equipment safety and waste disposal, and the willingness of the government to indemnify nuclear plant operators.

These favorable policies made nuclear power plants attractive to utility company planners who saw the demand for electricity increasing during the 1960s and who foresaw oil price increases and stiffer government regulations for coal-fired plants. Environmental groups were slow to object to the trend because some felt that nuclear plants would be less destructive of the natural environment than hydroelectric plants, coal- and oil-fired plants.

Suddenly, without having taken earlier opportunities to evaluate what the consequences would be of multiplying nuclear power production five or sixfold in the next ten years, federal energy officials are advocating this course of action. And they are being challenged by people who object to nuclear power on principle—who feel that it is wrong to expose future generations to the hazards of accumulating radioactive wastes and emissions when other ways to produce and conserve energy have not been tried as thoroughly.

Underlying this more obscure controversy is the question of whether nuclear power plants can be operated without the accidental escape of large amounts of radiation. The safety issue and the future of nuclear power are inescapably linked. If the public is not convinced that nuclear plants are safe, opposition to building more of them will inevitably increase.

The job of insuring plant safety rests with the Nuclear Regulatory Commission (formerly with the Atomic Energy Commission). The following case study illustrates how these agencies performed while supervising the construction of a nuclear plant in central Virginia and why people are not confident in the nuclear regulatory process.

In March of 1969, the demand for electricity in the Virginia Electric and Power Company (Vepco) service area was growing at a rate higher than ten per cent per year, and Vepco saw its future in nuclear power. On March 21, the utility applied to the AEC for a construction license for the first two of four planned pressurized water reactors which would each have an electrical rating of 892 megawatts (thousand kilowatts). The reactors, the steam supply systems, and the generators would be furnished by Westinghouse Electric Corporation and the rest of the plant would be designed by Vepco and the Stone & Webster Engineering Corporation.

Vepco had already picked the site for its plant, about seventy-five miles southwest of the nation's capital and a hundred miles northwest of the company's first nuclear plant, then under construction near Surry, Virginia, on the James River. The site for the new plant was 1075 acres of woods and gently rolling pastures in Louisa County. There family beef and dairy farms spread across the landscape, interrupted by small, less prosperous settlements and an occasional mobile home.

To operate the plant, Vepco needed a large water supply which it proposed to create by damming the North Anna River and backing up the water into a 13,000 acre impoundment. About 9,600 acres of the artificial lake would serve as a reservoir from which the plant would draw cooling water and the remaining 3,400 acres would be a series of lagoons into which the plant would discharge hot water containing legally permissible amounts of radioactive contamination.

When residents got word of Vepco's specific plans for the site, many were disturbed. About sixty had joined in an unsuccessful petition to the state court of appeals to halt the taking of their land, but most property owners had sold willingly, excited by Vepco's assurances that the lake development would raise the value of surrounding property. Some of the original opponents accepted the inevitability of the power plant once the land condemnation battle was lost. But others were distressed, not only that the plant was going to be built, but that it was going to be a nuclear powered one.

"We are begging you," Mollie Rogers wrote to the AEC on May 28, 1969, [1] "not to allow them to put this atomic plant in. We feel that we need a lot more research done to make it safe before it should be built. Our home is right on the cooling pond, and we fear for our very lives." Mrs. Rogers had noticed that Vepco was preparing the site for its plant and wondered why, since the AEC had not held public hearings or granted the requisite construction permit.

"The Commission's rules and regulations," answered Peter Morris, AEC director of reactor licensing, "permit a company to begin site preparation and construction which does not relate directly to the nuclear portion of the facility, prior to the issuance of a construction permit, but this work is performed entirely at the risk of the applicant and has no effect on subsequent granting or denial of a construction permit for a' proposed plant."

Another resident whose land would border the cooling lagoons was worried about the release of radioactivity from the plant. "I am troubled with the thought that our cattle will have to drink water from the cooling lagoons," wrote Bertha Boxley. "Will you promise me that this water will be free from atomic pollution?"

"Small amounts of radioactive material," the AEC official responded, "are permitted by AEC regulations to be released into the environment at controlled rates and in controlled amounts, provided there is monitoring."

The information was not reassuring. Several residents turned to their representatives in the state legislature and Congress for help in stopping what seemed to them the irresistible forces that would take their land and threaten their way of life. On behalf of a constituent, U.S. Congressman David E. Satterfield (D-Va.) of Richmond queried the AEC about the suitability of the site Vepco had chosen on the North Anna River.

"In reviewing the application," Harold L. Price, AEC director of regulation, assured Satterfield, "one of the principal items evaluated by the Commission is the suitability of the site from the viewpoint of the public health and safety."

● SITE GEOLOGY: IGNORING THE OBVIOUS

By September 18, 1969, the AEC had reviewed Vepco's Preliminary Safety Analysis Report, the basic technical document in the permit application, and had found it incomplete. On that day, Morris, the AEC's licensing director, sent a letter to Vepco asking for further information on hundreds of items. The list of questions filled thirty-eight pages and many of them had to do with the suitability of the site from a geological point of view: the stability of the foundation rock and the susceptibility of the site to geological movement.

"On page IIA-13 of the preliminary safety analysis report," said one of the AEC's questions, "a fault which would project to about 4½ miles northwest of the site is mentioned. Provide information regarding the strike, dip, length, maximum displacement, age, and history of the fault. Have any earthquake epicenters been localized along this fault?"

The AEC's question was not trivial, not a matter of a federal regulatory agency bothering a company with unnecessary detail. About 130 earthquakes had been recorded in Virginia since official tallies were begun in 1774, many of them in adjacent Albemarle County, thirty-five or forty miles southwest of the plant site. The AEC was responsible for assuring that no sign of earthquake activity—particularly no recent faulting, or slippage of rock masses— could be found at the North Anna site. Little, however, was known about the geology of the Piedmont, that ancient, folded region of the country that lies between the Appalachian Mountains and the tidal plain of the Atlantic.

Two months after the AEC sent its long list of questions, Vepco responded to the one about the fault. According to utility officials, the fault was exposed in a privately owned mine near Mineral, Virginia, a small town about five miles southwest of the plant site. Though mine officials, Vepco said, would not permit utility people to examine the fault within the mine, Vepco provided the following information: The fault extended in the direction of the plant site only one thousand feet, then turned southeast for a total distance of "no more than a few miles." The age and history of the fault could not be determined, but there was no evidence of earthquake activity related to it and the fault "has probably been inactive for millions of years." Vepco mentioned no other known faults in the area, though it came to light much later [2] that the utility's engineering contractor, Stone & Webster, had identified one the previous February on a geologic map they prepared of the lake and dam area.

Vepco also failed to point out, in response to the official inquiries, that a Dames and Moore Associates study prepared for Vepco in May of 1969, [3] mentioned that "stability problems may exist" in certain portions of the excavations for the concrete reactor buildings. Dames and Moore geologist Joseph Fischer had recommended in the report that an experienced engineering geologist "thoroughly and continually inspect the excavation as it progresses."

Then it happened. In late January or early February of 1970, according to documents and statements produced years later, [4] the lip of the excavation for reactor unit number 1 caved in. Cleanup operations exposed a seam in the earth that was filled with weathered chlorite rock and that was responsible for the instability of the rock above it.

Robert J. Henry, Stone & Webster's geologist on the North Anna site, reported the rockslide to his supervisor in Boston who quickly dispatched John Briedis, another geologist with the firm, to North Anna. Henry and Briedis inspected the site together and Briedis returned, after the slide was cleaned up, to map the geological features in the excavation.

Four days before Briedis' return on February 23, inspectors from the AEC's Office of Compliance in Atlanta showed up at North Anna to make a routine check on the status of construction and to have an introductory meeting with Vepco management. The inspectors were told of the problem in the excavation and so reported; but none was a geologist and they identified the cause of the rockslide simply as "unstable strata." [5]

By coincidence, on the day Briedis returned to map the excavation, another geologist, not connected with the power plant project, had come to inspect the site out of academic curiosity. John Funkhouser, a member of the faculty at John Tyler Community College in nearby Chester, Virginia, wanted to see if the excavation presented geological features that would warrant a student field trip. The geology professor was amazed at his findings. There in the middle of the excavation was the chlorite-filled seam which he immediately identified as a geological fault—and it was to be the foundation for a nuclear reactor. According to later testimony, he told his guide, Vepco resident engineer Herbert L. Engleman, that he had "a very unusual geologic feature" in the excavation, and asked if he could return at a later date and bring another geologist.

Two days later, William F. Swiger, a Stone & Webster civil engineer, arrived at North Anna to discuss the significance of the chlorite seam with project geologists Briedis and Henry. The three later admitted under oath that they considered the possibility that it might be a fault. Briedis took rock samples to the Virginia Division of Mineral Resources for identification.

According to later testimony from State Geologist James L. Calver, Briedis was informed orally that the chlorite in all the samples and smooth abrasions on some of them could indicate faulting. [6] The geologists, nevertheless, abandoned the theory without tracing the seam beyond the excavation to determine conclusively whether it was or was not a fault and without notifying the AEC of the possibility. The AEC, however, soon received a copy of the mineral analysis, which Calver put in writing to Briedis on March 19. The copy was not furnished by Calver but apparently arrived at AEC headquarters in a letter from Dwight Taylor, the Louisa County landholder on whose behalf Congressman Satterfield had written earlier.

On March 23, 1970, Professor Funkhouser returned to North Anna with Bruce Goodwin, chairman of the geology department at the College of William and Mary, a third colleague, and two students. Funkhouser wanted a structural geologist's opinion on whether or not the chlorite seam was a fault. Goodwin agreed that the feature was, indeed, a fault. The three professors discussed the fault with Engleman, the Vepco engineer in charge, and asked him if he were not concerned about it. [7] Engleman later testified that he did not think the discussion was significant enough to report to superiors, and those above him have sworn that he did not report it to them.

The geology professors used photographs of the fault in their lectures but never considered making an issue of it to the AEC. "We assumed geologists were being consulted and figured they knew what they were doing," Goodwin said in a recent interview. "But apparently they [Vepco] got some bad consulting work." The geologic feature was so obvious, Goodwin said, that a freshman geology student "should be able to identify it as a fault." [8]

At the end of April, the AEC licensing director in Washington notified Vepco that answers to some questions about the preliminary safety analysis report were still lacking and were necessary for a proper evaluation of the project. In the same letter, Morris told Vepco, "We have concluded that for your site, diagonal reinforcement of the containment will be required."

By the time of Morris' letter to Vepco, AEC inspectors from Atlanta had made three more trips to North Anna and had reported on the special efforts of construction workers to stabilize the walls of the excavation with rock bolts. Walter Butler, who was the AEC's North Anna project manager at the time, said in September of 1977 that he had never seen the inspection reports and never knew any inspections took place prior to construction licensing. [9] How such a failure of communication between the compliance and the licensing divisions could have occurred is one of the mysteries of the North Anna case. But some word of the stability problems must have gotten through to the licensing staff for Morris to conclude that special reinforcement requirements would be necessary. It appears that licensing division officials simply failed to make use of the inspection reports, not that they were unaware of the reports, as Butler says he was. Butler's superiors definitely knew the previous reports existed when, in October of 1970, a compliance official in Atlanta sent copies of a July inspection report (marked as the sixth that year) to Morris and three others in licensing, plus Edson Case in the regulatory branch. The July report gave Vepco particularly bad marks on its quality assurance plans.

The early reports tell explicitly of the problems in the excavation for unit 1 and emphasize that the inspectors had repeatedly told Vepco of the need to volunteer information about any problems at the site. During inspections on February 20 and July 21, 1970, the compliance officials even interviewed Engleman, the Vepco site engineer, but he apparently did not mention anything about the comments of the academic geologists that the plant was being built astride a fault.[10]

Summary

Despite the web of regulatory procedures which the nuclear industry finds so burdensome, the AEC failed, at that timely stage, to catch the fact that Vepco was building its reactors on a fault. AEC officials had a report of the rock slide and the unstable layers below it. They also had a mineral analysis that suggested the possibility of a fault to state geologists. But the AEC geologist never inspected the excavation. The regulators depended on Vepco to volunteer any bad news about their project, even if it was counter to the company's interests to do so. Vepco's contractors examined the excavation in detail after the cave-in and considered the possibility of faulting but did not report it to the AEC nor, apparently, to Vepco. If any Vepco official other than Engleman was informed directly about the possibility of faulting in 1970, the secret has been carefully guarded. The AEC, for its part, succeeded in keeping its own inspection reports out of the public record, though NRC public information officials today say they should have been filed in 1970. These missing reports were added to the public files on November 23, 1977—seven years late—after NRC public information officials cooperated with this writer's efforts to determine whether any inspections had taken place prior to construction license approval.

• THE FIRST CONSTRUCTION LICENSE HEARING

On June 15, 1970, Stanley Ragone, a Vepco vice-president, wrote to Morris, the AEC's licensing director, to forward the answers to the remaining AEC questions and to inform Morris that the reactor containment buildings were designed to withstand a force 12/100 times the force of gravity due to shaking from an earthquake, as then required by the AEC. But that was not the main point of Ragone's letter.

What Ragone wanted was an exemption for Vepco to build the floor and walls of the containment for reactor units 1 and 2 before the construction license was issued. The exemption was needed, Ragone said, so that the units could be operating by the spring of 1974 and 1975, respectively. Vepco estimated that, by then, a ten per cent annual growth in demand for power would approach the company's ability to generate electricity and would leave an insufficient reserve to use during routine maintenance, repairs, or emergencies.

The Advisory Committee on Reactor Safeguards (ACRS), a group of technical advisors to the AEC, met August 13-15 to review Vepco's documents in support of the regular construction permit application. On August 17, 1970, before the advisory group could make its report to AEC Chairman Glenn T. Seaborg, however, Seaborg got a letter from John N. Nassikas of the Federal Power Commission supporting Vepco's claim that the North Anna plant would be needed by 1974 if Vepco was to have sufficient reserve generating capacity. "There is no doubt," Nassikas said, "that the North Anna plant is needed as planned if the Company is to meet its obligation to its customers during the summer of 1974." Nassikas' message conformed with the general position of the Nixon Administration on nuclear power, that licensing of plants should be expedited.

When the advisory committee reported to Seaborg three days later, it recommended approval of the construction license, if Vepco would follow certain recommendations. Of major concern was that the plant have a source of cooling water that would be available even if the worst postulated earthquake occurred in the area. Structures designed to withstand this hypothetically-chosen force are called Class I structures. The ACRS was not certain that the North Anna lake and dam would qualify as Class I, so the advisory group recommended that Vepco build a small, Class I emergency reservoir. Other recommendations were that Vepco's environmental monitoring plan be improved to detect any buildup of cesium and other radioactive isotopes in the cooling lagoons, and that Vepco participate more directly in the quality assurance program of its contractors.

Five days after the advisory committee report, Vepco's Ragone wrote again urging that the AEC grant the requested exemption by September 15, so that construction could proceed. On September 4, AEC regulatory staff director Harold L. Price granted the exemption for work on the containment structure up to ground level. Price reminded Ragone that the exemption would have no bearing on subsequent approval or denial of a construction permit, nor did it signify AEC approval of construction work prior to licensing. The action did, however, grant Vepco permission to pour concrete over a foundation of questionable stability without any investigation by government geologists into the cause of the rockslide.

Vepco's preliminary environmental impact statement, meanwhile, was getting bad reviews from other federal agencies to which it had been circulated. The Public Health Service complained that the proposed radioactivity monitoring program was not adequate, that the plant design did not make use of the most up-to-date radioactive waste treatment technology and that Vepco had proposed no emergency plan for evacuating residents in the event of a serious accident.

Perhaps the most critical comments came from Charles J. Orlebeke, deputy undersecretary of the Department of Housing and Urban Development. "After reading the company's letter," Orlebeke said, "we have concluded that the material submitted does not afford even a minimum response to the format of environmental impact statements . . . Accordingly, we believe the AEC should reject the current statement as inadequate and require that a proper environmental statement be prepared and circulated for comment."

On September 9, 1970, two and a half months before the scheduled construction license hearing, Virginia Governor Linwood Holton wrote the AEC: "The Commonwealth of Virginia will urgently need the electrical output of North Anna in the summer of 1974. Every effort should be made to expedite the schedule of proceedings. Certainly there is no reason for the Atomic Energy Commission to delay plans for a public hearing or issuance of a construction permit." Holton had, apparently, been advised that there was some local opposition to the plant.

The residents needed legal help just to get the AEC to hold the hearing in Louisa County, where the plant was being built and where most of them lived. But, eager for an opportunity to express their views, they made no attempt to delay the proceedings. The hearing took place as scheduled, November 23, 1970, before the Atomic Safety and Licensing Board (ASLB), a triumvirate which traditionally includes an attorney who serves as chairman, a nuclear physicist with experience in one of the federal laboratories, and an academic physicist. The board has the power to grant or deny a license. In doing so, it takes into consideration summary reports from the AEC regulatory staff, which is the legal arm, and the licensing staff, which is the technical arm, plus any reports which the applicant wishes to submit for the record.

Theoretically, the AEC and the applicant are adversaries in this proceeding and the applicant has the burden of showing that its plans meet all the regulatory requirements for nuclear power plants. The AEC represents the government, and is supposed to represent the public interest; and the company represents its own interest.

The board, however, can only base its decision on documents and testimony in the hearing record. Opponents of the plant were concerned that because of the political and economic pressure to get on with construction, the AEC would not raise all the safety questions that were troubling them. They were worried that the actual interests of the AEC and the utility were so similar that the hearing would not be a contest between conflicting interests but rather, as one plant opponent later called it, "a pageant for the peasants." So the residents and the county board of supervisors had applied for legal status to intervene in the proceedings. The ASLB had granted them that status and likewise had invited state agencies to participate directly in the hearing.

The opening remarks confirmed the anxieties of the local people that the process was not going to be an adversary one. "We have received from the applicant," began AEC attorney David Kartalia, "what we consider to be satisfactory responses to the questions that we feel have to be resolved at this point in the history of the facility. Consequently, we don't expect to engage in cross-examination of the applicant's witnesses at this hearing."

"Normally," ASLB Chairman J.D. Bond explained to the residents, "the applicant goes forward and assumes the burden of proof. A recurring abnormality is that an early step is a jointly proferred exhibit." From that point, the AEC's Kartalia proceeded to present the joint evidence on behalf of the government *and* Vepco.

The summary statement of the regulatory staff was signed by Harold Price who, two and a half months earlier, had approved Vepco's construction exemption. Price gave Vepco good marks on its plant design and its technical and financial qualifications to build the plant. And he certified that construction would not be "inimical to the common defense and security or to the health and safety of the public." The summary report of the licensing division reiterated the concerns of the Advisory Committee on Reactor Safeguards about the integrity of the cooling water supply in the event of an earthquake and Vepco's quality assurance program, among other things. Walter Butler, the AEC's North Anna project manager, testified that the construction license would be contingent upon Vepco's meeting the concerns of the ACRS, as described in the staff report.

AEC staff lawyers gathered no testimony at the hearing about the suitability of the location of the reactor units or the dam, though the AEC knew of the stability problems in unit 1 and the fault under the dam was on the contractor's geologic map. Neither the AEC staff attorneys nor the licensing board sought any testimony from Joseph Fischer, the Dames and Moore geologist who first determined that "stability problems may exist" in the reactor excavation, though Vepco had registered him as a witness in case any such questions arose.[11] And the state Division of Mineral Resources, whose geologists had found evidence on rock samples that the rock in the reactor foundation might be faulted, did not participate in the hearing, though all state agencies were invited to do so.

According to Butler, no testimony was sought on the geology of the site because "it was not an issue" in 1970. The subject of the fault under the dam, he said, "just never came up." There was an issue about the dam, he said, and that was, "Is it seismic Class I?" That issue, the quality assurance issue, and the stability issue, however, were all raised by AEC compliance division officials during site inspections. Why license staffers and the ACRS considered two of these problems important and ignored the other is unclear unless they considered the geological problem—like the problem of radioactive emissions—insoluble.

Any concerns that were not considered "an issue" by the licensing staff were left to the intervenors to bring up at the hearing. The local intervenors, however, did not have a shred of information about the geology of the site or news of the cave-in, so they asked nothing about the stability of the foundation. Their questions centered around the amount of radioactivity that would be permitted to escape from the plant and how it might build up in the lake during periods of drought. They were told by an attorney for Vepco that radiation in the lake would never exceed three per cent of the maximum permitted by AEC regulations existing at that time. The residents, like the Public Health Service before them, argued that better radioactive waste treatment technology was available and that tougher standards for radioactive pollution were actually being met by utilities in other states.

The intervenors issued their findings soon after the hearing.[12] "Grave radiological danger," they concluded, "will exist as a result of the installation and operation of the proposed facilities. Although the applicant has sought to minimize the potential danger, it appears to the intervenors that the staff evaluation by the Division of Reactor Licensing of the United States Atomic Energy Commission has done little more than to support the applicant's position regarding the installation." This feeling—that the AEC's review was neither independent enough nor rigorous enough to catch problems and prevent unnecessary risks—was at the crux of the intervenors' complaint.

The construction permits for units 1 and 2 were granted initially on February 27, 1971, but an AEC inspection three weeks later turned up deficiencies in welding procedures at the plant which could jeopardize the quality of work. Construction, including the extraordinary work to reinforce the excavations, had been underway by special exemption for six months without the deficiency coming to light. By March 29, however, the AEC was again satisfied that Vepco and its contractors were adhering to proper construction practices, and the construction license became final.

The question whether the design of the dam would meet earthquake standards was still unanswered. In the early spring and late summer of 1971, there was considerable correspondence from Vepco to the AEC on the subject. By August 5, Blume and Associates, engineering consultants to the AEC, had reviewed the documents and had raised additional questions for the AEC to put to Vepco. Within a month and a half, the AEC advised Vepco that the service water reservoir planned for the site would satisfy the seismic design requirements for an emergency source of cooling water. Thus Vepco was relieved of the obligation, which had been the AEC's major issue at the construction license hearing, to prove that the dam was seismic Class I, or to build an emergency reservoir.

Butler, by that time, had turned over the job of project manager to someone else at the AEC. His recollection in 1977 was that Vepco had applied for relief from the requirement on grounds that other utilities were not being required to build their main reservoirs to Class I standards. "The staff may have found out that indeed different projects were being handled differently," Butler said. "Anyhow, subsequent to issuance of the CP [construction permit], the Commission adopted a uniform policy statement on seismic design, and Vepco's service water reservoir satisfied the new requirement."

Meanwhile, Vepco site consultants were going through the same process of studying the environmental and geological conditions for reactor units 3 and 4 that they had gone through two years before for units 1 and 2. This time Dames and Moore reported to Vepco that they had found rock strata filled with chlorite or clay and showing "movement up to one and one-half feet." [13] The news must have hit the Stone & Webster geologists hard because their opinion that the seam in the excavation for unit 1 was not a fault rested heavily on the fact that no conclusive signs of movement had been found. The project geologists, however, were spared the embarrassment of being proved wrong, for the time being, because the same Dames and Moore report that told of the movement somehow also concluded that "the site is apparently free of faulting and structural anomalies."

In a much-delayed supplement to its environmental impact statement, filed with the AEC on March 15, 1972, Vepco stated, "Faulting at the site is neither known nor is it suspected. Site conditions reveal that all safety Class I structures will be founded on hard crystalline rock or on dense residual soil." [14] The latter statement was made despite test borings for the foundation for units 3 and 4 that showed "highly fractured zones with chlorite coating." [15]

Despite the fact that the suitability of the site is one of the major items in the AEC's safety review, no AEC staff geologist paid serious enough attention to the mounting evidence in Vepco consultant reports during this period to determine that the company's conclusions about the site were ill-founded.

- ## OPPONENTS ORGANIZE FOR THE SECOND CONSTRUCTION LICENSE HEARING

The local opposition to the power plant died down soon after the intervenors' views were rejected by the AEC and the construction permits issued. Some residents were still opposed to the plant but were discouraged because they no longer had the support of local officials.

Among them were Phyllis and J.B. Vaughan, whose home soon would be overlooking one of the cooling lagoons. In March of 1971, the Vaughans had noticed a letter, printed in the local newspaper, opposing nuclear power in general and federal insurance for nuclear plants specifically, and sympathizing with people living near the North Anna site. The letter was written by Margaret Dietrich, who lived in Gordonsville, twenty miles from the plant, and who was a stranger to the Vaughans. "We were delighted," Mrs. Vaughan said later.[16] "Until then, we hadn't heard that anyone outside the immediate area was interested in this." Mr. Vaughan made a special trip to Gordonsville to thank Mrs. Dietrich for writing the letter and, finding her out for the day, asked her husband to convey his thanks.

Three days before Christmas of 1972—the dam and lake now completed and the reactor containment buildings for units 1 and 2 rising above the landscape—the Vaughans saw a notice in the Charlottesville newspaper that the AEC was going to have a hearing the following May on Vepco's application for construction licenses for units 3 and 4. Phyllis Vaughan fired off a letter to the AEC asking to be informed about the hearings and any other developments. Margaret Dietrich also saw the notice in the paper and decided to join forces with the opponents of the plant. The two intervening years since J.B. Vaughan's thank-you visit had brushed the name from her memory, but Mrs. Dietrich combed the telephone book until she recalled it. She telephoned the Vaughans and asked if they and their neighbors were interested in meeting at her house to plan for the May 1973 hearing. Then she wrote a letter to the Charlottesville paper about the hearing, hoping it would catch the attention of others.

Among the people who saw Mrs. Dietrich's letter were William Warren, a physics graduate student at the University of Virginia in Charlottesville, and June Allen, a teacher with a particular interest in ecology. The two had written to the AEC, asking to make statements at the hearing. They called Mrs. Dietrich and she invited them to the meeting she was planning. On January 27, 1973, in Mrs. Dietrich's living room, the North Anna Environmental Coalition was formed.

"I was really a greenhorn—I guess we all were," recalls Mrs. Dietrich, who is old enough to be a grandmother and young enough to be a crusader. "I had been reading about nuclear power and was all upset. It's the kind of thing that you think one person can't do anything about and you feel like throwing up your hands. But you can and learn a lot about it if you try," she said.[17]

Whether or not the people in the North Anna Environmental Coalition could "do anything about" nuclear power in their part of the country, however, would take years to find out.

In January of 1973, Vepco began the excavation for unit 3, and in March, the excavation for unit 4. On April 16, according to an AEC investigation report issued a year later, Robert Pastuszak, a Stone & Webster geologist on the site, reported to superiors that he had observed offset rock strata in the unit 3 excavation which suggested possible faulting. Lyndon Rosenblad, Pastuszak's supervisor, flew to North Anna the next day, according to the later testimony, and reached the same conclusion about faulting. He asked that Briedis, the geologist who had been on the project since 1968 in various capacities, visit the site. Briedis did so, returned to Boston to talk with superiors about the problem and then notified Vepco engineer Clifford Robinson on April 24 that there was possible faulting at the site.

By coincidence, a routine request from the AEC for information necessary to evaluate the company's application for units 3 and 4 had arrived at Vepco a few days before Briedis' message. Among the twenty-one pages of questions, the AEC asked many about the geological conditions of the site: its behavior during prior earthquakes, identification of active faults, description of active faults, surface faulting, stability, and other details.

Further excavation in unit 3 revealed other offset strata along a chlorite seam. Vepco initiated an extensive study of the suspected faults on April 24, but apparently did not report the developments to the AEC. The only word the AEC got from Vepco about faulting during this period was in an April 30 letter from Vepco vice-president Ragone which accompanied the final safety analysis report on units 1 and 2. "Faulting at the site," said Ragone's letter, "is neither known nor is it suspected."

According to testimony and documents later obtained by the Coalition, including the Vepco engineer's work journal, Vepco and Stone & Webster personnel spent the following week discussing how to disprove Pastuszak's theory that the site was faulted. Briedis and Swiger, both of whom had determined three years earlier that the chlorite seam in unit 1 was not a fault, insisted that the same feature in unit 3 be shown not to be a fault. On May 2, they outlined a plan with Dames and Moore's Brian Ellwood to keep the whole problem under study until after the construction license hearing. The Vepco officials involved also agreed not to take any action until the consultant's study was finished.

Construction license hearings for units 3 and 4 were held as scheduled May 7-10, 1973. Vepco and its contractors succeeded in the effort to keep the geological problems of the site quiet until they could be shown to be of no consequence. The record of the hearing shows no mention that a fault was suspected at the site and no questions from the AEC staff lawyers about site geology. Vepco's plant engineering manager, W.C. Spencer, testified to the truth and accuracy of the preliminary safety analysis report for units 3 and 4 that said faulting was not suspected. But the secret was difficult to keep.

There was some pressure from within Vepco ranks to report the geologic findings to the AEC. Project engineer R.P. Wessel, for one, recommended in a May 9 letter to vice-president Ragone that the AEC be told. And a geologist from the University of Massachusetts at Amherst, Donald U. Wise, whom Vepco had recently hired as a consultant, reported on May 14 that the site was faulted and it would be impossible to argue otherwise.

On May 17, 1973, Vepco executive E. Ashby Baum telephoned the AEC to advise that "there was a possible zone of geologic faults at the North Anna site," as AEC legal documents later put it. The notification came the day the hearing record was closed to parties other than Vepco and the AEC. Vepco did not put the notice in writing, as was the practice required by the AEC; thus it did not appear in public files.[18]

The first mention of the fault in the public record appeared on June 21 in the form of a memo, about a visit to the site, written by AEC's Robert L. Ferguson, who had succeeded Butler as North Anna project manager. "On June 18, 1973," the memo said, "representatives of Vepco met with the regulatory staff to discuss a 'chlorite seam' in the excavations for units 1, 2, 3, and 4. The seam is associated with a fault which has been traced from the excavation for unit 1 through excavations for the other units." The memo said that the excavation for unit 3 showed movement "in the order of inches to several feet, possibly as much as 20 feet." The memo also mentioned the "comprehensive program" which Vepco had initiated two months earlier to study the fault, and Vepco's conclusion that the fault was inactive.

Vepco staff and consultants had been working for more than a month to turn up evidence that would satisfy the AEC safety criteria for locating power plants near faults. (The regulations are, basically, that a plant cannot be located near a fault that has been active within 500,000 years—a very recent fault on a geologic scale which goes back hundreds of millions of years. The regulations do not include criteria for siting reactors directly on faults, because this event and its associated problems were never contemplated.) The company investigators had discussed all sorts of ways to test the age of the fault and its potential to be reactivated, abandoning those methods that would leave open the possibility of a young or active fault. They were apparently most concerned that the analysis done by their own consultant from the University of Massachusetts failed to rule out a young fault. An entry in Robinson's journal on June 6 even mentions that Swiger of Stone & Webster wanted to "recall the Wise report and change the wording." The same entry notes that testing the age of soils on either side of the fault might suffice to prove the company's case. But, the journal entry said, "what do we do if soil test don't show what we want it to show?[sic]"

The soil tests *did* show what Vepco wanted them to show, at least the AEC visitors to the site on June 18 were convinced by the evidence presented to them that the fault was more than 500,000 years old. Examining the excavation with Ferguson were AEC staff geologist A.T. Cardone and U.S. Geological Survey staffer Fred Hauser, none of whom had inspected the site since the digging started for unit 1. After meeting with the Vepco officials, Ferguson decided there was "no reason to alter the staff's previous conclusion regarding the issuance of a construction permit for units 3 and 4."

Ferguson might have felt different if he had read the report of yet another consulting geologist, Paul J. Roper, of Lafayette College in Pennsylvania, a specialist in Piedmont geology. But the report was not submitted to the AEC. "Unfortunately," it said, "the region of greatest tectonic activity in Virginia as well as one of the most active regions in the central Appalachians lies approximately at the intersection of Neuschel's lineament and the 38th parallel fracture, which is only a few miles southwest of the North Anna nuclear power station."[19] Neuschel's lineament is actually a geological dividing line between rock types on the East Coast. There is much debate among geologists about its current significance and whether it represents some kind of fault line. Some geologists theorize that it has to do with the ancient dividing of continents, a theory which has attracted much attention to this previously little studied region of the country.

Meanwhile, high ranking officials in the regulatory division—including the current (April 1978) deputy director of the Department of Energy, John O'Leary, and the current NRC director of regulation, Edson Case—were debating whether to report the fault to the Atomic Safety and Licensing Board, about to issue a construction permit for units 3 and 4. According to a memo from a Justice Department investigation four years later, Case persuaded the others that it would be premature to have the ASLB reopen the hearings. Vepco officials were almost certain the AEC staff would not press them on questions of regional geology, regardless of the fault. As Robinson put it in his journal, "If AEC should shoot down NA site, then would have to shoot down all Piedmont sites."[20]

• THE SHOW CAUSE HEARING

While Vepco was gathering evidence to prove that its fault met the official criteria for safety, the North Anna Environmental Coalition was showing a film, "How Safe Are America's Atomic Reactors?" at the local high school. A construction worker at North Anna who had come to watch the film told the group that project officials were worried about earthquakes because workers had drilled through rock and hit clay. Word that the problem might be a fault reached the Coalition on July 24 from a Louisa county resident who had information which seemed to verify the worker's comment. The resident, who has asked not to be identified, urged the Coalition to raise the question with the AEC. The Coalition called the AEC and attorney Kartalia confirmed that there was a fault running through all four excavations.

Realizing that the word was about to get out, the top ranks of the regulatory staff agreed to handle the matter by inserting an affidavit from AEC geologist Cardone in the hearing record, rather than by reopening the hearings. The sworn statement notified the Atomic Safety and Licensing Board of the fault and asserted that an upcoming Vepco report would resolve any safety questions they might have about it. The affidavit was made available to Vepco, too.

On August 4, the Coalition issued a news release on the discovery of the fault. Four days later Vepco held a news conference in Richmond and read Cardone's affidavit to indicate publicly that the AEC agreed with Vepco that the site was safe, despite the fault.

On August 24, Vepco submitted a Dames and Moore report, *Supplemental Geological Data, North Anna Power Station,* stating that the fault was inactive and would present no safety hazard. Draft reports on the geology underneath units 1 and 2 were ordered destroyed, according to a mid-August entry in Robinson's journal, apparently because they would reveal in graphic fashion what was known in 1970 and never brought to the attention of the AEC.

The Coalition wrote the AEC's Ferguson on September 4, urging an independent investigation of the safety of the site. During his visit to North Anna on June 18, Ferguson had seen some photographs of unit 1 taken by Vepco's contractors in 1970 and, though he was now convinced that the fault was inactive, his trust in Vepco had been eroded to the point that he was willing to seek outside opinions.

AEC records show that Ferguson was in touch, during September of 1973, with Funkhouser and the other geology professors who had identified the fault in the unit 1 excavation in February-March of 1970, and with Virginia state geologist James L. Calver whose office had done the mineral analyses that same month.

The three geology professors, according to Bruce Goodwin, the William and Mary geology department head, met with Ferguson September 7, 1973, after reviewing the Dames and Moore data and agreed that the fault was more than 500,000 years old and was not capable of being reactivated by geological pressure, for example, from Lake Anna. But the professors did not endorse Dames and Moore's explanation of the formation of the fault nor did they agree that the site was necessarily suitable for a nuclear power plant. There was a general feeling, Goodwin said more recently, that the geologic study which was produced in August of 1973 "should have been done when the fault turned up in unit 1" in February of 1970. Though earthquake activity is more common on the West Coast, careful geologic study is also necessary when plant siting decisions are made in the East, Goodwin said, because so little is known: "Piedmont geology is a big blank spot in all the books."[21]

Meanwhile, the Coalition was pushing for an investigation by the AEC to determine whether the site would now be considered safe. Their cause was aided when, on September 27, *Washington Post* reporter Hal Willard wrote a story on the North Anna fault which caused some embarrassment for the members of the Congressional Joint Committee on Atomic Energy because they were caught unaware of a problem the AEC had known of for months. On October 17, 1973, AEC lawyers sent a letter to Vepco asking the utility to show cause why construction should proceed while an official investigation was underway. On November 6, Vepco officials responded that they wanted a "show cause" hearing in order to present their case publicly. The Coalition wrote to the AEC urging that Vepco not be allowed to do any work in the excavation for unit 3 that might obscure the geological formations there, until the public hearing was over. Vepco agreed. In November, realizing that they were handicapped by their lack of access to information, the Coalition requested that a full set of public documents on the North Anna plant be made available to area residents. After three months of negotiations, the request was filled and a public document room was established in the Alderman Library of the University of Virginia in Charlottesville.

The show cause hearing was held March 20 through April 4, 1974, in Louisa County, before a licensing board made up of members not previously involved in the North Anna case. Documents produced for the first time at this hearing included sworn depositions and reports secured by the AEC during its investigation, as well as other records secured under the federal Freedom of Information Act by the Coalition's lawyer, Professor William H. Rodgers, Jr., of the Georgetown University Law Center. Under a system of legal discovery, the Coalition was able to get additional information from Vepco. It was while preparing for this hearing that Professor Rodgers discovered the suppressed report by Lafayette College geologist Paul Roper.

The purpose of the show cause hearing was simply to determine whether or not the North Anna site met AEC safety regulations, considering the existence of the fault. But the regulatory division went out of its way in the written investigation report to clear Vepco of suspicion that the utility knew of or suspected faulting as far back as February of 1970. Under pressure from AEC staff attorneys, the show cause board ruled the subject of suppressed information out of order at the hearing. Before the show cause board made its ruling, the Coalition charged the AEC with issuing a fraudulent investigation report. The charges were levied April 11, 1974, at a meeting of the Advisory Committee on Reactor Safeguards which was reviewing construction problems in units 1 and 2. To support its charges, the Coalition pointed out sworn depositions that faulting under the dam was mapped as early as 1969, that Vepco's resident engineer, Engelman, had the fault in unit 1 pointed out to him in February and March 1970, and that Briedis, the Stone & Webster geologist, was alerted to the possibility of faulting by state geologists in February 1970.

On June 27, 1974, the show cause board ruled that the site was safe, under AEC regulations, for construction to proceed. The Coalition appealed the ruling but the appeal was denied, and the board's decision was later upheld in federal court.

The Coalition was given thirty days to request a hearing on the concealment issues that had been ruled out at the show cause proceeding. They requested one, and it was finally held on January 29, 1975. During the investigation for this disclosure hearing, AEC attorneys learned there was not one but a dozen faults under the lake and dam and that other geologic information had been withheld by Vepco. The Atomic Safety and Licensing Board determined on April 14 that there were twelve of these omissions which met the definition of "material false statements" in AEC regulations.

The Coalition was given thirty days to request a hearing on the under provisions of Nuclear Regulatory Commission rules that provide for revocation if a utility makes *any* false statements in its application or if civil penalties prove to be ineffective in getting a utility to adhere to regulations. Vepco had been fined twice before—

$38,000 in May of 1973 and $10,000 in January of 1975—for not taking sufficient and timely action to prevent recurring safety violations at its Surry plant.

Another hearing was held in May of 1975 to determine the appropriate penalty for the twelve false statements and the staff recommended a $5,000 civil penalty for each. Vepco appealed the ruling and the appeals board determined that Vepco had made only four false statements. Subsequently, the NRC commissioners set the fine at $32,500 and the number of false statements at seven, and in March 1978, the U.S. Court of Appeals for the Fourth Circuit in Richmond ruled that the commissioners' action should stand.

Summary

Vepco Chairman of the Board John McGurn contends that his company has been unfairly maligned for failing to notify the AEC of the fault before licenses were approved because the fault was not discovered until after the licenses were approved. His position is that the site, despite the fault, meets the current NRC safety criteria and that Vepco did not intend to deceive the AEC, a view endorsed by all federal court rulings in the matter.[22]

The NRC's position, obviously, is that Vepco did not always uphold its responsibility to report safety-related problems, but that the violations of the past are not significant enough to suggest that the plant will not be operated safely. "Whether Vepco determined that the problem in unit 1 was a fault or not," NRC's Ferguson said, "they should have notified us. Whatever they chose to call it, the problem they had in 1970 was basic to the suitability of the site. They should have notified us then. But that doesn't mean the site is a bad one. Even with the fault, the site is better than some others. And it meets our requirements because we were able to determine that the fault was inactive and could not be reactivated."[23]

The Coalition contends that Vepco had important geological information which it failed to report and that such concealment is grounds for revoking the plant licenses. The NRC's reluctant action in 1974 and subsequently has been too little and too late to assure that the plant foundation will be sound, the Coalition argues. Should people trust their safety, it asks, to a less than scrupulous operator, governed by a regulatory agency which refuses to revoke permits regardless of repeated violations of its regulations?

"For years," Coalition president June Allen told a Congressional subcommittee during hearings in July 1975, "NRC accepted Vepco's statement on North Anna that faulting of rock at this site is neither known nor is it suspected. Once it did become undeniably suspected and painfully known, Vepco was allowed to return to those same consultants—the very people who said the fault was not there at all—to return to those same consultants now for them to prove that, although the fault was there, it was ancient, benevolent and harmless."[24]

The hearings were called by the late Senator Lee Metcalf (D-Montana), then chairman of the subcommittee on reports, accounting, and management of the Committee on Government Operations. Senator Metcalf had become interested in the North Anna case from the point of view of how well information was flowing from the utility to the AEC and to the public. The senator's staff was interested in whether close financial ties between the utility and the contractor might be inhibiting the contractor from disclosing information necessary for proper evaluation of the project by the NRC. Senator Metcalf's queries confirmed information dug up earlier by the Coalition, of interlocking management and financial relations between Vepco and its prime contractor, Stone & Webster, specifically that Whitney Stone, a principal owner of the contracting firm, formerly owned Vepco and was still the largest individual holder of Vepco stock.[25]

• CONTINUING PROBLEMS AT NORTH ANNA: THE SHOW MUST GO ON

Throughout 1975 and 1976, the North Anna Environmental Coalition kept close watch on the problems that cropped up as construction progressed. One of these was that the service water pump house for units 1 and 2 settled so severely and so abnormally that its concrete walls cracked and pipes had to be relaid and rehung to avoid stress and possible rupture. Though Vepco had asserted all along that the pump house, like other Class I structures, would be set on bedrock or dense residual soil, the company had to admit its mistake when the settling problem became obvious. The pump house, Vepco said, was apparently resting on saprolite, a general term for rock that has been fractured and weathered by chemical processes.

Vepco had been warned of the saprolite problem in late May of 1973 by Professor Roper. He suggested either deepening the excavations for units 3 and 4 or digging new reactor pits to avoid the zone of weathered rock. "This region," Roper predicted, "will also be the site of intense chemical weathering in the future and may result in an unstable base under the reactors. Unless this problem is dealt with it could be a source of constant trouble in future years."[26]

Another Vepco consultant reported in June of 1976 that "most of the clay in the saprolite is halloysite."[27] The North Anna Coalition asked an independent geologist about the suitability of holloysite as a foundation material and was told that it has a tubelike structure which, when wet, acts like "a pile of roller bearings," and moves.[28]

Another problem at North Anna has been that very sensitive earthquake monitoring equipment, in operation between January 1974 and May 1976, has revealed a pattern of microearthquakes—movements usually too slight for human senses to detect—around the lower part of Lake Anna, between the power plant and the dam. The microearthquakes have been particularly frequent near the point where the postulated geologic feature called Neuschel's Lineament would intersect with Lake Anna.

Dames and Moore, Vepco's geological consultant, attempted to discount this "spacial coincidence," as they called it in a 1976 seismology report,[29] but NRC seismologists thought the correlation between the lake and the microquakes was significant enough to require Vepco to continue the monitoring program for an additional year. The NRC staff then recommended that the monitoring be discounted but, as of April 1978, the Advisory Committee on Reactor Safeguards was urging its continuation.

A third serious problem, discovered at the plant during construction of units 1 and 2, was that supporting equipment for the steam generators and reactor coolant pumps had defects which caused them to crack. The supports are intended to protect the equipment above them from damage in the event of an earthquake or other movement.

"No penalty other than revocation [of the construction license]," the Coalition said in a January 25, 1976, press release after the defects were discovered, "can really protect the public from the undue risk of technologically questionable equipment astride a geologically questionable site."

The defective supports for the generators and pumps had cost Vepco a reported $24 million in repairs. The utility sued the manufacturer, Sun Ship, a subsidiary of Sun Oil Company, for damages from the ensuing construction delays. On March 26, 1976, Sun filed a petition with the NRC to intervene in the upcoming operating license hearings for units 1 and 2. Sun alleged that it had suspected defects in its support equipment, but that Vepco and

Stone & Webster would not allow the manufacturer to do necessary tests after the equipment was installed. The petition further alleged that there were other defects in construction, including welding defects, which would compromise the safety of the plant.

The operating license hearings began on November 30, 1976, but there were so many unresolved safety questions that the hearings were continued. The list of problems was so long that Professor Max W. Carbon, a nuclear engineer at the University of Wisconsin and member of the Advisory Committee on Reactor Safeguards, said the North Anna plant was "an exception or worst case" among plants under review. In January, Vepco was fined $31,900 for violating NRC regulations on procedures for certifying welds and for other failures in quality assurance that were brought to the NRC's attention mainly by workers. Meeting that same month, the Advisory Committee on Reactor Safeguards acknowledged the uncertainties of East Coast geology and recommended that future reactors be designed to withstand .20 gravities, rather than .12 gravities of horizontal force from earthquakes. In the same letter, however, the committee recommended approval of the North Anna operating licenses, despite the fact that the reactors were designed to meet the lower standard.

The main issue at the operating license hearing, which finally resumed on May 31, 1977, was whether Vepco's quality assurance program had improved enough to satisfy the Licensing Board that violations of the past would not recur. In their presentation, Vepco officials testified that a management consulting firm had recently reported favorably on the quality assurance program. Licensing Board Chairman Frederick J. Coufal interrupted the presentation to ask whether the management consultants were available for questioning. Finding they were not, Coufal told the Vepco officials that he found it strange Vepco had not decided to have them testify on the company's behalf, if their report was so favorable.

Under questioning by an attorney representing the Commonwealth of Virginia, Vepco officials testified that they had increased their on-site quality assurance staff from six to thirty-five. Further questioning revealed, however, that the supervisory staff was increased after construction on units 1 and 2 was virtually completed.

Richard Foster, an attorney who represented a member of the Coalition, without payment, established for the hearing record what seemed to the layman to be a devastating case against Vepco's general competence to operate a nuclear power plant. The points he established included an admission by Vepco Board Chairman

McGurn that the Virginia utility had received more fines from the NRC than any other utility in the country.

By contrast, NRC attorneys did not press Vepco officials on their past or future quality assurance programs. They asked the utility officials only if they were prepared to meet new NRC regulations on plant security. The Vepco officials said they were.

Margaret Dietrich and Phyllis Vaughan were in the audience shaking their heads. They had heard it all before. "This has been one continuous hearing," Mrs. Vaughan said. "Despite all opposition, the construction persists. We actually once thought if we could show that the public safety was endangered by this plant, we could stop it. But we were mistaken. The question at these hearings," she said, "is not whether Vepco will be able to operate, but under what conditions they will operate."

Mrs. Vaughan said, however, that she does not think the work of the Coalition has all been in vain. If the plant is just a little safer than it would have been had the Coalition not intervened, she said, it will have been worth the effort. "Already we have gained three years without the risks of an operating plant," she said. "You know, they were going to start operation in 1974. They were in a great hurry."

In July 1977, the Advisory Committee on Reactor Safeguards met to review all new information on the North Anna plant and, once again, recommended that the operating license be approved. In August, just before the license was to be granted, however, Vepco discovered a problem during a computerized test of emergency cooling water pumps. The pumps are located in the reactor containment building and are responsible for flooding the building with water if the normal reactor cooling system fails. The test revealed that the pumps had not been designed to do this job adequately.

That same month, the NRC adopted stiff new regulations for the reporting of safety-related problems. The new rules make utility contractors and consultants, as well as the utility itself, responsible for notifying the NRC of problems or regulatory violations. But the new rules have not suceeded in getting Vepco contractors to report problems directly to the agency, nor have they altered Vepco's apparent habit of reporting its safety-related problems to the NRC after licensing decisions have been made. The NRC staff is apparently no longer cooperating with Vepco to keep potential problems hushed up—the NRC has in fact been meticulously open about them since early 1977—but the regulators have not developed a way to find out about new problems until Vepco decides to disclose them.

On December 9, 1977, for example, Stone & Webster advised Vepco that there was an error in computer codes used to determine whether certain pipes would function properly, if needed during an emergency. The error did not mean that the emergency system would fail, only that its proper function could not be verified, but the error in the codes was the kind of problem that must be reported promptly to the NRC. On same day, Westinghouse notified Vepco that some electrical equipment could short-circuit during vibrations. Vepco proceeded to investigate both the problems but did not report them until several days after the Atomic Safety and Licensing Board had approved the operating license for units 1 and 2 on December 13. As a result, the NRC staff asked that the license be withheld once again and the hearing reopened. But the collective problems at North Anna and Vepco's repeated reluctance to admit them in a timely fashion have not been sufficient to cause the staff to recommend denial of the permit. Final approval of the operating license was given December 29, 1977, by the Atomic Safety Licensing Board and April 1, 1978, by the NRC staff.

• EPILOGUE

In 1975, petitioned by the Coalition, the U.S. Justice Department began to investigate the events leading up to and following the 1973 discovery of the fault at North Anna to determine whether the government could make a criminal case against Vepco for concealing information. A Justice Department summary of findings, written in May 1977 but not released until October of that year, confirmed earlier findings that Vepco had withheld pertinent information and had made misleading statements which had the effect of keeping the public in the dark during the 1973 construction license hearing.[30] The Justice Department summary, however, concluded that the government would not be able to make a very strong case against Vepco because Atomic Energy Commission officials actually helped keep the fault secret for almost three months after Vepco reported it—until the North Anna Coalition made inquiries and issued a press release the first week in August 1973.

"We would have a much stronger case against Vepco," said the Justice Department memo, "but for the actions of the NRC in sanctioning the continued construction by Vepco and concealing on its own part from the Atomic Safety and Licensing Board the discovery of a fault." The memo predicted that, if prosecuted, "Vepco would call as witnesses virtually the entire Office of Regulation of the Nuclear Regulatory Commission to testify that they were well aware of the fault and had determined not to take any immediate action to halt construction or to reopen the hearings." The memo called the government agency's actions at the time "ill considered and inept" and said they demonstrated "a pervasive bias against the scrutiny which a project of this importance deserves and is entitled to under federal law."

The Justice Department memo raises more questions about the process of nuclear regulation than it settles. The one point that it unequivocally settles is that the goals and interests of Vepco and the AEC in 1973 were so similar that high-ranking AEC officials actually perpetuated the utility's public fraud. The memo also makes it clear that the utility cannot be successfully prosecuted by the government because of the agency's complicity; nor, of course can Justice act against the agency officials who failed to make an issue of the fault once Vepco reported it. What recourse, then, does the public have now for assuring that North Anna is safe and what certainty that the NRC will perform better in the future?

The question is especially significant when one considers how similar the goals of the government and the nuclear industry will be as current and future administrations look to nuclear power to supply a greater share of the country's energy. Under these conditions there will be great pressure to avoid delays in the licensing process just as there was in the early 1970s. The pressure may even increase. The "pervasive bias against the scrutiny" of power plant projects, which the Justice Department found in the North Anna case, will certainly recur unless something is done to require the NRC to search for potential safety problems and resolve safety issues before plant construction is underway.

If the Justice Department cannot require the NRC to follow its legal mandate, who will? Who will regulate the NRC? Right now, the job is left to small, self-financed, citizen organizations, like the North Anna Coalition, which depends on voluntary legal help, and larger organizations, like the Union of Concerned Scientists, which offer technical assistance to citizen groups. These organizations have had some success at getting the NRC to tighten up its regulations and procedures. Partly because of the North Anna experience, for example, the NRC now requires a public hearing on the suitability of a plant site before even limited site work can begin and NRC geologists now routinely inspect reactor excavations before construction permits are issued.

But many citizen groups, who have started out naively, perhaps, thinking they can halt a nuclear plant project if they can demonstrate its dangers, have learned some bitter lessons. They have learned that the laws and regulations which the NRC enforces often allow a higher degree of risk than they find acceptable. They have learned that utilities can take advantage of NRC regulations which are made more lenient during safety review—as the structural standards for the North Anna lake and dam were—but do not always have to comply with rules which are tightened during review, as the East Coast earthquake design standards were. And they have learned that the NRC has not always been successful in enforcing the regulations that do exist.

Many citizens have, therefore, come to the conclusion that the government cannot be trusted to protect them from the hazards of nuclear energy. Some of the regulators, in turn, have become defensive about their work and unsympathetic toward citizens who are pushing for safety. The antagonism that certain regulators feel towards citizens who have intervened in regulatory proceedings is so great that these officials absolutely refuse to help the intervenors dig out the information they need to determine whether their safety concerns are legitimate.

This writer encountered a striking example of this antagonism when interviewing Walter Butler, who was the AEC's North Anna project manager in 1970. Butler said he suspected the interview was instigated by the North Anna Environmental Coalition and he made it clear that he would not cooperate with members of the Coalition in their attempt to discover how licensing decisions were made for the North Anna plant. And yet, the objective of regulatory officials and citizens concerned about nuclear plant safety should be one and the same. The members of the North Anna Environmental Coalition and their neighbors bear the risks of a power plant which will service millions of people. Those millions, through the NRC, therefore, have a special obligation to those relatively few who are put at greatest risk. The government takes the liability for nuclear accidents off the shoulders of the utilities and imposes a regulatory system in its place, designed to anticipate problems and prevent accidents.

At the very least, it would seem, the NRC is obligated to ferret out and make known any potential or actual safety problems at plants. This was not the case at North Anna or at who-knows-how-many other plants where concerned residents are less persistent in their inquiries or where residents have not organized at all. If the nuclear regulatory process is to be improved, if people are to have confidence in it, the fundamental safety questions are going to have to be investigated and resolved *before* a plant is built. The way the process works now, many safety issues—both the "generic" issues common to all plants and specific issues—are allowed to go unresolved until after a plant is built. The bulk of these are never independently investigated by the NRC or its consultants who still rely on information provided by the utility. Had regulatory officials actually investigated every problem that AEC inspectors found in 1970, and had they made Vepco resolve each one prior to issuing construction permits, the safe operation of North Anna could have been far less subject to chance than it is now.

Vepco, too, could have avoided years of delays and millions of dollars in extra expenses that likely will be passed on to customers, if utility officials had been a litle more conscientious. In their haste to complete the project, however, utility officials have worked not only against the interests of public safety, but against their own interests as well.

*   *   *

Problems caused by the unstable foundation at North Anna have, predictably, worsened and one serious new problem has come to light since the preceding chapter was written. The pumphouse has sunk to within about a third of an inch of the 1.8 inches allowed by the NRC for the plant's entire forty year lifespan. And, once the plant began operating, radiation levels inside the reactor building were found to be eighteen times greater than Vepco anticipated. If these problems persist—no way has been found in three years to stop the pumphouse from settling—the NRC will have to lower its standards to accommodate Vepco or the utility will have to shut down prematurely. Vepco can reduce the radiation hazard to workers inside the containment by limiting the repair and maintenance work that would ordinarily be done while the plant is operating. That "solution," however, would increase the risk that other equipment failures will go unnoticed and would have the effect of compounding all the other problems at North Anna, known and unknown.

IV.

The Case of the Saccharin Studies: Public Protection and Individual Choice

Not until 1968, when the Congress and the White House began looking into the relationship between the American diet and health, did the government acknowledge that malnutrition flourishes in this land of plenty. The malnutrition problems exposed at that time are not caused by too little food, but by the wrong kind of food, often too much of the wrong kind of food.

The problem of poor nutrition in rich America is complex because, in addition to poverty, it involves personal living and eating habits: what and how much a person chooses to eat. It involves the economics of the food industry: what and how much a person is persuaded to eat. And the problem of poor nutrition involves the government: what non-nutritious substances food processors are permitted to sell as food and what nutritious substances they are permitted to remove during processing.

By law, the Food and Drug Administration (FDA) in the Department of Health, Education and Welfare is responsible for setting standards so that foods on the grocery shelf are basically what they appear to be. Except by restricting the amount of extraneous ingredients a manufacturer can put in a product, like cereal in frankfurters, and still call the product frankfurters, however, the FDA has no control over how nutritious a food is. Many food standards actually permit the nutritional value of foods to be reduced during processing. Even the Department of Agriculture's food grading system for fresh fruits, vegetables, and meats—which many consumers believe has something to do with nutrition—is based solely on the color, flavor, and texture of these foods. Most high grade meats, for example, contain more fats than lower grade ones. This means that a prime cut may be more tasty to someone accustomed to fatty meats, but that the lower-grade cut may be more healthy.

The FDA has regulations designed to prevent foods from being adulterated with filth or contaminated with germs during manufacture, storage and shipping, and the power to take such foods off the market. Likewise, the FDA is responsible for seeing to it that anything the manufacturer adds to food—to preserve it or to make it more attractive or tastier—is safe.

The average American has relied on the government's food standards as if they were some objective index of the relative wholesomeness of foods. And he believes that past regulatory efforts have succeeded in protecting the public from harm. But consumer advocates who have looked into the matter a little more carefully have found that food standards have usually been set by the manufacturers and endorsed by the government, that the food grading system is based on the sales appeal of foods rather than their wholesomeness, and that regulatory officials have relied, to a great extent, on the findings of manufacturers that substances added to foods are safe.

The historical reliance of government regulators on the food manufacturers would probably not cause much of a public stir were it not for two things: evidence gathered in the past decade that many serious diseases are diet-related and evidence gathered in the past few years that manufacturers skimp on the quality of foods and the safety of additives when company economics create pressure.

The ill effect of too much cholesterol on the arteries, the relationship between sugar consumption and poor health, the effect of salt consumption on blood pressure—medical researchers have found that these effects can often be avoided and the risk of disease reduced by dietary restrictions. Cancer specialists believe that certain vitamin deficiencies, food additives, and even too much animal fat in the everyday diet of most Americans is responsible for many forms of cancer. Gio B. Gori, deputy director of Cancer Cause and Prevention at the National Cancer Institute says that diet is related to half of all cancers in women and at least a third of the cancers in men. Evidence for this conclusion was presented at a professional conference sponsored by the National Cancer Institute and the American Cancer Society and reported in the November 1975 issue of *Cancer Research.* [1]

In the early 1970s, legislators heard rumblings of popular discontent with the FDA's tendency to let food manufacturers set their own standards and regulate themselves. In 1972, the Senate Select Committee on Nutrition and Human Needs held hearings to determine what legislative steps might be taken to help Americans improve their diet. Beginning in 1974, the committee, under the chairmanship of Senator George McGovern (D-S.D.), focused the hearings on legislation to establish a national policy on nutrition. The public interest and the interest of other legislators in a comprehensive food policy was so slight, according to a McGovern aide, that the committee concentrated its subsequent hearings on the relationship between diet and specific diseases.

In January 1977, the committee released a report, based on its hearings, called "Dietary Goals for the United States." Among the goals recommended in the report were that Americans, on a national basis, eat twenty-five per cent less fat, forty per cent less sugar, reduce cholesterol intake by fifty per cent, and salt by fifty to eighty-five per cent. The report was hailed by health-minded organizations around the country, including the Center for Science in the Public Interest, a Washington, D.C., group known for its annual sponsorship of Food Day. The Center gathered the signatures of health professionals in a petition to President Carter to adopt the goals. The Senate Select Committee report, however, hit a sensitive nerve in industries whose products were high in fat, sugar, and cholesterol. Industry representatives objected fiercely. Lobby groups representing the beef industry asked for hearings to present opposing views. Senator McGovern held additional hearings and later announced he would modify the wording of the report so it would be clear that the committee was not recommending that people eat less meat, but less high-fat meat.

• "SAFE" FOOD ADDITIVES AND HEALTH

As long as the FDA permits food manufacturers to add ingredients to foods other than what the name of the food strictly implies, the agency has to have a system for determining which additives are safe and which are unsafe. The very basis of this system is a group of substances that are "generally recognized as safe" (GRAS) by the FDA because they have been in the food supply for so many years or because food manufacturing associations certify that they are safe. Substances which fall into the GRAS category do not have to be approved by the FDA for use in food and most of them do not have to be mentioned specifically on the product label. If the food standard for orange juice, for example, permits manufacturers to substitute other ingredients for ten per cent of their product, that portion can be added water, sugar, flavoring, preservatives—anything the manufacturer wants to add that the FDA considers safe.

In 1969, President Nixon called for a re-evaluation of the safety of the substances generally recognized as safe. At that time, no one, not even the FDA, knew exactly what they all were or how prevalent they were in the American diet. In 1970, therefore, the FDA asked the Food Protection Committee of the National Academy of Sciences (NAS) to find out. The committee sent out surveys to food manufacturers asking about their use of 251 substances listed as safe in the Code of Federal Regulations, 83 substances presumed to be safe by the FDA, and 1,596 flavorings published as safe by the Flavor and Extract Manufacturers Association. Responses came in from companies which, according to the committee's estimate, represented sixty to seventy per cent of the processed food business and ninety per cent of the baby food business. The data were compiled and presented to the FDA in September 1972. [2]

The substances presumed to be safe in 1970 and included in the survey ran the gamut from vitamins and minerals to saccharin and monosodium glutamate. The sheer number of additives included in the Academy survey was an impressive revelation of how many things people eat without knowing it. But perhaps the more startling revelation was the volume of additives consumed. The data in the survey indicate, for example, that more than nine pounds of salt for every American was added to foods by manufacturers in 1970 and more than thirty-two pounds of sugar per person. If a person buys reconstituted rather than fresh vegetables, the Academy committee found, he can expect that 7.3 per cent of what he is eating is added salt. Likewise, 2.5 per cent of all processed meat is added salt. An astounding eleven per cent of baby food was found to be sugar or corn syrup, added, consumer groups have concluded, to make the product more palatable to mothers. The FDA did not publish any conclusions based on this study but one suggests itself: if Americans want to cut down on salt and sugar and help the next generation do the same, a good way to start would be by cutting out processed foods and substituting fresh foods.

Re-evaluation of the safety of food additives in the GRAS category proceeded slowly, largely because consumers and government regulators had no reason to doubt that the additives people had been consuming for decades were safe. When pressure from consumer groups finally did cause the FDA to question the safety of "safe" additives, the agency began to act on the basis of evidence already accumulated against particular additives. Cyclamate, an artificial sweetener, was taken off the market in 1970. Monosodium glutamate was banned from baby foods. Saccharin was taken off the GRAS list and labeled for use only by people who had to restrict their sugar intake. It was classified as provisionally safe which meant that the FDA had to make a final determination on a priority basis. In 1975, the FDA acted to take red dye #2, a widely used food coloring, off the market; the ban took effect early the following year.

Action against other additives was somewhat hampered by the inconclusiveness of studies. By 1975, however, scientists had refined their techniques for determining whether chemical compounds cause cancer, genetic mutations or birth defects. That year, the FDA began systematically testing 116 GRAS substances for mutagenic effects and 64 for their effect on embryonic development. The testing program signaled a new era in regulatory practice. Previously the

FDA had been slow to act against additives that were suspected agents of cancer, though the agency's legal power to do so was very clear. Now, apparently, the agency was preparing for action against additives suspected of causing other problems besides cancer, though the legal grounds for doing so were not as explicit. Senator Gaylord Nelson (D-Wis.) tried to get the FDA on firmer legal ground by introducing a bill in the 1975 session of Congress to include additives which may cause mutations and birth defects in the clause that covers those which may cause cancer. Senator Nelson's bill was unsuccessful.

Legislators, food industry officials, and NAS scientists in fact had already expressed reservations about the 1958 amendment to the Food, Drug, and Cosmetic Act which automatically outlaws food additives that cause cancer in man or animals. The provision, known as the Delaney amendment, is the one that most precisely defines the grounds for declaring a food additive unsafe. "No additive," the law says, "shall be deemed to be safe if it is found to induce cancer when ingested by man or animal, or if it is found, after tests which are appropriate for the evaluation of the safety of food additives, to induce cancer in man or animal . . . " [3]

It was the Delaney amendment which, in October of 1969, was cited by the FDA and its advising scientists at the National Academy, as the reason for taking the chemical sweetener cyclamate off the GRAS list and later off the market. The cancer-causing potential of cyclamate was suspected as soon as it came on the market in 1950, and later tests on chick embryos showed it to be a potential cause of birth defects. Various Academy committees subsequently advised against its unrestricted use, but the FDA took no action. In 1969, the Abbott Laboratories, sole producer of cyclamate, brought to the FDA's attention new data from animal tests. The FDA asked the Academy's Committee on Non-nutritive Sweeteners to review the new findings. The committee did so and concluded that cyclamate is carcinogenic and falls within the legal definition of substances known to cause cancer in animals. [4]

The committee noted, however, that cancerous lesions had only occurred in test animals that were fed an amount of cyclamate equal to one-fourth pound of cyclamate per day for a human. The usual rule of thumb for establishing limits on the amount of a food chemical that a person should consume, the committee said, is one per cent of the amount animals can consume without ill effects. Following that rule, small amounts of cyclamate—about the amount one would use in two cups of coffee—would be considered safe for humans, the Academy scientists said. Because the Delaney amendment leaves the FDA no discretionary power to set a "safe" dose or to weigh the benefits of using a carcinogen in food, the committee urged that the Congress consider revising that part of the law.

Had there been good evidence in 1970 that cyclamate was essential for diabetics, effective for controlling obesity, or the only sugar substitute on the market, the public outcry would doubtless have been greater. Congress might have rushed through legislation to keep cyclamate on the market and the Delaney amendment might have been repealed. But the scant research available—primarily that reviewed in a 1962 report of the NAS Food Nutrition Board—indicated that cyclamate was not an effective weight regulator. Some scientists even argued that the sweetener could promote a dieter's appetite for other sweet foods. And people who had to avoid sugar could always fall back on saccharin.

● THE CONTROVERSY OVER SACCHARIN

On March 9, 1977, just days before a new FDA commissioner was to take office, the regulatory agency made an announcement sure to test his mettle and the popularity of the food additive law. The FDA proposed to ban saccharin from foods and beverages. [5] "My first press conference as FDA commissioner," said Donald Kennedy, a former Stanford University biologist, "unfortunately involves a subject that is bad news to a great many Americans. But I am learning that FDA does little that is not controversial." Though saccharin would be banned in foods, Kennedy said, it would be allowed as an over-the-counter drug if its medical effectiveness could be demonstrated. [6]

The FDA decision was based on a Canadian government study showing that high doses of saccharin fed to rats caused malignant bladder tumors in some of the animals. Previous tests on animals had raised suspicion about its cancer-causing potential, but the FDA had chosen not to act until the evidence against saccharin was more conclusive.

Seventy years earlier, in fact, Harvey Wiley, chief of the Agriculture Department's Bureau of Chemistry, suspected that the sweetener caused digestive problems. But Wiley got nowhere with his campaign to outlaw it. Theodore Roosevelt was President, and his doctor had prescribed saccharin to help the President control his weight. In addition to that, one of Roosevelt's science advisors was Ira Remsen, the chemist who had discovered saccharin. In 1912, a board of scientists headed by Remsen concluded that saccharin was safe in daily doses less than one gram (.04 oz.), an amount greater than anyone was likely to consume. The group conceded that more than one gram a day could lead to digestive problems.

During World War II, saccharin consumption increased, especially in Great Britain where sugar was scarce. But later surveys of saccharin users showed no unusually high incidence of cancer among them. Human epidemiological studies, as such surveys are called, are difficult to conduct and their results are often not convincing because the causes of cancer in humans cannot be isolated from one another and because the effects of carcinogens may not show up for decades.

The first systematic animal feeding experiments were done in 1951. Rats tested on a diet of five per cent saccharin for an extended period of time showed no signs that saccharin was a carcinogen, according to the FDA. In 1955 the Academy's Committee on Food Protection reviewed all the scientific literature and, basically, agreed with the Remsen board's findings forty-three years earlier. "The maximal amount of saccharin likely to be consumed is not hazardous," the committee concluded.

Then, in the 1960s, the consumption of saccharin in diet beverages increased dramatically, and the FDA asked for another review. Academy reviews in 1968 and 1970 turned up nothing new because animal studies had not produced any incriminating new data. Two important things did, however, occur during that period to make the FDA less sure that the unrestricted use of saccharin was safe. First, the evidence against cyclamate in the 1969 studies also implicated saccharin, because, as the Academy cyclamate review committee noted, "the most persuasive experiment [that cyclamate is a carcinogen] was done using a cyclamate-saccharin mixture." Second, cyclamate was taken off the market, causing a shift to saccharin by former cyclamate users. The Academy advisors recommended that longer-term animal feeding experiments be done.

In a study sponsored by the sugar industry and conducted by the Wisconsin Alumni Research Foundation in 1970-71, rats fed the five per cent dose for two years developed bladder tumors. But the experiment was done with only twenty-seven rats—four of which got tumors—and the FDA did not consider the findings conclusive enough to invoke the Delaney provision. The fact that a study done for the sugar industry had come up, rightly or wrongly, with new results about saccharin caused the FDA to question the objectivity of studies done for the promoters of the additive. The new evidence against saccharin persuaded the FDA to issue a regulation intended to restrict its use to people on low-sugar diets. The FDA conducted its own tests in 1973 and came out with results similar to the Wisconsin study after feeding fifty-four rats a diet that was seven and a half per cent saccharin, more than five hundred times the amount a person would consume. Instead of taking action at that time, however, the FDA referred its data to the Academy reviewers.

In December 1974, the Academy scientists said they could still reach no firm conclusion and recommended further research to see whether impurities in saccharin were the culprits in the rat tests and what the effects would be of feeding the sweetener to two generations of rats in a row. [7] The Canadian researchers were already investigating both these questions under careful test conditions and using two hundred rats. When the evidence came in that saccharin was, indeed, a cancer agent and that its effect was more severe in the second generation than in the first, FDA saw no alternative to acting under the provisions of the Delaney amendment. [8]

The prospect of regulatory action caused a public protest in Washington unparalleled since the 1973 Supreme Court decision to legalize abortion. Within five days of its March 9 announcement, the FDA had received sixteen thousand letters, many of them mocking the much-publicized fact that the test rats had consumed the amount of saccharin a person would get by drinking eight hundred cans of diet soda a day. Scientists caught the brunt of the public ridicule, which filled newspaper opinion pages for weeks. A cartoonist for the *Philadelphia Inquirer* depicted a saccharin researcher as Mickey Mouse dressed in laboratory garb. Bloated, belching rats writhed on the floor around him. "We fed these rats the equivalent of 800 bottles of diet soda per day," the cartoon character was telling eager news reporters, "and sure enough they got cancer by golly."

The mail on Capitol Hill was the kind no congressman could ignore. Saccharin, one writer said, enabled her diabetic son to drink soda pop like the other kids and was, therefore, essential for his normal social development. Other writers emphasized that saccharin was their only means for satisfying their craving for sweets and controlling their weight. Still others said their children would have more cavities if saccharin were banned from chewing gum and toothpaste. [9] Congress hastened to file bills—about eighty in all—designed to hold off the ban. They competed to see who, in the words of Representative Larry Winn (R-Kansas), would be the "saccharin saver."

Many of the bills called for a review, or for direct modification, of the Delaney amendment. The Calorie Control Council, a pro-saccharin industry group, lobbied hard for legislation that would modify the Delaney amendment without further review. The Council is headed by Royal Crown Cola Vice-president William Miller. Miller's company and all the other makers of diet beverages as well as the Sherwin-Williams Corporation, the sole U.S. producer of saccharin, figured the surest way to keep saccharin on the market was to get the law changed. Other food chemical companies see an advantage in modifying the Delaney provision. Abbott Laboratories, the cyclamate maker, and G.D. Searle, maker of an unapproved artificial sweetener called aspartame, also have executives on the Calorie Control Council.

Prospects for modification of the Delaney clause seemed bright—at least in the House, where nearly enough congressmen to pass the measure had signed their names to such a bill before the new FDA commissioner had even commented on the agency's proposed action. The bill, sponsored by Representative James G. Martin (R-N.C.), contemplated letting FDA officials weigh the value of a food additive against its risk, if the additive were shown to cause cancer in laboratory animals, rather than requiring the FDA to ban the substance.

By April 14, 1977, when FDA Commissioner Kennedy called his first press conference, the movement was well underway in Congress to do away with the Delaney clause. A counter-movement—to keep the law intact—was also gaining momentum. Legislators who thought it would be a mistake to drop the cancer clause charged the FDA with making an issue of saccharin just to generate opposition to the law. To clear up the motive for FDA action, Kennedy told the press and the Congress he would have acted to end the use of saccharin in foods even without the Delaney provision, simply on the accumulated evidence that saccharin carries a risk.

The exposure of test animals to high doses and the resulting tumors, Kennedy acknowledged, do not prove that saccharin, or any other tested chemical, *will* cause cancer in people. The high dosage is simply a scientific tool—and a reliable one, Kennedy said—for predicting that a chemical *may* cause cancer in humans, if it causes cancer in animals. People, he explained, consume much less saccharin but over a much longer period of time. Without the expedient of using high doses, researchers would have to feed thousands of rats low doses for a long period of time to demonstrate whether the chemical can cause cancer. If a chemical is not a carcinogen, Kennedy said, it will not cause animals to get tumors, "no matter how high the dose." He cited a 1969 study by the National Cancer Institute in which 120 suspected pesticides and industrial compounds were tested on mice, but only eleven of the chemicals caused tumors. So, Kennedy said, when studies show that a chemical food additive does cause cancer in animals, that is grounds enough for declaring it unsafe under the general provisions of the law, Delaney clause or no.

The FDA commissioner's statement dealt the Martin bill a serious blow because it said, in effect, that the contemplated change in the Delaney provision would not be sufficient to keep the FDA from acting against saccharin. By this time, health subcommittees in both the House and Senate had held preliminary hearings to decide whether the FDA was carrying out its legal mandate properly by outlawing saccharin and, if so, what legislative action should be taken to respond to the public outcry against the ban. The Senate subcommittee, hoping to stall the onslaught against the Delaney amendment at least until the Congress could examine the issues more rationally, requested the Congressional Office of Technology Assessment (OTA) to review the validity of the saccharin studies and any studies available on the health benefits of saccharin.

Both subcommittee chairmen—Paul Rogers (D-Fla.) in the House and Edward M. Kennedy (D-Mass.) in the Senate—introduced bills to delay the ban for eighteen months. Considering the public sentiment and the FDA's determination to act, a deferral of the agency's action was a politically attractive solution, if only a temporary one. For different reasons, this solution was satisfactory both to legislators who generally favor strong food protection laws and those who prefer the law to be more flexible than it is now. The former group was willing to exempt saccharin in order that other additives would be subject to the full weight of the law, including the Delaney amendment. The latter group felt the eighteen-month exemption would give industry time to prove, if it could be proved, that the benefits of saccharin use outweigh its risks and that future food additive legislation should take this into account.

While the two bills were still being considered by respective subcommittees, news broke of a new Canadian study—this one involving people rather than animals. The study concluded that men who use artificial sweeteners have a sixty per cent greater chance of getting bladder cancer than men who do not use them, but that female users have no greater risk than non-users. Canadian researchers from four universities, working cooperatively, compared a group of 480 men who had bladder cancer with a group of 480 other men, chosen because of their similarity to the first group except that none in this control group had bladder cancer. All the men were questioned about their use of artificial sweeteners and the group with cancer turned out to have a much larger percentage of users than the control group. Exclusive users of artificial sweeteners were found to be among the cancer victims in an even greater proportion. No relationship between the use of sweeteners and cancer was found in two similarly chosen groups of women.

The FDA's Kennedy attached great significance to the study, much more, he said, than to previous epidemiological studies, because the number of people surveyed was greater and because the findings actually showed a correlation with the findings of the animal studies on the sensitivity of males to the carcinogenic effect of artificial sweeteners. He said the findings indicated not only that chemical sweeteners can cause cancer in people who consume much less than test animals but also that the risk to humans may be much higher than the FDA had estimated based on the results of the animal experiments.[10]

The new scientific information, however, caused only a momentary delay in the legislative rush to exempt saccharin from regulatory action. Like the OTA study which, the week before, had confirmed the validity of the animal studies,[11] the new Canadian study on humans did not change many Congressional minds, if any, on how to vote. The OTA review and the new study only affirmed for the legislators that the scientific basis for regulatory action against saccharin was as solid as the political basis for it was weak. What little political support there was for the ban was further eroded when the American Medical Association, meeting in San Francisco that week, recommended that the FDA merely put a warning label on saccharin products. The fact that the public uproar about saccharin was causing his colleagues to ignore the accumulating evidence against the sweetener was not lost on Representative Andrew Maguire (D-N.J.), one of the few active supporters of the FDA ban in the House. "We don't want to act on the basis of scientific evidence, so why don't we just say we're countermanding the FDA and making a political decision," Maguire asked his colleagues on the health subcommittee. Representative Richard L. Ottinger (D-N.Y.), who also favored regulatory action to restrict the use of saccharin, tried to amend the subcommittee bill to allow the FDA to impose some limits on use, short of a ban during the eighteen-month delay. But Ottinger's amendments were voted down.

The differing points of view within the subcommittee and between the House and Senate subcommittees were obscured by the fact that both groups reported out bills calling for deferral of the FDA's action. But the underlying differences were apparent in some less publicized provisions of each bill. The Rogers bill, for example, provided that the Institute of Medicine of the National Academy of Sciences study whether scientists are really able "to predict the effect on humans of food additives found to cause cancer in animals and whether there should be a weighing of risks and benefits in making regulatory decisions respecting such additives . . . " The Kennedy bill provided, by contrast, that saccharin products could not be advertised during the eighteen-month deferral and that they would have to carry a warning label, advising that saccharin has been found to cause cancer in animals and "may increase your risk of contracting cancer."

Without abandoning his bill to modify the Delaney clause, Representative Martin decided to co-sponsor the Rogers bill, apparently realizing that its chances of passage were improved because of its similarity to the Senate bill. By mid-October 1977, the Senate had passed the Kennedy subcommittee bill and the House had passed the Rogers subcommittee bill, both by huge margins.

A House-Senate conference committee produced a compromise bill two weeks later. It provides for the eighteen-month deferral of FDA action, further study by the National Academy of Sciences on the propriety of using animal tests as a basis for banning food additives, and a warning label on saccharin products shipped in interstate commerce.

The most difficult problem for the conferees was how the warning label should be worded. The FDA has required a label on saccharin products since 1972, advising against their use except by people who are on sugar-restricted diets for medical reasons. But some of the conferees did not want saccharin labeled as a possible cancer hazard to humans without more convincing evidence and others felt the evidence was sufficient to warrant such a label. They finally agreed that the warning should say: "Use of this product may be hazardous to your health. This product contains saccharin which has been determined to cause cancer in laboratory animals."

The House and Senate passed the compromise measure in rapid succession and President Carter signed it into law on November 23, 1977.[12]

• CHANGING ATTITUDES: FDA AND THE PUBLIC

In 1969, the public cry, including the voice of big business, was for strict government regulation when the public health is at stake. A survey by social scientist Daniel Yankelovich, published in the January 1970 issue of *Fortune* magazine, showed that among three hundred executives of the country's largest corporations, more favored the FDA decision to ban cyclamate than opposed it, and forty per cent favored more stringent federal standards to protect consumers against health hazards. And this large percentage was among executives who reported, in the same poll, that they felt most government regulated industries were unfairly regulated.

Activist lawyer James Turner, in his 1970 book *The Chemical Feast,* charged the FDA with presuming, contrary to the law, that food additives are innocent until proven otherwise.[13] Within the bureaucracy, President Nixon's food and nutrition advisor Jean Mayer urged the FDA to require not only that a food additive be safe before it is approved but that it be less toxic than other additives used for the same purpose, that it improve the nutritional value of food, and that it hold promise for increasing the food supply and reducing the cost of food to consumers.

The prevailing attitude at the FDA has changed radically from eight or nine years ago when consumer advocates were clamoring for the agency to get tough. The FDA no longer presumes that food additives, generally recognized as safe all these years, are actually harmless and the agency is no longer accepting the word of food additive manufacturers that what they put in food is safe. If independent tests show that an additive cannot be presumed to be safe, the FDA is now acting to restrict or ban its use.

About the same time the FDA announced its action against saccharin, the agency contracted with the Federation of American Societies for Experimental Biology, of Rockville, Maryland, to evaluate the safety of all food additives on the GRAS list. In May 1977, on the recommendation of the federation, the FDA proposed to restrict any new uses of butylated hydroxytoluene (BHT), a synthetic compound used extensively to prevent oily foods from becoming rancid. The action, the FDA commissioner explained, was to keep consumption of BHT at current levels until appropriate tests either removed or confirmed the suspicion, raised by some early studies with rats, that the chemical might cause liver problems. Food manufacturers who want to continue using BHT were required to conduct the necessary studies; the results had to leave no doubt that

BHT was safe, or the FDA would act to remove it from the market.

Consumers can now expect the FDA to take action against some of the old, familiar food additives as systematic testing turns up evidence against them. Likewise, consumers can expect the FDA to take a more critical look at data submitted by food chemical manufacturers in support of their applications for approval of new additives.

In recent years, petitions for new additives or new uses in foods have been arriving at the FDA at an average rate of about two hundred a year and the FDA has approved an average of about sixty a year. About ninety per cent of the time the FDA has no second source of information with which to verify or refute the information it gets from an applicant on the effects of a new additive; the agency depends on the honesty of the applicant and the accuracy of his tests.

Recently the FDA and other government regulatory agencies have discovered that an alarming number of the studies done in support of applications for new food additives, drugs and pesticides have not been as honest and accurate as the regulatory process demands. The first food additive case that put the FDA on its guard occurred when G.D. Searle and Company of Skokie, Illinois, a pharmaceutical firm, applied for approval of aspartame, an artificial sweetener which was to be used in desserts, breakfast cereals, sodas and chewing gum. The FDA reviewed the company's supporting data and gave initial approval in July 1974. Attorney James Turner and physician John W. Olney of the Washington University School of Medicine in St. Louis filed objections to the approval on the grounds that, contrary to Searle's claims, the actual data raised rather than resolved questions about the hazards of aspartame to infants and young children. Searle agreed not to market aspartame until the safety questions were settled.

Meanwhile, the FDA's Bureau of Drugs had been re-examining test data submitted by the same firm in a petition for a drug called Flagyl, because an independent study indicating that Flagyl caused cancer in test animals had, by chance, come into the FDA's hands. The agency undertook a special investigation of the Searle applications during which officials discovered "numerous problems" with eleven studies submitted by the company in support of its petition to market aspartame. On December 5, 1975, the FDA stayed its approval of the sweetener and subsequent petitions have failed to win agency approval. According to FDA officials quoted by *Science* magazine and the *Washington Post*, [14] the agency has referred its findings in the Searle case to the Department of Justice, recommending that the government prosecute if criminal violations are found.

The pharmaceutical company's practices were the subject of hearings in April 1976, before the Senate health subcommittee and the Senate subcommittee on administrative practice and procedure. The hearings caused the FDA and the Environmental Protection Agency to begin investigating the practices of other research laboratories which do animal tests under contract to chemical and drug manufacturers. This investigation turned up, after the fact, discrepancies and irregularities in scientific reports that had been the basis for government approval of hundreds of chemicals and drugs now in use. So many discrepancies were found that the FDA decided to impose strict new rules for laboratory testing nationwide. In two cases, in addition to Searle, agency investigators found such a pattern of discrepancies that they turned the evidence over to the Justice Department. The companies in question are the Industrial Biotest Laboratory, of Northbrook, Illinois, and Biometric Testing, Inc., of Englewood Cliffs, New Jersey.

The overall effect of FDA's hard look at the safety testing business has been a fundamental change in the long-standing agency practice of relying on the data submitted by manufacturers and their contractors. The FDA will not only require now that laboratories follow stricter research protocols; it will check up on the laboratories through a system of internal auditors. Industry and laboratory officials have said that the intervention of federal inspectors and the increased paperwork will only lead to more mistakes and less honesty about them, and will discourage the better research teams from doing work for private companies. But the FDA thinks otherwise and the Congress added sixteen million dollars to the fiscal 1977 budget to get the agency inspection program underway.

Now that the FDA has gotten tough, the public is not so sure it wants as much protection from unsafe food additives as it bargained for. It might be a fair summation to say that the public wants protection from food additives which carry any risk, especially any risk of cancer, unless the additive is perceived, generally, to have beneficial effects as well as harmful ones. Then the consumer wants the right to decide for himself whether the risk is worth taking.

This is very different from the view that prevailed in 1958 when the Delaney amendment was adopted and which has served as grounds for refusal of new additives and the removal of several old ones from the food supply. That view, embodied in the law, is that no conceivable benefit from a food additive is worth risking even a slight increase in the incidence of human cancers because the incidence is already so high. The public has found an exception to that rule in saccharin. And the Congress has decided to make saccharin the exception which tests the rule.

One of the most intriguing questions that can be asked about the politics of the saccharin controversy is this: why did the public interest health groups, after pressuring the FDA for so long to act, not hasten to congratulate the agency on its bold move against saccharin? Were they concerned that the FDA either intentionally or unintentionally was jeopardizing the Delaney clause? Or do these groups also have some reservations about the existing food additive law?

The truth is, public interest health advocates do have mixed feelings about the existing law.[15] If strictly enforced, it guarantees that the public will be protected from food additives that carry any inherent health risk. But it does not guarantee protection from the unknown number of additives which, though apparently safe themselves, enable manufacturers to make foods which are not nutritional. If a law could be written which would allow consumers to weigh all the benefits of an additive against all its risks, public health advocates suspect that many additives now in use would be banned. As long as the law permits the use of additives which have no demonstrable benefit to the public health, however, public interest health groups will fight for legal guarantees against harmful additives.

The ideal public interest approach to food additive regulation was described by James Turner at a public forum held by the National Academy of Sciences in May 1973.[16] Safety, said the public interest advocate, is not a scientific question. It may be asked in scientific terms, but it cannot be answered by science. It is a policy question to be answered by the public. Ideally, he said, food additive regulation would be a three-step process. Scientists would establish what the discernible effects of an additive are. The public, with the help of scientists, would determine which of these effects are risks and which are benefits. And finally the public would decide what weight to attach to the risks and what weight to give the benefits in a decision to outlaw or permit use of the additive.

Thus the equivocal response of the public interest movement to the FDA's action: the public interest health advocates agree in principle with the opponents of the saccharin ban that there should be a weighing of the risks and benefits of food additives. But they generally disagree with industry that this kind of evaluation should be limited to additives which have a known risk, and some disagree with saccharin users that the medical benefits of saccharin outweigh the risks.

FDA Commissioner Kennedy was asked, at a meeting of the American Association for the Advancement of Science in February 1978, how he would feel if the agency were required by law to do a risk-benefit analysis on food additives. "Incredibly nervous," Kennedy said, only partly in jest. The FDA head explained that disputes, such as the one over saccharin and the Delaney clause, could probably be avoided if the Congress would regularly review laws that involve technologies that are changing rapidly. "I wish there were a review requirement on Congress," the Commissioner said, "so they could see whether what they said in 1958 still is what they mean, considering the changes in [cancer-testing] technology."

- **EPILOGUE**

Food manufacturers are now permitted to add some 2,500 substances to foods, counting additives that have been considered safe in the past. Most of these substances are synthetic chemicals intended to enhance the color or flavor of foods or to extend the amount of time foods can be marketed before they spoil or taste rancid. Some, though not the majority of additives, have nutritional value—vitamins and minerals, for example. But to meet government standards foods enriched with these do not have to be as nutritious as they were before processing. That is because government standards have nothing to do with the nutritional value of foods, processed or fresh.

Food additives are clearly beneficial to the manufacturer and the distributor. Use of preservatives allows a manufacturer to centralize production without worrying about the spoilage that would otherwise occur while his product is being distributed over large distances. Flavorings and colors enable a manufacturer to produce an apparent variety of food products using the same basic ingredients, to produce synthetic foods with the taste and appearance of natural ones, and to improve the appearance of fresh foods which otherwise might be rejected by consumers.

Food manufacturers say the use of additives means they can produce foods at lower cost and offer more choice to consumers. But they do not claim that additives have led to an improvement in the American diet. Additives are a mixed blessing to the consumer.

Without them, foods would spoil more quickly, certain foods would not be available, and meals would take longer to prepare. But how nutritious are synthetic foods, preserved foods, and prepared foods? Some research indicates that one additive—BHT, itself under suspicion by the FDA—may subdue the potential carcinogenic effect of another additive, namely the nitrate used to preserve meats. If true, that is comforting news for the consumer who happened to eat the two chemicals in combination. But it is hardly grounds for the meat processor to claim that his use of chemical preservatives has been beneficial to the public health. The individual and collective risks of food additives to the consumer, like the benefits, are very difficult to measure.

If there had been a correlation between the increased use of food additives in the past two decades and improved nutrition, people might assume that food additives are, on the whole, beneficial to health. But poor nutrition remains a national problem. The incidence of diet-related disease here is much higher than in countries where food is equally abundant but where the use of additives is kept to a minimum.

The ironic fact is this: as the problems of the American diet in general and the harmful effects of additives in particular have begun to concern government officials, the public has become less sure that it wants the government deciding, on the basis of scientific evidence of risk, what additives should be eliminated. The public objects only when the FDA acts to remove an additive which people feel they cannot do without. When the FDA acts against an additive for which there is an available substitute or which has little perceived value to the consumer, the public accepts the decision, regardless of how it was made. When cyclamate was available, for example, saccharin was restricted just as FDA Commissioner Kennedy proposed restricting it in his April 1977 press conference. It was sold as an over-the-counter drug. But because no other sugar substitute was available, the public this time fought the proposed restrictions on saccharin.

Public controversy forces people to look at how social decisions are made and to see whether the process can be improved. The saccharin controversy is no exception. It has forced the Congress to ask itself whether the food additive law is still a valid statement of how the public wants food additive decisions to be made. The companion question is whether a new law can be written to reflect public sentiment better than the current law does. The Congressional deferral of FDA's action against saccharin does not answer either of these questions, but it was not intended to. The deferral was to give the Congress time to deliberate over changes to the Food, Drug, and Cosmetic Act "without a gun at our heads," as several congressmen put it. The Congress can use this breather either to find out whether the people really want a change in the food protection laws, and if so what kind of change, or simply to find out what the current views of the National Academy committee are on the Delaney clause.

The current food additive law is based on the principle that the government is responsible for protecting people from harmful substances in the food supply, but not for providing people with beneficial substances. The government cannot make manufacturers put beneficial substances into foods nor keep them from removing beneficial substances from foods during processing. The FDA can only keep them from adding harmful ones. If, therefore, an additive is known to have harmful effects when fed to test rats or injected into chick embryos or tested for its effect on laboratory bacteria, the FDA is obligated to assume that the substance may carry some risk to humans. If it can be proved that a substance will not harm people when consumed in small quantities, the FDA can approve it as an additive with appropriate restrictions on the amount that can be added to foods.

Scientists have long assumed—and the FDA has followed this rule in the past—that people can safely consume one hundredth of the minimum amount of almost any chemical additive that causes harm to test animals. But the assumption that there is a tolerance level for certain toxic chemicals, including cancer-causing ones, has not been substantiated. And studies such as the Canadian survey of people with bladder cancer provide strong evidence that people are not all tolerant to the effects of carcinogens, even if they consume only one hundredth of the amount that causes cancer in test animals. The food additive law was written with the assumption that all carcinogens carry some risk to people, even in small doses; in its enforcement of that provision, the FDA is now taking the assumption seriously.

It is an increasingly popular notion now that government safety regulations prevent people from reaping the benefits of technical innovation, including innovations in food chemical technology. That notion leads to the conclusion that the harmful effects of a food additive should be weighed against its beneficial effects when regulatory decisions are made. The reason people ridiculed the saccharin studies and objected to the FDA's action was not because they believed saccharin to be risk-free but because, for them, the risk seemed far smaller than the benefit.

The dispute over saccharin is really a dispute over what the FDA should take into consideration when it acts to protect the public. Is it the FDA's job—as the current food additive law suggests—to guarantee that any substance added to food will not make a healthy person sick? Or is it the FDA's job—as supporters of the Martin bill suggest—to guarantee that any substance added to food will enable more people to stay healthy than it will make sick?

The importance of the proposed change in the Delaney clause is not that it would allow carcinogens in the food supply, though this could be the result in cases where the benefit to health clearly exceeds the risk. The importance is that it would introduce a new procedure into food additive regulation—a procedure which would establish as grounds for regulatory decisions the part food additives play in the maintenance of health as well as in the cause of disease. If the benefit-risk method should turn out to be a publicly acceptable way for the FDA to regulate carcinogenic additives, it may not be reserved solely for that class of additives. The view could become popular that every food additive should have a demonstrable benefit before the additive is permitted in food. If the FDA is responsible for evaluating benefits as well as risks, the hundreds of additives that have no demonstrable benefit will become conspicuous.

Without realizing it, the opponents of the Delaney clause may be opening the door for those public interest health advocates who have long argued that the only significant social value of food is nutrition and that additives should be judged strictly on the basis of what they contribute to nutrition and health.

V.

The Case of Recombinant DNA: Braving the New World of Bio-technology

Back when science was a lot less specialized than it is today, two rather unlikely fellows made two different discoveries that contributed in an important way to the modern understanding of living things.

One was Gregor Mendel, an Austrian monk, who was preoccupied with the characteristics of pea plants which he cultivated in the abbey garden. After systematically breeding and cross-breeding tall and short varieties, in 1866 Mendel laid out the mathematical evidence for the random inheritance of independent characters which we know today as genetic inheritance. Mendel's concept was diametrically opposed to the conventional view of inheritance, which was that parental characteristics blended together in offspring, like spices in a stew.

Before Mendel's clever work was accepted and affirmed by the similar findings of academic biologists in 1900, the second unlikely fellow had made his contribution. This one, a brewery chemist named Eduard Buchner, was trying to learn how yeast converts sugar into alcohol. The prevailing view of living things—a view which even the great Louis Pasteur held—was that vital processes, including fermentation, could only take place within living cells. Buchner ground up some living yeast cells and strained them so that no whole cells remained. But the purée of yeast still produced alcohol when sugar was added. Suddenly the chemical components of the cell, and not the cell itself, became the keys to unlocking the secrets of life.

Much biological research going on today is centered at the point where the path of genetic research from Mendel converges with the path of biochemical research from Buchner. At the convergence is the field of study known as molecular genetics, and advances in this field during the past five or six years have been remarkable.

• DEBUT OF THE RECOMBINANT DNA TECHNIQUE

"Scientists have shown," notes a 1976 Library of Congress report on the status of genetic research, "that they possess the tools to begin controlled manipulation of the very foundation of life itself."[1]

The report is referring to the ability of geneticists, biochemists, and molecular biologists, as they are variously called, to do artificially what nature sometimes does on its own: to insert a bit of foreign genetic material in a plant or animal organism in such a way that the organism responds as though the material were its own. This research technique was developed in 1973 and is known as the DNA recombinant technique.

Tools of the Trade

DNA (deoxyribonucleic acid) is the chemical substance considered fundamental to life because it is responsible for directing and controlling the countless tasks that cells perform to keep an organism alive and well. DNA is responsible for the fact that daughter cells are identical to their parent cell. In the case of organisms that reproduce sexually, DNA is responsible for transferring to offspring the genetic material that will determine their characteristics. Within the nucleus of a cell, DNA forms microscopic strands known as chromosomes. DNA can also be found in bacterial cells, for example, in thick, circular strands known as plasmids. Viruses are nothing but strands of DNA (or sometimes its chemical complement, RNA) protected by a shield of protein.

A virus can be thought of as the leader of a biological revolution. It invades the cell of a host and puts the cell under command of its viral genes. Not a drop of blood is shed during the coup. Were it not for the fever that a human body generates when it begins to fight back, a person victimized by this invader might not know an insurrection was underway. A virus is a piece of life struggling, like everything alive, against the forces of death. One of the first living things on the earth may have been a virus, though anyone suffering from an attack by its progeny is not likely to find much comfort in these thoughts.

Plasmids, the circular pieces of DNA found in cells but not part of chromosomes, and viruses, the protein-coated bits of DNA which invade cells, are the vehicles that biochemists have turned to in recent years to study the functions of specific genes. The plasmids and the viruses are used as carriers (the biochemist would say vectors) to transport a specific segment of DNA, a segment that includes the genes which the researcher wants to study, into a new host cell. The genes under study then have the host cell do their bidding, just as viral genes normally do. The researcher can measure and observe the way the transplanted genes operate, under the relatively controlled conditions of the laboratory experiment.

The host cell that researchers use when they perform DNA recombinant experiments is a cell which has been used in biological research for about fifty years. It is a single-cell organism, on the plant side of the great divide between plants and animals. It is a weakened variety of the bacterium known as *Escherichia coli* or *E. coli.* The normal strain of *E. coli* is found in vast numbers in the human colon where it is essential to the digestive process.

The term "recombinant," which is used to describe the technique used in this kind of research, refers to the fact that the researcher is able to put pieces of DNA together in all sorts of combinations, most of which probably have, and some of which may not have, occurred in nature. The piece of chromosomal DNA to be studied is cut off from the rest of the chromosome by the action of certain enzymes, organic chemicals which tend to break chromosomes apart at specific places. Researchers then recombine the severed piece of chromosomal DNA with a plasmid or viral DNA carrier which has also been severed at a specific place. To complete the recombination, certain enzymes which patch up the broken ends of the DNA are used. Through chemical treatment of its cell wall, or on its own, the host cell takes up the carrier DNA and with it the foreign bit of DNA under study and begins responding to the orders of all the new genes it has acquired. Usually there is a special gene on the carrier that the researcher knows about, like a gene for resistance to a certain drug which would ordinarily kill the host cell. When he applies the drug and the host cell culture thrives, the researcher knows that the host cell is responding to the commands of the genes it has absorbed.

The foreign DNA reproduces inside its host, sometimes when the host cell divides, sometimes much faster. The host cell may even attach the foreign DNA to one of its own chromosomes, thus altering its genetic make-up. In the case of a single-cell organism, recombination of this type makes the whole organism very different from what it originally was. One does not have to stretch his imagination too far to envision the day when a desired gene from a chromosome of a human reproductive cell can be successfully taken up by a functioning cell of the same type and passed on to the resulting child. Closer, probably, is the day when genes in certain body cells can be altered to make those cells perform functions they were failing to perform. Already E. coli have been put to work in the laboratory manufacturing organic substances they would not manufacture except at the command of foreign genes. DNA recombinant research, its practitioners say, will not only bring these practical benefits, but will also increase man's understanding of how genes work and how they are related to the cellular functions which they control.

Potential Uses of the Recombinant Technique

The potential both for increasing our understanding of genes and for gaining control over them has triggered excitement and activity in laboratories around the world. At this point, much of the activity could be considered basic research, that is, designed to increase scientific knowledge. But there is also in the laboratories a strong tendency, one might say a sense of urgency, about DNA recombinant research because of the practical uses foreseen for its results. Given the choice, for example, of whether to study the function of a gene that can cause a disability in the human population or another, less pernicious gene, researchers are choosing the problem gene. Particular interest is being shown in the genetic control of the production of insulin, an organic substance needed to break down sugars, and in the genetic control of hemoglobin, a protein which enables red blood cells to carry oxygen. When there is a problem with the body's production of insulin, diabetes can result. When there is a problem with the structure of hemoglobin, various kinds of anemia may result. Such disabilities are referred to as gene-controlled deficiencies.

When the genetic researcher describes a problem which he wants to examine, he does not do so in a vacuum. Of the several millions of genes which theoretically might exist on the twenty-three chromosome pairs in a human cell, researchers have identified and learned something about the function of approximately 120. Of the immense amount still to be learned, what is most immediately worth studying? When a university research team submits its proposal for funding to the National Institutes of Health or when a commercial laboratory signs a contract with a pharmaceutical manufacturer, the researcher has one eye on the test tube and one eye on the national health statistics.

With the new technique, basic genetic research can no longer be thought of as an end in itself. It is a stepping stone on the path toward controlling genes for specific practical purposes. Or, put the other way around, "It will only be possible to correct by genetic engineering a given gene-controlled deficiency when knowledge of the gene or combination of genes, or positional relationships of genes within chromosome pairs or even between pairs of chromosomes is known." [2] Whether medical, agricultural, or industrial, the areas of research opened up by the DNA recombinant technique are in the applied sciences, because the technique introduces certain efficiencies, speed, and economy previously absent from genetic research methods.

Agricultural applications that geneticists have postulated include the creation of edible plants which have very efficient growth characteristics and the creation of plants which can take the nitrogen they need directly from the air rather than from fertilizers. Ideas about altering the genetic make-up of organisms to suit certain human purposes are not confined to microorganisms and agricultural plants. Some researchers have suggested that recombinant techniques have the potential to enable man to improve the characteristics of animals which are important to agriculture and the national economy. This would mean making genetic alterations that would cause specific characteristics to persist in the breed, that is, altering the genetic make-up of the reproductive cells. If experiments of this kind in domesticated animals were successful, they would suggest that the same kind of alteration would be possible in human reproductive cells. Man has imposed changes on plants and animals for hundreds of years through genetic hybridization techniques. The potential of those methods and the potential of the recombinant technique, however, differ in two major ways: the *kind* of changes which may be possible, and the *rate* at which those changes may occur. DNA recombination may produce all sorts of genetic "hybrids" which cannot be produced by traditional hybridization techniques and may produce them at a much faster rate than the normal reproductive rate of the organisms involved.

Industrial applications postulated include the use of genetically altered microorganisms for treating industrial and organic wastes, that is, breaking down products like oil or toxic chemicals whose disposal poses a threat to the environment. One of the problems is that the altered organisms would not be able to distinguish between oil or chemicals that happen to be threatening the environment and those that are not. [3]

If the potential use of the recombination technique seems limitless, that is because the genetic combinations, theoretically, are limitless. Researchers doing some of the earliest work with DNA recombination observed that there were no limits on what new genetic combination might be produced in the lab, a fact which has both a good side and a bad side.

Potential Hazards of the Technique

Annie C.Y. Chang and Stanley N. Cohen, working at the Stanford University School of Medicine, and Herbert W. Boyer and Robert B. Helling, working at the University of California School of Medicine, were the first to conduct a successful DNA recombination in *E. coli.* The experiment was simple by today's standards for recombinant research. The researchers combined two different plasmids which occur naturally in *E. coli* and inserted the composite DNA into *E. coli* cells which then responded to the commands of the genes of both plasmids. The carrier plasmid was resistant to the drug tetracycline, a frequently prescribed antibiotic drug, so the researchers knew the plasmid genes were commanding the host *E. coli* cells when the tetracycline resistance showed up.

According to Cohen, before the results of these experiments were published, he and his associates became concerned about possible biological hazards that could arise from the new technique. "Investigators normally facilitate the free exchange of bacteria and other experimental strains they have isolated," Cohen explained in *Scientific American* two years after the experiment, "but Chang and I were concerned that manipulation of certain genes could give rise to novel organisms whose infectious properties and ecological effects could not be predicted. In agreeing to provide the plasmid we therefore asked for assurance that our colleagues would neither introduce tumor viruses into bacteria nor create antibiotic-resistance combinations that were not already present in nature . . ." [4]

Scientists discussed the potential hazards of the new research at a professional meeting, the Gordon Conference on Nucleic Acids, held June 11-15, 1973, in New Hampshire. They asked the National Academy of Sciences to make a more formal study of the hazards to ensure that experiments using the new technique would be safe. The Academy asked Paul Berg, chairman of the department of biochemistry at the Stanford University Medical Center, to form an advisory committee to set some standards for research.

Berg had been studying a virus that causes tumors in monkeys and wanted to use the recombinant technique to examine the behavior of the viral genes further. Slowly, he became convinced that experiments attempting to introduce genes from the tumor virus into *E. coli* could be risky. The risk, ironically, would come with a successful experiment. There was the remote possibility that the laboratory strain of *E. coli,* with its newly acquired viral genes, could make its way into someone's bowels and transfer a tumor-causing gene to the *E. coli* living there, which could conceivably transfer it to the cells of the intestinal wall. Berg abandoned his own plans to do experiments with the animal virus and discussed with colleagues concern over other experiments which might turn *E. coli* into a toxin-producing organism (like the bacterium which causes "food poisoning") or which might give *E. coli* unknown genetic traits.

By the spring of 1974, Boyer at the University of California

School of Medicine, and Ronald W. Davis and David S. Hogness, at the Stanford Medical Center, had demonstrated that DNA from the chromosomes of fruit flies could be recombined with DNA from a virus and that the composite DNA could infect *E. coli* cells and reproduce itself there. Berg assembled ten colleagues, several from the Stanford group and others, from other major universities like Harvard and MIT, who were interested in the recombinant technique for their own research. [5]

Under the auspices of the National Academy, this Committee on Recombinant DNA Molecules released a letter to professional journals [6] in July 1974, calling for a voluntary deferment of two types of experiments. The first type were experiments that might give antibiotic resistance or toxin-producing capability to bacterial strains which do not have such characteristics naturally. The second type were experiments that would introduce DNA from tumor viruses or other animal viruses into bacteria. The Berg committee also warned against introducing fragments of DNA from animal cells into *E. coli* when the precise genetic structure, or chemical sequence, of the animal DNA was not known. Such experiments, now known as shotgun experiments, caused concern because work by Edward Skolnick of the National Cancer Institute and others seemed to indicate that certain segments of animal cell DNA, when introduced into the cells of other species, could give rise to viruses made of RNA, perhaps because the new DNA would synthesize a complementary strand of RNA.

The overriding concern of the Berg committee was to find a way that research could continue without threatening to increase the incidence of cancer or other diseases in humans or any other species. The Berg committee letter urged the National Institutes of Health to establish a committee which could draw up more formal guidelines for the conduct of research with potentially hazardous recombinations. The letter also proposed that an international meeting be held early the following year to discuss the progress of research and its problems.

Such a meeting was convened at the Asilomar Conference Center in southern California in February 1975. According to Berg, who was in charge of organizing the conference and reporting on it later to the National Academy, the bulk of the 130 researchers present wanted only such restrictions on their work as would be necessary to assure safety to lab workers, the public, and the ecological system, generally. [7] Other participants, some of whom were not DNA researchers, favored formal restrictions on the work because of the potential risks, the fundamental nature of the changes that could be artificially imposed on organisms, the irreversible nature of the changes, and the ignorance of the consequences of such changes. But still others were equally opposed to the idea that use of such a promising tool of research should be encumbered by government regulation. Some were even unhappy with the voluntary restrictions outlined in the Berg committee letter, though they had honored the restrictions.

Emerging as one of the most convincing skeptics at the conference was Robert L. Sinsheimer, then a biologist at the California Institute of Technology in Pasadena. Sinsheimer is a soft-spoken and reflective man whose research credentials are admired by his academic colleagues. The fact that such a respected insider would have serious qualms about the research and the fact that their work was beginning to receive public attention persuaded the conference participants that they would have to make a special effort to ensure that their experiments would be safe.

At first the discussion centered on improvements that could be made in laboratories to ensure that the biological agents used in the research—DNA from chromosomes, the viral or plasmid DNA carriers, and the modified *E. coli* host cells—could not physically escape from the laboratory. Physical containment, as these precautions are collectively known, includes everything from rules against eating in the lab to intricate air circulation systems designed to prevent the escape of microscopic organisms into the environment. (The most sophisticated methods of physical containment are familiar to biologists who have been responsible for preventing contamination of the earth by organisms from outer space, and vice versa, and to scientists who worked with lethal germs at the Army's germ warfare center in Fort Detrick, Maryland, during World War II.)

Discussion at the Asilomar Conference soon turned to the idea of reducing the risk of biological hazard from DNA recombinations by making it virtually impossible for the organisms under study to survive except under the ideal conditions provided in the laboratory. The concept of biological containment includes the use of viral or plasmid carriers which are able to reproduce only in certain host cells and of weakened host *E. coli* strains which would die if they escaped from the laboratory. If such biological barriers to the spread of potentially harmful agents could be created, the researchers agreed, anxieties about even some of the more risky experiments could be allayed.

Meanwhile, the conferees decided, certain experiments would be deferred and others would be conducted based on the judgment of the investigator that the physical and biological containment he could achieve would be appropriate to the estimated risk of the experiment he planned to conduct. By establishing new categories of experiments to be deferred, the Asilomar conferees essentially lifted the voluntary ban on certain experiments and placed it on others. After Asilomar, experiments with many animal viruses, including the one Berg had refrained from using, were allowed again, provided the containment was suitable. Also no longer ruled out were experiments that could introduce antibiotic resistance in organisms which had not previously enjoyed such a trait. Still banned were experiments using DNA with genes for the production of toxins. Also banned by the Asilomar agreement were experiments using DNA from certain especially virulent disease-causing organisms and experiments that could produce large quantities of organic chemicals that might be harmful.

The National Institutes of Health, meanwhile, had provided for a twelve-member advisory group whose purpose was to develop ways of preventing the spread of recombinants and to draw up guidelines for researchers working under NIH grants. Membership was confined to researchers in molecular biology, genetics, and related disciplines. The NIH Recombinant DNA Advisory Committee, as it was called, had its first official meeting in San Francisco immediately after the Asilomar Conference. The committee suggested, and the NIH agreed, to let the recommendations from Asilomar govern NIH-funded work until the committee could draw up more specific guidelines.

• NIH RESEARCH GUIDELINES

Between May and December of 1975, various subcommittees of the NIH advisory group drafted and revised and redrafted guidelines. The revisions were an attempt to keep up with research activity and intensifying public anxiety over it. Finally the committee arrived at a set of proposed guidelines by voting item-by-item on the terms of three earlier versions. NIH Director Donald S. Frederickson wanted some advice on the proposed guidelines from people with a broader perspective. He, therefore, called a special meeting of a five-man standing committee whose purpose is to advise the NIH director on matters of social consequence. This committee is made up, generally, of administrative heads of academic and medical institutions. At the public hearing on the proposed guidelines, February 9-10, 1976, at NIH headquarters in Bethesda, Maryland, other people not involved in biomedical research participated, many of whom urged caution until the issues could be discussed more widely. The NIH Recombinant DNA Advisory Committee met again on April 1 and 2 to review the issues raised at the director's meeting and the public hearing and to make final comments on them. In June, Frederickson issued the official Recombinant DNA Research Guidelines, and they were published in the *Federal Register* on July 7, 1976. [8]

It was immediately apparent that the guidelines were stricter than what had been envisioned by most of the researchers at Asilomar, but not strict enough to allay public fears. Even if they had been free of compromises between people with differing views of the safety of the research, the guidelines alone were insufficient to assure public safety for they applied only to NIH-supported research. Privately supported research and work done in foreign countries legally could not be subject to the guidelines, though biological agents produced by those sources might pose as great a threat as agents produced by government-supported researchers.

These original NIH guidelines describe four levels of physical containment and three levels of biological containment and classify all permissible experiments according to what containment is required. The guidelines prohibit deliberate release into the environment of any organism containing recombined segments of DNA from even the most innocuous source. They also prohibit two kinds of experiments, in addition to the experiments involving potent disease organisms and toxin-producing genes ruled out by the Asilomar conferees: Researchers must avoid experiments using DNA from organisms causing plant diseases if recombination could increase the virulence or extend the range of the diseases; and they are prohibited from transferring a drug-resistant trait to micro-organisms which are not known to acquire it naturally, if transfer of the trait could compromise the use of antibiotic drugs.

The most stringent physical and biological containment standards are required for experiments which use DNA from the cells of humans or other primates, especially when the researcher does not know whether the DNA segment he is using may contain a harmful gene. Equally stringent standards are required for experiments using the DNA from animal viruses. Paul Berg, the Stanford Medical Center biochemist, thinks the requirements are excessive. As of early 1978, for example, there were no host cells sufficiently crippled nor laboratory sufficiently equipped so that Berg could do the recombinant experiments, which he once envisioned, on the harmful properties of animal tumor viruses. Though such an experiment is not outlawed under the NIH guidelines, the standards for doing it are so strict that it is not likely to be performed until a special federal laboratory is made available. The federal government is upgrading its World War II vintage germ warfare research laboratories at Fort Detrick, Maryland, to meet the standards for the high level of physical containment which such experiments require.

Many experiments can be conducted under far less stringent standards. Experiments using DNA from fruit flies, for example, can be done under conditions prevailing in an ordinary college laboratory and with the ordinary laboratory strain of *E. coli* acting as the host cell. Though such an experiment may alter the genetic characteristics of the host bacteria as radically as another type of experiment, it is considered safe because the risk of producing a harmful organism or toxic chemical is so slight.

In September of 1976, the NIH Recombinant DNA Advisory Committee approved a new, weaker strain of *E. coli* for use in experiments that would pose a "moderate" risk if the organisms escaped into the natural environment. This allows researchers to study the genetic characteristics of DNA segments from virtually any plant or animal, except humans and monkeys, and allows the study of human and monkey genes if the cells are taken from the embryo.

The advisory committee has certified that the new bacterial strain is so crippled that even if it were to escape the laboratory with a harmful gene, fewer than one in a hundred thousand cells would survive. The researcher who developed the new strain made it sensitive to human bile so that accidental ingestion would pose no health hazard, since the bacterial cells would die before they reached the colon where they might transfer a harmful trait to the *E. coli* there.

Many researchers, like Berg, think the biological safeguards are the answer. Many laymen, however, do not share their confidence. Some are unhappy with the advisory process which puts in the hands of the scientists involved in such a delicate line of research the responsibility for regulating it. Take the case of Roy Curtiss, III, for example, who is a microbiologist at the University of Alabama School of Medicine and whose work is supported by grants from the NIH. He serves on the NIH Recombinant DNA Advisory Committee and his role on that committee, the record clearly shows, has been one of urging stricter rather than looser standards for the conduct of research. Curtiss is also the researcher in whose lab the new, crippled strain of *E. coli* was developed. When it came time for the advisory committee to certify that the Curtiss strain met the requirements for use in moderate risk recombinant DNA experiments, Curtiss and another committee member who had submitted supporting data on the new strain had to leave the room. No doubt the *E. coli* strain would have been certified whether Curtiss served on the advisory committee or not. But concerns about the new strain might have been discussed more freely had Curtiss not been on the committee. As it was, two members of the committee abstained from voting on the question, one more than typically abstained on such decisions. The reason, apparently, was because there were so many unanswered questions about the behavior of the new strain. Experiments with it under natural conditions had fallen short of guaranteeing the degree of safety the review committee had expected. [9]

News of the crippled strain, with the historically significant name X1776, caused a minor revolution in Boston where citizens had already organized to challenge the right of local universities to conduct recombinant DNA research. The Boston Area Recombinant DNA Group had registered its objections to X1776 strain when a working group of the NIH committee had met in Boston in June 1976 to review experimental data on the new strain. The working group had agreed with many of the critical points raised by the Bostonians, except one: that the introduction of a plasmid into the weakened *E. coli* increases its ability to survive in a natural environment. The working group *did* recommend to the NIH committee, however, that future plasmid-host combinations include plasmids with specially developed biological limitations.

Other objections to the NIH guidelines arise not from the process which makes researchers both judge and defendant of their activities, but from the attempt to set safety standards without a concept of the possible risks involved. "How can one erect guidelines," asks Harvard biologist Ruth Hubbard, "when the risk is not known. What are they protecting us from?" If the DNA recombination experiments should produce novel genetic combinations that are able eventually to make their way into human cells and cause harm, Hubbard says, the mystery disease may start showing up as much as fifteen or twenty years after the experiments and may not even be traceable to the experiments that caused it. [10]

• ETHICAL DEBATE

To reduce the risk of accidentally spreading disease, causing ecological damage or inadvertent genetic change, is the goal of the NIH guidelines. But there are other risks associated with recombinant DNA research which the guidelines do not take into consideration. These are the risks to society and to humanity that that would arise from the intentional application of the recombinant DNA technique to human genes. In the recombinant DNA technique, researchers have a tool which may some day be refined enough to use to alter the genetic make-up of humans. Society, however, has no tool which it can use with the same precision to decide whether such genetic changes should be made and, if so, which ones. The scientists are interested in human gene modification. If they were not, they would not be bothered by the current restrictions in the NIH guidelines which apply to work with human cells and they would not have created a national repository for DNA fragments from human cells.[11] "Human eugenics is very much in the public mind," said Cambridge, Massachusetts, City Councilor Richard McKinnon in a March 1977 public television broadcast. People, he said, are concerned about the future of the species. They are concerned about the children that will be born once manipulation of human genes is a reality.[12]

NIH Director Frederickson says it is unfortunate that the issue of human gene manipulation entered the controversy over research guidelines for recombinant DNA experiments. He thinks the issues should be considered separately: one involving the safety of research, the other involving the uses to which research will be put.

Robert Sinsheimer, the Cal Tech biologist who emerged as the skeptical insider at the Asilomar conference in 1975, is sympathetic with those who see a relationship between today's basic research and tommorrow's social dilemma. Certain kinds of basic research, Sinsheimer believes, are inherently dangerous and the capabilities acquired through such research should be exercised with the greatest care. He says the potential danger of the recombinant DNA research technique is that it "introduces a quantum jump in evolution." It allows man to alter the rules of evolution beyond recognition without even knowing what the consequences will be. The public has watched before as some achievement of basic science has led to a particular technology and as the technology has had its unfortunate consequences for society. People are groping, Sinsheimer says, for a way to intervene between the stage where research simply advances knowledge and the stage where it begins to create more problems than it solves.

Researchers doing experiments with recombinant DNA object to having their work restricted for reasons other than safety. They say it is an infringement on their academic freedom, on the free pursuit of knowledge. People who disagree point to the work on nuclear fission which eventually led to the development of the A-bomb. Early fission research, they say, was done in the interest of acquiring knowledge about the structure of atoms. Scientists did not examine its implications, good or bad, until war was about to break out in Europe years later. By then it was too late for any public control to be exercised over the use of fission.

Sinsheimer thinks the analogy with nuclear research is a legitimate one: "I think if you assessed the social value of nuclear research to this point, you would have to say, on balance, it has been negative."[13] Sinsheimer said he believes generally that a scientist should assume responsibility for evaluating the possible effects of his research at an early stage and that the public has a right to do the same. But, he said, scientists have not usually taken this responsibility. "The scientists who differ with me philosophically on this point," he said, "feel confident that nature will take care of everything. They don't see how lucky we have been."

Joshua Lederberg, a Stanford geneticist, published an article in *Prism,* a journal of the American Medical Association, before the NIH guidelines were adopted, suggesting that public fear of the new research might rob humanity of its benefits. Recombinant DNA research, Lederberg wrote, "promises some of the most pervasive benefits for the public health since the discovery . . . of antibiotics." He said the research is likely to lead to ways of producing human proteins, like the globulins in blood, which are in great demand in therapeutic medicine but are in scarce supply. Lederberg's general concern was that the initial cautious approach scientists took could lead to ironclad government regulations which would reduce the benefits. "Those who consider themselves guardians of the public safety," Lederberg said, "must count the costs to the public health of *impeding* research as well as the speculative *hazards* of research." What is needed, he said, is a careful assessment of benefits and risks and, where risks can be identified, the creation of "ethical and operational safety standards."

Ethical standards for recombinant DNA research is a subject widely raised but as yet little discussed. The researcher is not accustomed to scrutinizing the ethical questions his work presents, sometimes because he believes basic research should not be subject to ethical judgments but more often, in this country, because he thinks the ethical question has been settled: he believes that all basic research is good and he thinks that the public should support it because of the benefits they eventually reap from it.

Some research scientists feel that the recombinant DNA technique is especially susceptible to being used in socially harmful ways. Take the case of Jon Beckwith who has been doing research for twelve years at the Harvard Medical School. "Over the last couple of years, we have been discussing in our laboratory how the recombinant DNA technique could make certain of our experiments much easier to do," Beckwith explains. "However, as a result of these discussions, we decided not to use this technique at all. This is not because the particular experiments we were talking about could be thought of as health hazards in any way. Rather, my reasons were that I do not wish to contribute to the development of a technology which I believe will have profound and harmful effects on this society.[14]

"There are still some barriers left to introducing genes into human cells, organs or embryos," according to Beckwith, "but these goals are not at all inconceivable and they may be achieved very rapidly." Beckwith says that the capability to alter human genes is not, in itself, bad. He asserts, however, that the power to alter genes can have bad consequences in a society that has not had time to decide whether it approves of artificial gene alterations and does not have the power, really, to object to these applications. Beckwith cites cases in which the political and social pressure is already great to find genetic solutions to problems which have little relation to a person's genes: companies, for example, which use genetic screening to weed out workers who may be especially susceptible to workplace chemicals rather than clean up the workplace. Beckwith's point is that, as genetic solutions to problems become cheaper or easier than other solutions, they will be used even in the face of strong social objections. Beckwith says it is inevitable that alteration of human genes, like other scientific capabilities, will be used by those with power in society against those without power in order to maintain the *status quo.* For that reason he is willing to forgo the use of the recombinant technique in his own work.

Erwin Chargaff takes a slightly different position but still objects to some of the research on ethical grounds. It was Chargaff whose work on the chemical components of DNA gave James Watson one of the main clues he needed to figure out the chemical structure of

DNA in 1953. Watson's conception of the double helix structure enables the researcher to envision what is happening when a fragment of DNA is severed by enzymes and then joined back together. Chargaff says that research with recombined DNA fragments has caused him to relinquish a life-long maxim: "Never say 'no' to an experiment." There are practical considerations, Chargaff says, for abandoning experiments with recombinant DNA, such as the possible risk to public health. But, he adds, there are also ethical considerations. "People all over the world have become extremely aware of the disastrous deterioration of the environment which industrial and scientific progress has brought them," Chargaff says. "I fear that there is a great likelihood that the research on recombinant DNA which is already being performed, and especially the direction in which it is going, will contribute to the impermissible load that our generation has been imposing on the future."[15]

Politicians, Chargaff says, are not able to represent the interests of the public on matters where science is involved because they have been paralyzed by the "myth of expertise," and allow scientists to make decisions that will affect everybody while policy makers look to less important matters. How, Chargaff asks, would the wise men of Plato's ideal republic have faced the prospect of recombinant DNA research? "They would certainly have said," Chargaff asserts, "that the genetic inheritance of mankind is its greatest and most indispensable treasure which must be protected under all circumstances from defilement."

In this view he is joined by Harvard biologist George Wald who has campaigned publicly for sanctions against genetic alteration, by any technique, of human reproductive cells. Wald believes that if society is as powerless as it seems to be to halt recombinant DNA research, then at least social sanctions can be established against undesirable purposes to which the research may be put. In Sinsheimer's terminology, Wald has decided that one way to intervene in the inevitable progression of science from basic research to undesirable social consequences is to establish early which consequences are socially acceptable and which are not.

● MICHIGAN REGENTS AND THE DNA DECISION

The issues raised by the advent of recombinant DNA research were not being discussed much beyond the confines of scientific meetings when the University of Michigan regents met to handle some routine business in November of 1975. On the agenda at that meeting was a request by the university's vice president for research for approval of a $300,000 renovation of research laboratories. The renovation would permit "ongoing faculty work with recombinant DNA techniques," among other things, and the National Cancer Institute was to provide the funds. The regents, who are elected state officials, did not notice anything special about the request and they gave it their approval.

Several faculty members who knew enough about the research to be concerned about its social implications read about the regents' decision in the local newspapers. They questioned it on procedural grounds, wondering whether all the pertinent issues had been considered when the regents decided to approve the lab renovation project. Regent Sarah Power talked with other members of the board about the faculty concerns and they agreed that they really needed to know a lot more about the proposed research before they could satisfy themselves that the laboratory renovation should take place.

The faculty members who thought the regents had acted prematurely, meanwhile, voiced their opposition during a meeting of the faculty assembly. The assembly passed a resolution asking the university to halt the building plans until a committee, called "committee B" and charged with reviewing DNA research policy, had made its report. Susan Wright, a professor of the history of science and technology, had been among the first to question the regents' hasty action. Professor Wright and a colleague now raised the same questions in a letter to the chairman of the research policy committee. The letter was signed by thirty-four other faculty members, some of whom obtained permission to speak at the next regents' meeting.

When the regents met in December, they realized that the recombinant DNA research technique was no ordinary scientific breakthrough. Frederick Neidhardt, chairman of the microbiology department of the medical school, described the potential risks of altering the genetic make-up of *E. coli* and emphasized that use of the artificial gene recombination technique could ultimately lead to fundamental changes in organisms. "In pursuing DNA research," said Henry Skolimowski, a philosophy professor, "we are actually beginning to tamper with the nature of life itself. In order to tamper with life in a fundamental way, we have to have wisdom and moral responsibility; whereas, in my opinion, we have neither."

Many of the faculty members were insistent that the regents hold off the laboratory plans until the issues could be discussed more widely in the Ann Arbor community and citizens could have an opportunity to express their views. The faculty organized a public forum for March 3 and 4 and invited some authorities on the research from other campuses, but the sessions were dominated by the questions and comments of the audience, now somewhat confused by the conflicting views of the invited experts.

The committee on research policy, meanwhile, was completing its report with the aid of the NIH guidelines which had recently been issued. In its report, the faculty committee concluded that the NIH guidelines would be "an acceptable basis for assuring the safety of experimentation in molecular genetics." The committee suggested, however, that experiments requiring the strictest containment under the NIH guidelines be subject to specific approval by the regents and that the most enfeebled strain of *E. coli* available be used by researchers.

Not everyone on the research policy committee felt that even with these restrictions the research should proceed. The dissent of Shaw Livermore, an historian on the faculty who had been instrumental in arranging the public forum, stressed that danger lay not so much in the limitations of researchers to conduct their work safely as in the limitations of society to cope with the new capabilities that would arise from success in the laboratories. "If [the research] is successful, man will have a dramatically powerful means of changing the order of life. I know of no more elemental capability," Livermore said, "including the manipulation of nuclear forces . . . "

In response to Livermore, law Professor Robert A. Burt cautioned against forestalling scientific inquiry on the grounds that it could change the relationship between man and nature or because it could increase mankind's capability for harm as well as good. "Value perspectives about various technologies," he said, "have changed over time . . . The Copernican view of the universe led to drastically revised views about human nature and destiny, but I am persuaded that the prospect of this revision was not an adequate reason to stop Copernicus' inquiries."

The debate continued at the April regents' meeting and the regents decided to seek opinions from people who had no apparent vested interest in the outcome of the Michigan decision. They invited Paul Berg of Stanford and two officials from NIH to attend a special session May 12 to answer their questions and debate the issues with members of the faculty. Some of the faculty had proposed that risky experiments be restricted to a single national laboratory.

Berg and the representatives from NIH explained the objections of university researchers to that proposal, which, incidentally, had been endorsed by Robert Sinsheimer of Cal Tech in a letter to the regents. A national laboratory, the NIH officials said, would isolate researchers from the university setting where their work could be encouraged or criticized by peers in other fields.

The regents convened for their regular May meeting a week later and passed a resolution approving the research, subject to the NIH guidelines and the additional restrictions recommended by the research policy committee. The regents further required that the research be constantly monitored by a faculty committee which would report to the regents at least annually. In addition to its faculty members, the monitoring committee was to include two members from the Ann Arbor community: the county public health commissioner, who is allied with the university through an appointment there, and a local cleric.

Only one regent, Gerald R. Dunn, voted against the solution that the others found acceptable after six months of deliberation. "I felt that the national laboratory approach was preferable . . . I'm afraid that our decision will bring about a proliferation of [this kind of] research," Dunn later explained.

Many universities have, indeed, upgraded their research facilities to enable investigators to do a variety of experiments with recombinant DNA, but not necessarily because of the Michigan regents' decision. The pressure, by this time, from researchers who wanted to get on with new projects was being felt in universities all over the country. And the universities were responding to it because of the constant battle they wage to keep and attract talented researchers. More than stimulating other university governing boards to make the same decision without public review, the action of the Michigan regents made universities, embarking on the same course, realize that they would have to hold public sessions because their actions would have significance far beyond the confines of their campuses.

- ## "O, YOU CITIZENS OF BOSTON": THE CAMBRIDGE CITY COUNCIL DECISION

There hadn't been anything like it in Boston area politics since Charlie, that victim of the subway fare increase, handed in his dime at the Kendall Square station and made for Jamaica Plain. But the citizens of Boston have a history of recognizing a good political issue when they see one, and the right of citizens to protect themselves from the sophisticated tamperings of university biochemists had all the earmarks of a good political issue.

Cambridge, Massachusetts, is an independent city in the Boston metropolis where Harvard University and the Massachusetts Institute of Technology are located. Some Harvard University scientists who were alarmed at the implications of the recombinant DNA technique confirmed for Cambridge Mayor Alfred E. Vellucci in June of 1976 that Harvard was going to upgrade its biology labs so that new kinds of experiments could be conducted there. The plans were for a $380,000 renovation of Harvard's depression-era biology building so that researchers there could conduct experiments with recombined segments of DNA from mammal cells, for example, or any other experiments that would require a moderate degree of physical containment, to satisfy the terms of the NIH guidelines which were about to be issued.

Vellucci saw the political possibilities. Protection of the public health is one of the fundamental responsibilities of local government, and, in this case, the city council held a trump card: its power to grant a certificate of occupancy for the new laboratory. If the mayor could establish himself as the champion of the public health, locked in combat against the force of intellectual arrogance, there would be some political benefits to reap. Vellucci called a press conference and told reporters that the level of hazard that Cambridge citizens would be willing to accept from the new research was "zero." He and the city council set up public hearings on the matter for the following week, the exact day, as it happened, that NIH released its guidelines.

Among those who brought the issue to Vellucci's attention and who testified at the June council hearing was Harvard biologist George Wald, a man slow of speech and quick of wit. He is fond of predicting that not even the strictest NIH requirements will do away with the red ants that issue from the food vending machines in the biology building, despite numerous attempts to thwart them: "We will have our fancy new laboratory and we will still have our ants."

The new technology, Wald told the Cambridge audience, places in human hands the ability to refashion, in an instant, what it took nature three billion years to design. He said the recombination technique can be used to cross any boundaries which divide living things, including the boundary separating the lowest organisms, bacteria and certain algae, which have a simple cellular structure, from the highest organisms. The recombinant technology, he warned, has the potential to make *E. coli* a disease agent, to breed new animal and plant diseases, new sources of cancer and novel epidemics.

Proponents of the research were angered at Wald's characterization of their work. Mark Ptashne, a Harvard researcher, took on the task of disputing point by point Wald's story about the spread of novel diseases. Despite years of trying, Ptashne said, no researcher has been able to turn the laboratory strain of *E. coli* into an agent of disease by transferring genes from a disease-causing strain to it. Even with no laboratory precautions against the spread of the bacteria, the probability of genetic recombination in *E. coli* ever causing disease is so slight that it might as well be zero. For this to occur, he explained, not only would the segment of foreign DNA, by some miracle, have to turn *E. coli* into a disease-causing organism, but the weak laboratory *E. coli* would have to survive in someone, which does not ordinarily happen, and also survive after leaving the initial host to infect another. The chance of any one of these things happening is small, Ptashne said, and the chance of all of them happening is "vanishingly small."[16]

Other researchers, notably Jon Beckwith of Harvard and Jonathan King of MIT who had decided not to use the recombinant technique in their labs, spoke in opposition to giving Harvard the go-ahead on its new laboratory. Matthew Meselson, chairman of the department of biochemistry at Harvard, and David Baltimore, a microbiologist at MIT's Center for Cancer Research, took the opposite stand. Letters from other biochemists around the country, most of them in support of the research, started piling up in Vellucci's office.

In spite of the pressure, and to some degree *because* of it, the Cambridge council voted on the evening of July 7, 1976, to ask Harvard and MIT to suspend for three months any recombinant DNA research that exceeded very low levels of risk. In the meantime, the council wanted to make an independent study of the potential hazards. In a way, the universities were relieved by the vote, because they had been anticipating a council-imposed moratorium on *all* research with recombined DNA, and because proposals by Vellucci and council member Saundra Graham for a longer moratorium on research had been soundly defeated.[17] The research moratorium, as short and as gentle as it was, was the first of its kind in the country. The University of Michigan regents had taken six months to make their decision but local elected officials had let the university officials handle the matter. With the Cambridge council action, researchers began to talk about how science was being dragged through City Hall.

The Cambridge City Council turned for technical advice to City Manager James Sullivan, who turned to Dr. Francis Comunale, acting commissioner of health and hospitals. Sullivan, it was decided, would appoint a committee of eight lay people whose job would be to review whether the proposed research would have any adverse effect on the public health. The committee would report to Comunale. The job of the Cambridge Experimentation Review Board, in other words, was to decide in three months what scientists had been debating for two years. Fortunately, the review board had the summary opinion of the nation's molecular geneticists available to them in the form of the NIH guidelines.

Among the citizen board members was Daniel J. Hayes, head of a small oil company and former Cambridge mayor whose coolness in the face of controversy eventually won him the board chairmanship and the gratitude of the city council. In addition to Hayes, Sullivan appointed to the review board a former city councilwoman who has a special interest in local health regulations, a doctor, a social worker, an urban specialist who is a professor at Tufts University, a secretary, a community welfare organizer, and a structural engineer.[18]

Throughout August 1976, review board members spent their evenings reading material on molecular biology, many just to get to the point that they could ask the right questions of expert witnesses and understand the answers. The board took testimony from thirty-five scientists, including some who agreed to act as advocates for their point of view in a mock trial. Board members also had phone conversations with officials at NIH, including a lengthy conference call with the NIH director.

On September 27, the city council extended the research moratorium in order for the citizen review board to be able to look over an environmental impact statement the NIH was preparing on the possible effects of DNA research subject to the guidelines. Representatives of Harvard and MIT were consulted before the review board requested the extension and were agreeable to it.[19] The second week in November, however, Harvard announced that it was going ahead with construction of the new laboratory. John E. Dowling, chairman of the department of cellular and developmental biology at Harvard, said the laboratory was needed for tissue culture research whether recombinant DNA work was allowed to proceed or not. This announcement, and rumors that Harvard and MIT researchers were going to defect to other universities where restrictions were not as tight on their work, reached the review board during the final days of its deliberations. On December 5, in fact, the *Boston Globe* carried an Associated Press story quoting Baltimore, the MIT microbiologist, that promising young researchers were avoiding Cambridge and quoting Philip Sharp, an MIT biologist, that his research was stopped in midstream because of the moratorium.

Apparently, the review board was little ruffled by the pressure. On January 5, 1977, as scheduled, it submitted a twelve-page report to the city council. The laboratory could be built and the research could proceed, the report said, if the researchers would follow the NIH requirements plus some additional safeguards to be administered by a local biohazards committee. Unlike many university biohazards committees which have a preponderance of researchers, the proposed Cambridge committee was to represent the whole community. It would monitor the health of lab workers on a regular basis, and would require use of only the most enfeebled strain of *E. coli*.

Review board members later told *Globe* reporter Richard Knox that they were not impressed by the claims that the research would bring enormous benefit to mankind, nor were they at all convinced of the possibility of dire diseases. They were convinced, however, by the testimony of Beckwith and King that the NIH guidelines were not sufficient, considering all the uncertainties. In its report,[20] the Cambridge Experimental Review Board (CERB) made several observations not directly related to its recommendations, but more related to the special problems of making decisions on behalf of the public when scientific issues are involved:

• "Decisions regarding the appropriate course between the risks and benefits of potentially dangerous scientific inquiry must not be adjudicated within the inner circles of the scientific establishment . . . Our recommendations call for more assurance than was called for by the NIH guidelines . . . We recognized that absolute assurance was an impossible expectation. It was clearly a question of how much assurance was satisfactory to the deliberating body, and, in the case of the CERB, the body was comprised of citizens with no special interest in promoting the research.

• "Throughout our inquiry, we recognized that the controversy over recombinant DNA research involves profound philosophical issues that extend beyond the scope of our charge. The social and ethical implications of genetic research must receive the broadest possible dialogue in our society. That dialogue should address the issue of whether all knowledge is worth pursuing [and] whether any particular route to knowledge threatens to transgress upon our precious human liberties.

• "In presenting the results of our findings, we wish also to express our sincere belief that a predominantly lay citizen group can face a technical scientific matter of general and deep public concern, educate itself appropriately to the task, and reach a fair decision."

The Cambridge City Council, and most of the antagonists in the debate, thought the review board did, in fact, reach a fair decision. On January 17, 1977, the city council passed three bills intended to incorporate the recommendations of the review board into a comprehensive city health ordinance. The bills were sponsored by council members Barbara Ackermann and David Clem who sponsored them despite reservations about the research on social and ethical grounds. Mayor Vellucci and Councilwoman Graham voted against every bill. "I am not in the mood to thank Harvard about anything yet," the mayor said, promising a last ditch effort to ban from Cambridge all but the lowest risk experiments. [21] On February 7, unable to get a majority to support the ban, Vellucci joined the rest of the council in agreeing to permit the research under the terms the review board had outlined.

• **WASHINGTON REACTS:
INTRODUCTION OF FEDERAL LEGISLATION**

By October of 1976, three months after final publication of the NIH guidelines and at the height of the controversy in Cambridge, HEW Secretary David Mathews decided that action needed to be taken to apply some safety standards to privately funded DNA research. He appointed an Interagency Committee on Recombinant DNA Research and asked the committee to make recommendations for federal legislation.

A week after the first meeting of the committee, Secretary Mathews received a petition from the Environmental Defense Fund and the Natural Resources Defense Council, on behalf of their sixty-four thousand members, calling for a public review of the NIH guidelines. The petition asked the Secretary to make the guidelines binding on everyone engaged in recombinant DNA research until the review could be completed. It noted that General Electric was interested in developing a bacterium that would degrade petroleum and, thus, could be used to consume oil spills and that drug companies were interested in the synthesis of medicines by recombinant techniques.[22] None of these companies, the petition noted, would be "effectively restrained from conducting any of the experiments which NIH deemed so dangerous that they should not be conducted at all."[23]

The petitioners said that little discussion during development of the NIH guidelines was devoted to whether or not experiments using recombined genes should be performed at all. The scientists who developed the guidelines, said the petitioners, assume "there is an intrinsic and even necessary good in recombinant DNA research" because many of them "are now doing recombinant DNA research and have a vested interest in its future."

On December 20, government attorneys for six federal agencies met at NIH headquarters to discuss whether the federal government had the power, under existing public health laws, to make the NIH guidelines binding on all recombinant DNA research, whether or not federally funded. To the surprise of many, including the Environmental Defense Fund which had petitioned under a section of the Public Health Service Act, the lawyers concluded that there was no single legal authority or combination of authorities in existence "which would clearly reach all such research and all requirements."[24]

The finding, carried by the Associated Press on February 20, seemed to justify the efforts just completed in Cambridge and underway in California and New York State to get safety regulations on the books. To complicate matters, on January 13, 1977, Betsy Ancker-Johnson, assistant secretary of commerce for science, issued a special patent order allowing firms or institutions seeking patents in connection with their recombinant DNA research to gain priority over other patent applicants "if they would certify that they were following the NIH guidelines or describe precisely why not."[25] The patent order was an unabashed last ditch attempt by the Commerce Department under the Ford Administration to stimulate possible commercial applications of recombinant DNA technology. "Where commercialization means that capital is going to be risked," Ancker-Johnson later said, "protection of proprietary interests is necessary. Biomedical research is likely to be impaired unless intellectual property is protected."

Ancker-Johnson explained that one of the purposes of the patent order was to encourage private industry to obey the NIH guidelines voluntarily if they wished speedy processing of their patent applications. Opponents of recombinant DNA research, however, saw the order as an invitation to industry to deviate from the guidelines and to ignore the consequences in a rush toward commercialization.

The events stimulated a flurry of legislation on Capitol Hill. Already Senator Dale Bumpers (D-Ark.) had introduced a bill which would extend the guidelines and enforce them with licenses, threat of loss of patents and strict civil liabilities. In early March, Congressman Richard Ottinger (D-N.Y.) introduced the same bill in the House of Representatives.

Congressman Stephen Solarz (D-N.Y.) and Senator Howard Metzenbaum (D-Ohio) introduced bills which, by contrast, would establish a national commission to regulate recombinant DNA research and to keep an eye on the direction of research for the public.

Senator Edward Kennedy (D-Mass.) and Congressman Paul Rogers (D-Fla.), chairmen of influential health subcommittees in the respective houses, introduced bills with various control provisions. Kennedy's bill called for licensing and inspection of research facilities and Rogers' bill anticipated confining certain high-risk experiments to specially equipped national laboratories.

On March 6, 1977, the *Washington Post* reported that, despite restrictions and the public demand for caution, recombinant DNA research was being conducted at eighty-six universities and research centers and at least nine private companies. Exactly that number of companies had joined funds with government agencies to sponsor a public forum on the issues that week at the National Academy of Sciences. Critics of the research said they were skeptical about the objectivity of the information that would be produced at the forum, considering its sponsorship. Then, on March 15, the federal interagency committee announced that the federal government had made 180 different grants in which recombinant DNA research was involved. The committee said it did not know how much privately funded research was underway but had asked the Industrial Research Institute and the Pharmaceutical Manufacturers Association to survey their member firms.

Congressman Rogers opened the health and environment subcommittee hearings the next day. Betsy Ancker-Johnson, the assistant secretary of commerce who had issued the special patent order in January, was on the hot seat, defending her action as an attempt at full disclosure of information by firms with commercial interests in DNA research. She was not asked by the committee, but confirmed in a conversation outside the hearing room that no private firm had applied for a patent under the special order, which had been repealed shortly before the hearing.

C. Joseph Stetler, president of the Pharmaceutical Manufacturers Association, testified that member companies were following the NIH guidelines, even though not required to by law. Though the drug industry was initially opposed to federal regulation of their recombinant DNA experiments, Stetler said, they now thought it would be a good idea. The firms, apparently, had assessed the public mood and decided it would be easier to work under existing federal guidelines than more stringent ones that might be drawn up by local and state governments. Stetler testified, however, that the industry objected to provisions in the Rogers bill which would virtually confine work with human DNA to centers designated by the secretary of HEW. "The bill," Stetler stated, "would favor governmental and non-profit centers over industry facilities." He also said that industry opposes federal licensing of research projects and prefers a system of registration, as proposed by the federal interagency committee.

Testifying at the Kennedy hearings, April 6, the new HEW secretary, Joseph Califano, announced that he supports federal licensing of DNA research projects. He said that he also disagrees with the recommendation of the interagency committee that federal standards for the research should pre-empt local ones. The Administration position, he said, is that HEW "must permit States or local governments to impose more stringent standards in their jurisdictions."

David Clem, the Cambridge city councillor whose legislation had established the standards for research in Cambridge, was heartened by Califano's testimony. Mr. Clem had come to Washington. He had testified before the House subcommittee and here he was testifying before a Senate subcommittee. "I urge the Senate not to exclude any vehicle for lay review of scientific decision-making that may impact the public health . . . Issues of scientific expediency and convenience should not outweigh informed consent at the local level," he said. "The real issue before us is not recombinant DNA research; the basic issue is the right of the public to know and the right of the public to decide. Our institutional models for decision-making falter when complex issues such as recombinant DNA arise . . . We must experiment with ways to achieve a comprehensive consensus on profound issues of our time. The Cambridge model is one example. It is probably not perfect or even adequate, but it is a beginning."

● EPILOGUE

The Senate subcommittee reported out its laboratory licensing bill in June 1977, with provisions to allow states or cities to set stronger regulations if they can show good reason for doing so. The action evoked a powerful response from researchers who met in Falmouth, Massachusetts, to review the status of research and plan political action. Sherwood Gorback of Tufts University chaired the meeting and reported to the NIH two weeks later that attendants had unanimously agreed that the dangers originally envisioned had virtually been eliminated by the use of enfeebled bacterial strains. Another 137 scientists wrote an open letter to the Congress saying that laboratory experience during the past four years had demonstrated that there is no "actual hazard" from the research. Finally, a group of scientists headed by Stanley Cohen of Stanford, many of whom were among the first to call the voluntary moratorium on certain experiments, met with Senator Kennedy on July 18.

In September, Kennedy withdrew support from his own bill, advocating instead a one-year extension of the NIH guidelines and a study of the issues by a commission to be appointed by the National Academy. He said he had been persuaded by the researchers who opposed tighter controls that their work was not as hazardous as originally imagined. In the House, Interstate Commerce Committee Chairman Harley M. Staggers (D-W.Va.) blocked a full committee vote on the Rogers subcommittee bill.

Congressional attention turned in the fall to energy legislation and the recombinant DNA regulatory bills were left in limbo. Then, on October 6, 1977, the issue came briefly back into the spotlight when the U.S. Court of Customs and Patent Appeals ruled that a company can patent new forms of life which it develops. National Academy of Sciences president Philip Handler told a Senate subcommittee, November 2, that scientists from university and private research institutions had artificially produced a brain hormone by using the recombinant technique. He simultaneously reported that a National Academy committee had determined that the hazards of DNA research, which was obviously leading to useful results like the one described, were negligible.

In the absence of Congressional action, the White House asked private firms if they would comply voluntarily with the NIH guidelines. Senator Adlai E. Stevenson (D-Ill.) told Presidential science advisor Frank Press at subcommittee hearings November 9, 1977, that he did not think the Administration was pushing hard enough for a research control bill. Press responded that the Administration had modified its view somewhat on the risk of the research.

The subcommittee heard testimony that already one university researcher had violated the NIH guidelines by using an unapproved plasmid in an attempt, which was later successful, to duplicate a rat insulin-producing gene. A month later, the NIH was forced to order a Harvard researcher to suspend his research for an apparent violation of the guidelines. The Environmental Defense Fund publicized the case, but these events had little effect on the Congress, now feeling less pressure from worried constituents than from annoyed researchers.

The NIH, meanwhile, held hearings on proposed changes to ease the guidelines. It appears as a result of these hearings that the original restrictions will be lifted from about a hundred of the three hundred recombinant DNA projects now being conducted with federal funds.[26]

VI.

Science and Human Progress: Summary and Prospectus

By the time Congress voted against the SST in 1971, social goals in America were changing discernibly. One of the clearest expressions of the change was the emerging public attitude toward the use of technology. As long as national goals had been preoccupied with military superiority and prowess in space, the public attitude toward big technological projects was quite positive. Technology held the key to meeting those goals.

As national attention shifted back to intractable domestic problems, however, the limitations of technology became more obvious. "If this country can land a man on the moon," social reformers of the early 1970s often asked, "then why can't we do such and such?" The "such and such" usually had to do with some basic social or ecomomic goal like housing and feeding people or getting them jobs, or transporting to work those who had jobs. People began to realize that these problems were not the kind that could be solved by crash research and development programs.

At least two major social changes of the 1960s led people to question whether technological advance was an accurate measure of human progress.

One extremely important change was brought on by the quest of young, relatively well-off college students for fundamental values in a world which espoused certain values, but seemed not to practice them. "Love thy neighbor," except if he is a different color, then don't even let him into the neighborhood. "Thou shalt not kill," unless the war is against communists, and then the more the better. And so forth. As these students looked for the source of contradiction in the generation that preceded them, they found it in a hypocritical moral code, a social system that divided instead of uniting people, an economic system that put profits ahead of people, and a political system which promoted social differences by concentrating power in the hands of the wealthy.

Big technology was a symbol of what these students considered the immorality of the American system. It allowed the wealthy to increase their wealth. It depersonalized society. It allowed the country to wage war in new and awful ways. And its ill effects were visited disproportionately on the poor and powerless. One could predict whose neighborhood the next superhighway would go through and whose school would be downsteam from the new chemical plant.

These young people embraced an ethical code that stressed personal relations, especially intimate relations, among peers, and de-emphasized the work ethic. Social responsibility for them involved getting the national house in order before overcrowding it with more people whose future would be even less certain than their own. The national birthrate began to drop noticeably.

But a second change was occuring in the larger society during this period that was to have an even greater effect on the public concept of progress in the 1970s. People were prosperous. Business was reaping the benefits of innovation, ploughing money back into research, and expanding. More people had more money to spend on non-essential items—home appliances, travel, entertainment—during the 1960s than at any previous time in the country's history. That meant greater production and more consumption of goods—and inflation. Planners began to extend the lines on their graphs and see that the national economy could not sustain such rapid growth, especially if one put into the equation the "real" future cost of energy and other limited resources, and the "hidden" costs of environmental pollution. The predominant concern of policymakers became that of limiting growth without causing economic recession.

Yet industry, agriculture, education—the whole structure of American life was built on the technical advances of the past thirty years. The country could not go back and start all over, but it could not continue to consume scarce fuels at a rapid rate nor defer its debt to the environment any longer, either. The federal government would have to exercise more control over technology, especially those technologies which affected the public health adversely. Even business leaders, who were traditionally against government regulation of the market, saw a need for government action when a product or practice threatened the public health.

One of the side effects of the general prosperity of the 1960s, it should be noted, was that a significant number of people, having achieved material success, realized that money was not the key to happiness that Depression-era fables had said it would be. They realized the truth in G.K. Chesterton's quip: "Nothing fails like success." They began looking inward to understand themselves and learned how to encourage what they found valuable within and to discourage what they found undesirable. The same principle, they found, could be applied to political choices. People began to think of government projects in terms of their human value, encouraging those which elevated the individual and discouraging those which further depersonalized.

People who were concerned about the adverse effects of

technology and the tendency of government to support technological development noticed—particularly after the initial successes of the anti-war movement, the consumer movement, and the environmental movement—that government policies could be altered if enough pressure were exerted by informed citizens who could document their case. This was the age of Ralph Nader, citizen advocacy, and public interest research; and of John Gardner and public interest lobbying. Organizations, supported by individual donations, pleaded the common cause before Congressional committees, flooded the federal courts with class actions, conducted seminars, demanded public disclosure of technical information, and pushed for broader representation of views on governmental science advisory committees. Their cause was aided by a new seriousness on campus toward the social sciences, a trend in government to adopt the techniques of private enterprise for long-range planning, and the growing sophistication of methods for detecting harmful substances in the environment and for measuring the effects of environmental change on living things.

By 1971, legislation to protect the environment was on the books and it was commonly agreed that even the most desirable technical advances have drawbacks. The problem of air pollution from automobiles illustrated how certain drawbacks do not become obvious until a technology is widely used and how difficult the problems are, at that late date, to rectify. The SST decision marks the beginning of official recognition that the disadvantages of a particular technological development might, in the long run, outweigh its advantages. The Congress, convinced that it had a responsibility to anticipate both the good and bad effects of government-supported technologies, established the Office of Technology Assessment in October of 1972.

Late in 1973, the Arab oil embargo and recession in the midst of inflation began to create political pressure against the new environmental policies. President Nixon, and President Ford after him, deferred pollution control efforts, encouraged energy production, and loosened regulatory controls on energy supplying industries. People who no longer believed that a technical solution was always the best solution to a national problem were dismayed. To them the energy crisis should have been taken as a warning that energy consumption and energy consuming technologies would have to be curbed, not that energy production would have to be increased. The relaxation of controls, however, was welcomed by many people, including some very influential scientists who remain convinced that technological innovation is the key to social progress and economic health, and who were becoming concerned that government controls were stifling innovation.

In 1974, for example, Freeman J. Dyson, a theoretical physicist on leave from the Institute for Advanced Study at Princeton, New Jersey, gave a speech on the subject to the International Meeting on Scientific Research and Energy Problems, convened in Madrid. In his talk, Dyson compared the hidden social costs of technological innovation with the hidden social costs of saying no to technology. He concluded that the risks of technology were being more carefully documented by the government than were the benefits. Legislative curbs on technological innovation, designed to avoid those risks, he stated, could result in devastating social costs in the long run.

Sentiment against science and technology and the changes they bring is nothing new in human history. Researchers are quick to point out that political repression of scientific inquiry has occurred even in this century. A favorite example is the repression of genetic research that occurred in the Soviet Union when Joseph Stalin adopted the views of geneticist Trofim D. Lysenko because they were compatible with Stalin's views of the communist state. The most recent *popular* movement against basic science took place in nineteenth century England when intellectuals became concerned that science could erode social values and argued that the sciences should be kept out of the curriculum. The precursor of the English humanistic movement, as it was called, was Jonathan Swift. One need only recall his satirical images—the mathematician who had to be interrupted from his thoughts to greet a visitor and the physicist who collected energy from cucumbers—to understand why researchers are on the defensive.

The current movement, in the U.S. and elsewhere, which holds that technological advance does not always bring social progress has some similarities to the English humanistic movement a century ago. The differences, however, are more striking. The current movement is a reaction to the convergence of science and technology, particularly the dominance of technology, in this century. It is not intent on preserving any political or religious or even educational regime. The challenge is not so much to preserve a particular way of life as it is to avoid the sometimes excessive social burden that technology imposes—both the direct costs that Friedrich Juenger and Rachel Carson wrote about and the more subtle dehumanization that captured the thoughts of young Henry Adams and Aldous Huxley. [1] This movement is not anti-scientific. Its adherents are not concerned with what goes on inside the lab, except for the possible creation and escape of pathogens. They are concerned with how the technologies developed there are applied. They point the finger not at the discovery of uranium fission but at the government-supported development of the atom bomb. The current movement is more prudent than it is dogmatic. It does not hold that all technologies are bad, but that some are potentially more harmful than others and could affect mankind in profoundly undesirable ways.

Some clever person summed up the viewpoint, that finally emerged as a popular one in this country in the late 1960s, this way: "When you have come to the edge of a giant precipice, the only progressive step is a giant step backwards." The analogy is a good one because a person's attitude toward technological progress is bound up with his notion of social progress. The person who believes that recent technological developments have helped society along a difficult, but progressive, path also believes that the precipice society has come to is just another chasm that technology can bridge. The person who believes society has already followed its technological impulse dangerously far, believes it is time to step back and perhaps to take another route.

The U.S. government today still strongly supports development of technological solutions to national problems, but more cautiously than in the 1960s. The government is paying more attention to the immediate risks of certain technologies, as more is learned about the risks. To complete the analogy, government policy today tends to favor building a bridge, but a safe one, over the chasm. The bigger question in people's minds—whether mankind is headed in the right direction—is often debated today. But policy decisions are influenced by the fact that government-supported technology often provides a bridge, and using it is easier than taking another route.

The conflicting views of the place of technology in human progress have made the job of the conscientious government decision maker much more difficult. He seeks advice from experts and they disagree. He picks up reports from two government agencies and they contradict each other. He gets conflicting views from citizens. How does he decide?

The following parts of this section provide a summary of how government is organized to make decisions when science or technology is involved, criticism of the decision-making process, and some recent ideas for changing it.

• GOVERNMENT ORGANIZATION: WHO DECIDES AND HOW?

The Congress

Technical developments that can be applied to national needs come about decades after research efforts begin. And the effects of technical applications often do not show up for decades. Their long life cycle is not one that fits well with the term of the average congressman. Members of the House, of course, run on a two-year cycle and the Senate, a six-year one, with a third of the members running for re-election every two years.

Subcommittees. Each house of Congress has a committee which nominally has jurisdiction over scientific and technological matters. But most of the work on scientific issues of public concern goes on in the dozens of subcommittees that have jurisdiction in a particular field, like health, or which have jurisdiction over a particular federal agency, like the Food and Drug Administration or the Nuclear Regulatory Commission. And often a specific technical development project flourishes or dies finally based on the support it gets from members of the appropriations subcommittee with jurisdiction over it. Funds for a demonstration plutonium breeder reactor, for example, were stripped from one energy bill last session only to be restored in an appropriations bill a few weeks later.

The chairmen of congressional subcommittees are a breed which has survived in office by developing a constituency. Each stands to become one of the few really powerful members of Congress depending on how well he builds on and broadens that support. The competition among subcommittee chairmen for influence among their peers and for attention from voters can be fierce. One of the best ways a chairman can achieve both is to determine what issues are of the greatest public interest, introduce legislation on the subject, issue press releases, and then hold hearings on the legislation. The development of new technologies and the control of existing ones, of course, are subjects of increasing public interest.

If the action of a particular regulatory agency is too tough for the public taste—as was the FDA's proposal to ban saccharin from food—the chairman can introduce a bill to head off the agency's action and hold hearings on it. If, on the other hand, public groups begin to criticize a regulatory agency for being too lax—as they have the NRC recently—a subcommittee chairman also may find it advantageous to hold a hearing to investigate those complaints.

In the past, hearings on government-supported technical development programs often amounted to a mutual effort between legislators and administrators of executive branch agencies to build Congressional and public support for a specific project. The motive of the legislators was to make a national reputation or channel government money to the voters back home and the motive of the administrators was to expand agency programs. Retired bureaucrats are full of stories about how they would get word of a prospective hearing, complete with a list of questions they would be asked, and in plenty of time to collect information justifying some new program or other.

As constituencies developed in opposition to various development projects, like the supersonic transport plane, hearings were often held by one subcommittee to counter the information generated during the hearings of another subcommittee. Lobbyists, representing both public and private interests, quickly learned which congressmen would be sympathetic to their position, which of these would be most influential, and which were undecided on an issue that might go either way in committee, or later, in a full House or Senate vote, or even later, in a House-Senate conference committee vote. This kind of activity, of course persists in the Congress and, probably, to the benefit of all of us who have neither the time nor inclination to inform ourselves fully on each of these issues and to write our congressmen.

Most legislators, however, have come to realize that issues involving the control or encouragement of technology are complex and not resolved by legislation which takes an extreme position in favor of or against a particular technical development. As a result, subcommittees tend now to invite testimony from spokesmen representing all discernible viewpoints. These include not only university researchers working in the particular field and funded by the government, and industry researchers and spokesmen, but also laymen who have become more or less expert in the particular field out of a sense of public responsibility. Typically, they have already expressed their views publicly. By the time of the hearings, bills have already been introduced reflecting the legislators' early reactions to the issue at hand. After the hearings, bills are withdrawn or amended until one reflects a consensus of the subcommittee's considered judgment. On the other side of Capitol Hill the same process is going on in another, or several other, subcommittees. If the bills finally reported out are markedly different, serious lobbying begins.

It was at this point, for example, that research biochemists and geneticists who opposed legislative curbs on their use of the recombinant DNA technique, were able to bring pressure to bear against the Kennedy subcommittee bill, which had relatively strict control provisions, in favor of a bill which provides for a National Academy of Sciences study of whether legislative controls are necessary.

Scientists, who are at the forefront of research and its emerging applications, have a stake in government-supported programs and are in a good position to persuade legislators of the value of these programs. The built-in bias of a scientist involved in a research or development project, however, may cause him to discount problems which other citizens might consider serious, if they knew about them. Two years ago, the Congress enacted a Kennedy bill designed to reduce the gap between what the average citizen knows about technical developments that may affect him and what the scientist knows. The assumption behind the Science for Citizens program, created by the bill, is that lay citizens are at a disadvantage when trying to influence government research and development policies and regulatory policies unless they understand the technical side of the issues. The program, however, is very circumscribed, because of fears in Congress that the money will be used not to educate but rather to propagandize against specific government research and development programs. More will be said about this program in the following discussion of the National Science Foundation.

The OTA. The Congress does have one way, in addition to hearings, to get information about technical developments from scientists and non-scientists alike. Its Office of Technology Assessment is charged with identifying the potential good and bad effects of technology early enough so that considered legislative action can be taken to support, manage or regulate a particular development.

The law that created the OTA in 1972 acknowledged that technical applications were increasingly pervasive and were affecting the natural and social environment in profound ways, beneficial and adverse. The problem was that the legislators had no way to get an objective evaluation of these effects. Hearings were not adequate for this purpose. Agency officials could not be expected to testify critically about the effects of technical development programs they were responsible for administering. In the words of the Technology Assessment Act: "The Federal agencies presently responsible directly to the Congress are not designed to provide the legislative branch with adequate and timely information, independently developed relative to the potential impact of technological applications, and the present mechanisms of the Congress do not [provide that information]."

The OTA is, by law, to act as a kind of early warning system, to anticipate the effects of technology before they actually occur. The basic function of the office is, according to the Act, ". . . to provide early indications of the probable beneficial and adverse impacts of the applications of technology . . . "

Technology assessment, as applied to the Congress, is a systematic method for enabling legislators to see what options they have for managing, regulating, or supporting given scientific or technical developments and what the consequences might be of various legislative actions, including the unforeseen effects that so often accompany government support or regulation of technology. Technology assessment borrows methods from planners, market analysts, policy analysts, and social forecasters. The OTA intentionally solicits public participation in its assessments because, as one staffer put it, "part of our job is to find out ahead of time whose ox is going to be gored."

Congressional committees initiate assessments and they are undertaken if approved by the director of the office and a bipartisan board of directors, six members from the House and six from the Senate. The judgments of the OTA director and the Congressional board are, in turn, influenced by an advisory council whose members are people eminent in the physical, biological, or social sciences or otherwise distinguished for their public service.

In practice, and particularly since requests for assessments have exceeded the number that can be undertaken, considerable power over whether an assessment is done has fallen to committee or subcommittee chairmen who either serve on, or have friends on, the OTA board. The influence of the senators on the board has been considerable because, in the past, they have virtually been able to place someone of their choosing on the staff of an OTA program—transportation, energy, food, health—in which the senator is particularly interested. That practice has been ended under the new OTA director, Russell W. Peterson.

The result of all this is that the OTA has been valuable to a limited number of committees, particularly Senate ones, in their day-to-day task of overseeing the work of executive branch agencies. At the same time, the office has been frustrated in trying to live up to its promises to anticipate the more subtle and longer-term effects of government supported technology.

One of the problems has been the difficulty of making technology assessment, with its intended long-term view of the future, fit the needs of legislators who are working on more narrowly defined problems and whose view of the future may be limited to their term of office. Retired Representative Charles Mosher (R-Ohio), former vice-chairman of the OTA board, told a group of professional technology assessors in 1976 that he couldn't name more than about a half-dozen colleagues in the House who agreed with him that technology assessment was valuable to their work.

Former Congressman Emilio Q. Daddario (D-Conn.), author of the legislation which created the OTA and first director of the office, was under constant pressure to justify continued funding for the fledgling institution. He, therefore, emphasized short-term studies with direct relevance to Congressional hearings and longer-term assessments that could be done in phases. Peterson, who took over the OTA directorship early in 1978, has said he tends to favor assessments which take a broad look at future trends. If he can demonstrate the value of this approach to members of the Congress, Peterson, who was most recently involved with the founding of a national citizens' lobby called New Directions, may set the OTA on the course originally charted in the founding legislation.

Some examples should suffice to indicate the kinds of assessments that have been done, and what the results have been. A story about assessments that were conceived, but never undertaken, should illustrate the current limits of the Congressional technology assessment process.

In the fall of 1974, when the interrelated problems of automobile pollution, energy consumption, and unemployment were on the minds of city officials, some communities began showing an interest in advanced urban transit systems. The prototypes of these computerized, automobile-like systems were on the drawing boards of Department of Transportation contractors. The transportation subcommittee of the Senate Committee on Appropriations, aware of problems with new systems in San Francisco and Morgantown, West Virginia, wanted to know if the more advanced systems were economically or socially desirable. The OTA did an assessment [2] which, among other things, questioned the economics and the social acceptability of certain of the systems. The result was that the Appropriations Committee modified the urban mass transit budget to require further investigation of the social and economic aspects of these systems before the DOT proceeded to develop them.

Likewise, an OTA analysis of the Energy Research and Development Administration program for fiscal 1976 resulted in a major shift in emphasis in energy research and development. ERDA was required to increase its program on energy conservation and to pursue a broader range of energy options, for example, nuclear breeder technologies that might subsititute for the plutonium breeder, and non-electric solar technologies.

In March of 1977, the OTA did an assessment called "Cancer-testing Technology and Saccharin," which the health subcommittee of the Senate Committee on Human Resources requested in order to evaluate the FDA's proposed ban on saccharin. By the time the draft came out three months later, public pressure on the Congress to keep saccharin on the market was so great that the OTA's work was of little real consequence. The saccharin assessment basically confirmed the FDA's finding that the sweetener is a weak carcinogen and a potential cause of cancer in humans, and that the exact risk cannot be estimated from scientific experiments. The study also noted that many saccharin users perceive it as a benefit, though medical studies are lacking to demonstrate whether use of saccharin by diabetics and other people has resulted in improved health.

The near uselessness of the saccharin assessment is testimony to the fact that purely rational methods for weighing the benefits and risks of technology and the products of technical innovation are not a sufficient basis for decision making in a democratic society. The technology assessors, of course, know this. And one of the important things they have found is that the removal or control of a product of technical innovation is often perceived as a disadvantage, whether the intrinsic benefits outweigh the risks or not.

All the greater, one might conclude, is the need to find out whether new technologies harbor future problems *before* the technology is widely used. The OTA, however, has not had much demand for assessments of new and emerging technologies. A fall 1976 request by Senator Clifford P. Case (R-N.J.) raised some hopes for improvement of that situation.

Senator Case, who serves on the OTA board, asked the staff to explore the question of how to fulfill its early warning function better. Two staffers took an informal poll of twenty-six administrators of research at universities and private companies to get a feeling for what lines of research or technological trends were likely to affect society most in the future. The research directors identified three items most frequently:

- advances in medical biology, including technologies which might eventually allow man to alter his genes
- the spread of computer technologies into new phases of human activity
- breakthroughs in communications technology

The staff members reported their findings to the OTA advisory council in November 1976, adding a fourth item—a trend toward production of synthetic food. They told the council that some of the people interviewed had raised the question whether OTA should not concentrate its early warning activities on emerging national needs rather than emerging technologies.

Advisory council member Frederick C. Robbins, dean of the Case Western Reserve School of Medicine, commented that OTA might want to investigate not only the effects of technology on society but also the effects of society on technical innovation. Jerome Wiesner, the council chairman, endorsed Robbins' suggestion. He speculated that, by the 1980s, technical applications may have slowed down to the point that national problems, now associated with technology, may then be associated in the public mind with a lack of technical innovation. Other OTA advisors, not so concerned with the speculation about a technological slowdown, were nevertheless intrigued with the idea of an OTA study on changing social values.

The advisory council met again on the question of OTA's long-range assessment capability in February 1977. Hazel Henderson, co-director of the Princeton Center for Alternative Futures, Inc., said she was excited about the prospect of the OTA studying social change because it might have the effect of the bringing some coherence to public policy. "The feedback [government is getting from people] says that the system has a problem. The scientists don't hear the feedback," Henderson said. "They are good at innovation and change but not so good at handling limits . . . Members of the scientific community were the last holdouts among people recognizing the limits to growth." Henderson is hopeful that OTA might get at questions like the moral inhibitions to recent developments in genetic research and other questions that highly rational analyses tend to overlook.

The advisory council gave the OTA staff the go-ahead on a study of public perceptions of technology. The study is underway now and it will be investigating some fascinating hypotheses: Do changing perceptions of technology affect what kinds of technologies will be applied to national problems? Do changing values influence whether technology is considered an appropriate solution to these problems at all?

The immediate effect of the advisory council's action, however, was to put off assessments of the long-term social consequences of recently developed genetic research techniques and the other items identified by research directors in the informal poll. The deferral came at a time when social controversy over recombinant DNA research was reaching such a pitch that members of Congress were beginning to introduce legislation to regulate research. Thanks to the conscientiousness of some of the scientists doing this research and some of their peers who questioned it, the public became well enough informed so that public safety issues have been aired for the legislators.

But the more profound issue—whether the purposes to which the recombinant DNA technique may be put are socially desirable—has received very little attention in Congress, nor does there exist any national policy on biomedical practice that might be used to regulate future applications of the technique. This is the kind of issue that OTA is supposed to present, in all its complexity, to the policy makers. The OTA exists because dramatic new technologies like recombinant DNA have arisen and will continue to arise and will be used, to understand the world and to change it. The OTA was to be the voice of prudence among all the others on Capitol Hill clamoring for expedience. On the subject of recombinant DNA, however, the OTA's voice has been silent.

So great is the influence of a few people in Congressional advisory positions that their views can determine what becomes an issue, demanding resolution, and what is passed over in the legislative rush. Had the advisory council not steered the OTA staff away from the issues raised by the advent of recombinant DNA and other emerging technologies, a study of these issues could have been completed at this writing and could serve as an objective basis for legislation in the next few years.

The Executive Branch Agencies

The government agencies which spend the money Congress appropriates for research and development are called mission agencies because they have a defined purpose. These agencies have come into being as the Congress and the President perceived a need for them. Most have been created since World War II when government officials learned that even the most esoteric research can lead to highly practical results. Other mission agencies, whose origins, like those of the NIH, antedate the war, really began to flourish after it.

The Atomic Energy Commission was born with twin objectives: to develop peaceful and military uses of atomic power. The National Science Foundation soon came along so that university research, in general, would have a source of government funds; NASA, to answer the Soviet challenge in space; the National Cancer Institute, to find a cure for cancer; the Urban Mass Transportation Administration, to make the cities accessible again; the Energy Research and Development Administration and, now, the Department of Energy, to find new ways to produce energy and to use it more efficiently.

The government agencies whose main job is to protect the public from hazardous uses of technology are regulatory agencies. They are, in a sense, mission agencies, too, but their mission is to crack down on individuals or industries which violate federal standards designed to protect the public interest. They have the obligation to enforce regulations that are spelled out in federal laws, and when the law is not explicit, to develop standards that will carry out the intent of the law.

The post-war mission agencies are a result of intense cooperation between government and science and they have produced equally intense cooperation between government and industry. The regulatory agencies are a result of public fears that these relationships can lead to undesirable, even collusive, results.

The Food and Drug Administration, for example, came into being only after the public was outraged by graphic reports of the practices of the meat packing industry at the turn of this century and after a crusading Agriculture Department chemist began warning people about the chemicals being surreptitiously added to their food. Even after the exposés, the federal government was reluctant to crack down on food packers and processors. Renewed public pressure has been necessary in recent years to get the FDA to investigate the safety of the hundreds of chemicals now used in foods. The Environmental Protection Agency was not formed until years after Rachel Carson and other warned of the hazards of pesticides and other chemical pollutants.

The Nuclear Regulatory Commission was not created until eighteen years after the first nuclear power plant was in commercial operation. Before that, the safety of nuclear plants and materials was the responsibility of the AEC. Now it has become obvious, even to many people in the atomic industries, that the public is raising legitimate safety issues, ignored for years in favor of development.

Who influences executive agency decisions about scientific research and technical applications today, and what are the trends in decision making?

Some answers might be found by looking first at the NSF to understand the general trend, at the Department of Energy and the NRC for trends in nuclear energy decision making, the FDA for regulatory decisions on foods chemicals, and the NIH for policy decisions on recombinant DNA research.

National Science Foundation. The NSF spent something in the neighborhood of $750 million in fiscal 1977 on research and development (R&D), much of it for basic research in traditional fields (biology, chemistry, physics) and in space, atmospheric, and ocean sciences. The outlay was an increase over the previous year's funding except in fields like energy resources and environmental research, where the decrease was compensated for in the programs of other agencies. [3]

The increased support was a result of political pressure from researchers and other people concerned about an apparent decline in government R&D spending since the mid-1960s. The leadership of the American Association for the Advancement of Science and of the advisory directors of NSF, the National Science Board, were among those pushing for more liberal funding. These people have watched federal R&D funds increase only three to four per cent per year (to about $25 billion in fiscal 1977), less than the rate needed to stay even with inflation. So they went to work on the Congress for the NSF, and the pressure had some results.

Meanwhile, another office of the NSF—though still a very small branch—has been enjoying increased support since fiscal year 1976. This is the Office of Science and Society, which runs three programs, two of them quite new. The programs are the Public Understanding of Science, Ethics and Values in Science and Technology, and Science for Citizens.

When the public understanding program began in 1960, its purpose was not to enlighten people about social issues relating to technological change. The program was stimulated by the launching of Sputnik and its purpose was to rally public support for scientific activities, especially the space program. "We even approached the Advertising Council," explained George Tressel, the current program director. [4] The thrust of the program changed somewhat between 1964 and 1974, but funding remained pretty constant—a few hundred thousand dollars annually—and the emphasis was on the positive changes technology would make in people's lives.

The program in 1977 operated on a $2.1 million budget but, according to Tressel, it still reached only about fifteen per cent of the potential audience. The program director said it is his goal to find ways to reach far more people because he believes that people who understand science and technology have an advantage in sorting out all the conflicting information they hear in day-to-day news accounts and can make better judgments as citizens. The public, Tressel said, has a right, for example, to know how much (ten per cent, he said) of federal research money is going to basic research and how much to applied research and to question whether it is being spent on the right things.

Tressel said he thinks most people—the eighty-five per cent who take little interest in programs such as the NSF has sponsored in the past—have little reason to be interested in scientific issues until something hits home, like a power failure or the breakout of a strange disease or the discovery of toxic chemicals in the drinking water supply; and that is when people need some background to understand the problems involved and how they might be avoided in the future. Tressel, therefore, is going to extend his public education campaign to issues which are of local or regional interest in order to reach people where they live.

The NSF program on ethics and values had its origins in the early 1970s when trends in biomedical research and the use of artificial life-sustaining equipment began to raise an increasing number of knotty legal and ethical questions. [5] In October 1971, a group of twenty-one scientists, philosophers, doctors and lawyers meeting at Georgetown University in Washington, D.C., issued a statement calling on the federal government to support inter-disciplinary research·and instruction on science and human values. The scholars, as a *New York Times* reporter put it, "urged that wisdom—and not just knowledge—become a determining factor in the direction of technological advances affecting human life."

Senator Kennedy endorsed the statement during health sub-committee hearings on a resolution introduced by then Senator Walter F. Mondale (D-Minn.) to establish a national commission to study the "ethical, social and legal implications of advances in biomedical research and technology." Mondale's commission did not survive as envisioned; it became a commission to protect human subjects used in research. But the idea survived. In 1974, the Congress appropriated half a million dollars for an NSF program on ethics and values in science. The agency was flooded with applications for proposed research projects and, in fiscal 1976, the funds for the program were doubled.

More projects have been awarded grants to explore the effect of changing ethical and social standards on the conduct of scientific work than the effects on people of specific scientific developments. This fact is not too surprising when one considers that NSF grantees are mostly research scientists whose work could be threatened by public opposition to certain lines of research. But the NSF also has a growing constituency of social scientists, political scientists, and historians, and about two hundred of the universities served by the NSF have developed programs in science and human values. So several projects have gotten directly at the question of social responsibility among scientists and have documented some of the *ad hoc* methods in use today for resolving ethical questions. One of these has been a project by Charles Weiner, an expert in the use of oral history, to document the response of scientists and the public to recombinant DNA research.

A fundamental question that the NSF ethics program is attempting to explore is this: Against what ethical and social standards are developments in science and technology to be evaluated? Obviously social standards change and people disagree over them. But are there constants, perhaps having to do with the control one has over how he lives and dies, that could serve as a framework against which the prospective uses of technology could be judged?

One way that policy makers have found to enable social and ethical values to play a part in decisions is to open up the once carefully guarded process of science policy-making to as many people as possible. A few years ago, government regulatory agencies began developing new channels for direct citizen participation in decisions and modifying old methods so that citizen involvement could take place early enough to have a significant effect on decisions.

In support of this trend to enable lay citizens to play a greater part in resolving scientific issues, the Congress appropriated $1.2 million in 1976 for an NSF program called Science for Citizens. The original bill, introduced by Senator Kennedy, would have allowed direct aid to citizen groups which often depend on *pro bono* legal help and free technical advice just to secure the information they need to participate in public hearings on complex issues. The compromise legislation which created the program, however, outlaws direct aid and further requires that each grant awarded under the program is first approved by the NSF's advisory group, the National Science Board.

The Congressional compromise was reached and the restrictions imposed when influential members of the House Committee on Science and Technology refused to support legislation which might promote rather than reduce public controversy over established government programs. To some legislators, public interest groups represent the opposition, and giving federal funds to them would be like feeding the enemy. A view more prevalent in the Senate is that public interest groups tend to spring up where the bureaucracy has fallen down or when it has gotten out of touch. This view holds that citizens who are willing to take such an active part in the political process should be encouraged.

Rachelle Hollander, director of the Science for Citizens program, suggested in a 1977 report [6] that the NSF may someday get into the business of financing technical advisors for citizen groups but that such a program would have to be administered with care: "I think what the program's new constituencies want more than anything," she said, "is the ability to respond intelligently to policy dicta and recommendations. For example, an environmental impact statement comes out and a citizen group indicates they don't know whether to believe it or not. Are vested interests lying behind it? They want a scientist to look at the statement critically, appraise it, and tell them whether they really have something to fight about. This kind of critical appraisal . . . potentially involves us in a more shadowy range of activities which, I think, we have to be very careful in considering." Hollander said the Science for Citizens program "flatly rules out" applicants who want support in order to advocate specific views.

Because of the sensitivity in Congress on the question of direct aid to organized citizen groups, the NSF is not able to provide technical assistance to those very citizens who are hungriest for it and who often cannot afford to buy it. The situation puts a greater burden on those citizens who are scientists and who, because of their training, might be aware of advantages and drawbacks of a particular technical development that lay citizens, including the members of Congress, might overlook. If these scientists are involved in a research and development project, however, their ability to appraise it critically may be limited. More and more scientists are risking their reputation among peers, possibly their chance for future federal funding, and some are even leaving secure jobs to help citizen groups make sense out of complex technical issues.

NSF programs, so far, have not been able to provide the lay citizen with this kind of issue-oriented technical help, but the potential now exists within the Office of Science and Society. If the Congress fears greater opposition to certain government programs and policies from citizens who are well informed about the technical aspects of those programs and policies than from citizens who are ill informed, then something is amiss. Programs and policies which may generate public opposition are precisely the ones that should be formulated after the most open public discussion of issues. If decisions are made on the basis of information that could have been made public, but was not, or on the basis of information that was distorted or incomplete, the public will find out sooner or later. Under these circumstances, even the desirable aspects of a given program might be overlooked.

It would behoove the Congress to encourage executive branch agencies to make technical information more accessible and more intelligible to citizens. If government agencies are unable to do this, citizen groups will increase their demand for technical assistance, especially if they have no outside funding or affiliation through which to secure help on their own. Pressure will bring Congressional action. When the Congress acts to enable citizen groups to evaluate the technical aspects of government programs, one can hope that the views of the group—for or against a particular government program—will not be the criterion for granting or denying technical assistance.

Department of Energy and Nuclear Regulatory Commission. Political leaders have paid considerable attention, since the Arab oil embargo of 1973-74, to the growing gap between the amount of energy produced from domestic resources and the amount consumed in this country. Particularly worrisome is the fact that almost half of the oil used by the U.S. is now imported. Domestic natural gas is likewise limited and massive importation of this fuel, in its liquid state, is about to begin. As if dependence on the fuel-exporting countries for commodities so basic to the U.S. economy were not enough to trouble them, federal energy officials and their advisors say even the fuel exporters, someday, will not have enough to meet the worldwide demand. That someday could be ten years away or fifty—the estimates vary—but all of the estimates suggest a problem that seems imminent, relative to the time it will take to develop new technologies and substitute fuels.

Technological solutions to the energy supply problem, that is, technologies which hold the promise of supplying energy on a large scale, are the kind which the federal government tends to favor. A single large development effort is easier to administer than thousands of small ones. The structure of the energy supplying industries likewise demands the kind of technical innovation which promises to be increasingly economic when used on a larger and larger scale. This puts pressure on the government to support the kind of research and development effort that is too expensive for individual companies, or even groups of companies, to undertake, but which promises to yield high returns in the future. These are the developments which take thirty, forty, even fifty years between initial research and commercial application. Thus the sense of urgency on the part of federal energy officials.

Until the early 1970s, when the drawbacks of conventional nuclear fission power plants became a public issue, federal energy research and development programs concentrated, almost exclusively, on nuclear technologies. The energy program anticipated the following development sequence: Conventional fission reactors would be succeeded by breeder reactors sometime near the year 1990 and, if desirable, breeders could be replaced with nuclear fusion reactors toward the early or middle part of the twenty-first century.

By 1975, however, federal officials began to acknowledge that the energy program was insufficient for several reasons. Not only were there increasing questions about the safety of conventional plants and the breeder, but there were questions about the capacity of nuclear fuels to substitute for oil and natural gas. They could substitute as boiler fuels in electricity generating plants. Homes could be converted from gas and oil heat to electric heat. But what about industrial processes that require oil and gas and the transportation system which relies heavily on oil?

The Congressional response to all of these questions came in two laws that took effect in 1975: The Energy Reorganization Act and the Non-nuclear Energy Research and Development Act. The reorganization did away with the Atomic Energy Commission. Its research and development responsibilities went to the Energy Research and Development Administration and its regulatory duties went to the Nuclear Regulatory Commission. The purpose of this was to give nuclear regulators some independence from administrators responsible for promoting nuclear development. The legislation on non-nuclear programs had the effect of increasing federal support for technical processes that might provide better substitutes for oil and natural gas than nuclear technology provides— processes that could produce synthetic gas and liquid fuels from coal, oil from shale, gas from organic wastes. Federal support for solar energy technologies also increased as did the effort to develop energy-saving technologies.

Before the reorganization, between sixty and seventy per cent of federal money spent on energy research and development was spent on nuclear technologies, the largest chunk of it on the plutonium breeder. Since the reorganization, the share between nuclear R&D and all other energy research and development has been about fifty-fifty. A comparison of solar and geothermal energy development spending with fission reactor development spending tells the story. In fiscal year 1974, $10.3 million was spent on solar and geothermal R&D, compared with $411.9 million on fission reactor R&D (most of this for the plutonium breeder). In fiscal 1977, $232.2 million was spent on solar and geothermal and $703.4 million on fission reactor development. During the same period a separate program was begun to investigate the potential for using other nuclear fuels, besides plutonium, in future breeder reactors. [7]

All of this suggests that the government has taken the first, necessary steps to increase the variety of technologies among which we must choose in the future. But if the need to choose is as imminent as President Carter and the chiefs of the newly created Department of Energy say, the variety of energy R & D programs is more apparent than real. The choice falls automatically to technologies that are already in an advanced state of development, particularly conventional nuclear technologies. President Carter has already called for a dramatic increase in nuclear power production by 1985—more, probably, than the utilities could get on line under the best of circumstances, and without any public opposition to nuclear power. The President is also counting on cooperative government-industry development programs to produce synthetic fuels, made from coal, economically enough so that these fuels will increasingly be used instead of oil and natural gas by 1985. And he is counting on the Congress to enact taxes and incentives which will encourage people to use less gasoline. The goal of the President's plan is to limit the amount of oil imported from abroad to the amount being imported in April of 1977, when he announced the plan, thus minimizing the U.S. trade deficit, the chance of abrupt oil shortages, and the potential for a severe economic recession.

The Government Accounting Office and other energy analysts reported that the legislative steps the Administration has proposed to meet its energy goals will not actually result in as much production and conservation of energy as the President envisions, even if the public and the Congress adopted the Administration plan. But the public remains unconvinced of the wisdom of the plan, and the necessity for it, and the Congress has adopted only parts of the Administration's energy bill. The result is not likely to be a comprehensive policy designed to meet specific goals, but rather a collection of additions and modifications to the patchwork quilt which now serves as U.S. energy policy.

Much of the public resistance to the Administration's energy plan arises because the plan attempts to incorporate several approaches to the problem of the energy deficit, but follows no one approach to its conclusion forty or fifty years hence. Attempting to use everybody's ideas in the formulation of the plan, the Administration has satisfied few people. Many (about half of all Americans, the polls say) for various reasons, do not buy the Administration view that energy is scarce enough to warrant conservation measures now. Among those who do see a need for conservation, about half favor it as a means for buying time so that the country can eventually switch from nuclear technologies to solar ones. But they feel the President's conservation proposals are not strict enough, and the solar development program not strong enough, to accomplish this. The plan appeals directly only to that remaining twenty-five per cent, or so, of the people who feel that energy conservation and greater reliance on conventional nuclear power and coal are the steps which must be taken now. Most of these people feel that development of the plutonium breeder reactor is a logical step and a necessary one for the longer-term, and so even their support of the plan is limited by the President's opposition to development of the breeder.

The Nuclear Regulatory Commission, because of its power to approve or deny construction and operating licenses, is caught in the middle of the policy debate over the future place of nuclear power in the energy supply picture. The NRC is caught between Administration initiatives to get more nuclear power plants into operation by speeding up the licensing process and public initiatives to prevent greater use of nuclear power unless the government improves its process for assuring the safety and security of plants and the safe disposal of nuclear wastes.

Since about 1975, when the regulatory arm of the Atomic Energy Commission was made an independent agency, nuclear energy regulators have been more attentive to the problems of nuclear power than they were in the past. No longer does the NRC's licensing division recommend approval of a construction permit without first making a geological inspection of the reactor excavations. No longer does the agency permit a utility to begin construction without a public hearing. The utility still may start work before the construction license hearing, but to do so, the applicant must now get from the NRC a limited work authorization, which requires a public hearing.

The NRC also will now review the suitability of a proposed nuclear power plant site before the utility even applies for its construction license, if the utility requests such a review. This enables the NRC and state officials to influence the choice, before money is committed to a particular site. In addition to these procedural changes, the NRC began requiring, in August of 1977, that companies which operate nuclear plants, and also their suppliers, builders, and consultants, must immediately report any defects they discover in equipment or any failure to comply with NRC regulations that they might know about. Officials on the North Anna project, however, have been able to violate the strict reporting requirement without jeopardizing NRC approval of their plant, thus the effectiveness of the new regulations is questionable.

Despite the stiffening of regulations and the attempt to include state government officials and affected citizens early in the licensing process, the NRC has not been able to satisfy its public critics. There are two main reasons for this. The first is that many safety issues are not finally reviewed until after construction is well underway, sometimes nearly complete, raising the questions of whether the NRC can really review the safety issues objectively and, if serious problems are found, deny an operating license to a utility which has probably already invested half a billion dollars in the plant. If a utility knows its operating permit will not be denied, a serious deficiency or a serious violation of NRC rules is no more important to the company than a minor deficiency or violation. Neither will bring the project to a halt. The situation leaves the impression that the NRC is working in cooperation with the utilities to smooth over problems and to get plants into operation, despite safety problems.

The second reason the licensing process is still vehemently criticized is that some major issues in the nuclear power controversy are not addressed at all during the entire ten or twelve years that a license is being reviewed. How, for example, does nuclear power—its safety, dependability, and economics—compare with possible alternative energy sources for the particular region where the plant is to be built? Where and when will the radioactive wastes be disposed of? Is the plant designed to keep radioactive emissions to the lowest possible level or will it simply meet federal standards for acceptable pollution levels? Are these amounts really safe?

The NRC is not responsible for answering many of the questions that are of extreme importance to people who expect to live in the vicinity of a nuclear plant and to people who are concerned that the unresolved problems of nuclear power are compounded with each new plant that is approved. The NRC's limited authority leaves people with the impression that the agency does not adequately represent their interests even when it has the opportunity to push for safer plants prior to the approval of each new construction license.

Not until the federal government and the nuclear power industry fulfill their long-standing commitment to resolve the known problems of nuclear power, including the waste disposal problem, will the government be in a position to talk about safety and expedited licensing in the same breath. Administration initiatives to make nuclear power plant licensing swift are meeting with especially fierce opposition because regulatory delay is the only legal method that nuclear power opponents have to make government and industry .re-examine the wisdom of linking the country's future to the future of nuclear power.

Realizing that inaction on the nuclear waste disposal problem has jeopardized its own energy plan, the Administration proposed, in October 1977, a new policy for storage of spent fuel from commercial reactors. The policy would allow the government to take title to the used, but still radioactive, fuel that has been piling up for twenty years in commercial plants in anticipation of the day when it would be reprocessed for use in plutonium breeder reactors. The utilities would pay the government a fee for storage and could regain title to the fuel if, in the future, the government should decide that commercial reprocessing can be accomplished economically and without serious risk of mishap or misuse of the plutonium.

Support for the new policy will likely come from opponents of nuclear power only if the government finds a way to store the spent fuel permanently—that is, until the fuel loses most of its radioactivity, thousands of years from now. Unless the option exists to dispose of spent fuel permanently, the only other realistic option, nuclear opponents fear, is to use it in breeder reactors which actually produce more nuclear fuel than they consume. Though the fuel-breeding technology could be a long-term solution to the energy supply problem, dependence on this technology would mean that the waste disposal problem would be perpetuated, as would the risks of accidental pollution and intentional diversion of materials for hostile uses.

The American people have had thirty years to evaluate the government's performance in the nuclear energy field. During that time, people have learned about the link between the peaceful and the military uses of nuclear power. They have learned about the biological hazards of radiation. And they have come to realize that public resistance is a more effective way to avoid the risks of nuclear power than government control mechanisms when, for whatever reason, the government favors nuclear power development. The resistance is not likely to die down until the federal government has tried equally hard to develop non-nuclear energy sources or until energy shortages are so severe that bystanders in the nuclear power controversy take sides with the proponents of the breeder technology.

Food and Drug Administration. In May of 1975, Commissioner of the FDA Alexander M. Schmidt published in the *Federal Register* a proposal to establish a new hearing procedure which could be used to resolve disputes over FDA regulatory action. The new procedure was to be used in place of the traditional hearing before an administrative law judge in cases where all parties to a disputed FDA decision agreed that an informal inquiry into the scientific basis for the decision would be more appropriate than a formal inquiry into the legal basis for the decision.

The FDA had some legal problems of its own just trying to establish the new hearing procedures, but by October 1975 the agency was ready to try out the new concept. It was called the Public Board of Inquiry. [8] The idea was to bring a disputed issue—FDA attorneys thought the safety of aspartame would be a good one to start with—before a board of three scientists who would review all the experimental data on the artificial sweetener and eventually render a scientific judgment as to its safety. Under the new procedures, the antagonists in the dispute, in this case those who wanted aspartame approved for use in foods and those who wanted it banned, would both have to agree to a hearing before the scientific panel and would have to waive their right to a hearing before an administrative law judge. Both parties would have the right to nominate five prospective members of the scientific tribunal and the FDA commissioner would pick one from each list of nominees and a third scientist, none of whom could be prejudiced about the issue or have an interest in the outcome of the dispute.

G. D. Searle and Company, the manufacturer of aspartame, was not too enthusiastic about participating in such a hearing, according to the recollection of one FDA attorney. Coincidentally the FDA's investigation of the data Searle had submitted with its aspartame application was turning up evidence enough for the FDA to ban the additive. Thus the issue was resolved before the FDA could get its new procedure established.

Not until November 1976 was all the red tape out of the way so that the FDA could, if it had agreeable parties, actually use the new hearing procedure. By that time, public health groups had already succeeded in getting the FDA to declare red dye #2 an unsafe additive, so they never requested a hearing before the new board on that issue, either. When the FDA felt compelled to act quickly against saccharin on the basis of the Canadian findings, and the Congress countermanded that action, it became clear that the saccharin issue, too, was out of the hands of the FDA or any Public Board of Inquiry that the agency might want to convene.

FDA sources can recall only one time, since the new hearing procedure has been available, that a food or drug manufacturer has requested a hearing before the new board. In that case, Ciba-Geigy, a manufacturer of phenformin, a drug used by diabetics, requested a hearing after the drug was declared an "imminent hazard to public health" and removed from the market. The hearing request was rejected, according to an FDA attorney, [9] because the FDA is required to hold an evidentiary hearing before an administrative law judge whenever a drug is declared an imminent hazard.

It is difficult to evaluate whether the FDA's new public hearing procedure is an improvement in the regulatory process, because no issue has actually come before the board of inquiry. Regulatory officials hoped that the procedure would enable them to make decisions faster and that the decisions would be more widely accepted by the public because the scientific information on which they were based would be certified in public by independent scientists. The procedure also appealed to FDA critics who felt the agency was not fulfilling its responsibility to review safety data thoroughly. But industry attorneys have not been enthusiastic about the prospect of a hearing record based on scientific, rather than legal, arguments.

Although it has never been used, the existence of the scientific inquiry procedure has had an effect on regulatory activities. During recent discussions with the manufacturer of a new drug, for example, FDA officials listed the reasons why they would not approve the drug. The agency, according to an official there, told the manufacturer it would be willing to convene a Public Board of

Inquiry to review the company's data. Wishing to avoid a hearing of any kind, the manufacturer agreed, instead, to reformulate the drug so its safety would be beyond question, according to the FDA source.

National Institutes of Health. The NIH is the mission agency which Presidents and congressmen depend on when they announce a new program that will bring an end to this or that disease. When President Nixon announced his war on cancer, what it meant in practical terms was that the budget of the National Cancer Institute would rise dramatically. Today, according to NIH budget officials, the agency spends about $2.3 billion on biomedical research—more than a third of it in search of cancer cures and treatment methods.

In recent years, successive presidents have tried to hold down the NIH budget and equalize expenditures among various program areas, realizing that big spending does not always increase the chances that a breakthrough will be achieved in the cure or treatment of disease. The Congress, however, responding to various public advocacy groups concerned about specific ailments, tends to raise the NIH budget in its appropriations bills.

Some research scientists object to this approach to the cure of diseases and they are letting the Congress know why. "We think it's a mistake to target money for diseases such as cancer," the chief of surgery at a Boston hospital told a House appropriations subcommittee recently. "It's more important to fund the study of the cell wall or the cell membrane which in the long run may provide you with the clues you need to fight cancer," he said. Money for this kind of basic research, several researchers testified, has actually been declining during the past ten years because of the public desire for quick cures and disenchantment with research that may have no immediate payoff. President Carter and some members of Congress have already responded to the researchers' appeal not to neglect basic science. On January 19, 1978, the President announced that he would increase the basic research budget by eleven per cent and several congressmen have said they will support bills to provide increased funding for research training grants at universities.

The NIH spends far less than one per cent—closer to one-tenth of one per cent—of its research budget on recombinant DNA research projects. Though the three hundred or so recombinant DNA projects now funded represent a small part of the NIH research effort, the number has doubled in only a year.[10] NIH officials are excited about the work because it allows researchers to do the most fundamental investigation of living things and, at the same time, has important potential payoffs of the kind that the public is looking for.

The problem is that many people are not convinced that the payoffs of this research will be as much a blessing for mankind as they will be a curse. The decisions about which projects to fund and what safety restrictions to impose rests entirely with the NIH and its advisors. This situation—one in which the promoters of a new technical capability are also the sole regulators of its use—is reminiscent of the situation that existed when nuclear technologies were being developed. Many people feel that the lesson to be drawn from past experience is that society should lay down its rules for governing the use of technology rather than letting the use of a new technology determine the rules by which society will operate.

So far, no policy guidelines have been established for determining which of the potential applications of recombinant DNA research are to be encouraged and which are to be avoided. In short, there exists no statement of public policy against which NIH officials can evaluate whether the funding of a particular project is consistent with the goals of society or not.

Even the degree of risk to which people will be exposed by the research has been established by the researchers themselves, acting as advisors to the NIH. Regardless of whether the NIH guidelines are overprotective or not protective enough, the point is that if the Congress pre-empts states and localities from adopting stricter guidelines, the judgment of scientists will effectively be substituted for the judgment of citizens on the safety issues, as well as the ultimate social value of the research.

The Federal Courts

Class Actions. Until the latter part of the 1960s, civil actions in federal courts were mainly a matter of an individual complainant in contest with an individual defendant. The exceptions, or course, were constitutional actions like voting rights or desegregation cases, brought on behalf of large numbers of people, many of whom did not know they were party to a complaint.

Strict legal procedures for defining the offended group in class action suits discouraged lawyers from bringing all but the most clear-cut cases into court. In 1967, however, a California Supreme Court decision opened the class action route to consumers by ordering a Los Angeles taxicab company, accused of overcharging customers, to adjust the meters in the cabs so that future riders, as a group, could recover their losses. At about the same time, the U.S. Congress slackened the rules under which federal courts could admit class actions. By 1969, the public interest law business was booming and the little guy, without legal or financial resources to sue on his own, was getting his day in court. The result was that civil dockets in federal courts became crowded and court decisions began to exert great influence over matters that were previously left to the other two branches of government.

In February 1970, a newly chartered environmental law group called the Natural Resources Defense Council applied to the Internal Revenue Service for tax-exempt status. The IRS ruled that the new organization would be exempted from tax only as long as it refrained from litigation. The ruling appeared to be discrimination of the first rank because of the large number of tax-exempt legal organizations already in existence. Lawyers for the new group therefore asked the IRS for a clarification, and in October the IRS announced it was investigating the tax-exempt status of all groups engaged in public interest litigation—except organizations acting on behalf of the poor, and educational organizations. The careful distinctions made by the IRS seemed designed to crack down on lawyers who were having some success taking business and government to court over consumer and environmental issues. President Nixon was silent on the IRS announcement, which led to speculation that he and big business were the forces behind it. Elsewhere in the Administration, the IRS action was denounced. William Ruckelshaus, head of the newly created Environmental Protection Agency, praised the accomplishments of public interest law firms in a speech soon after news of the IRS action broke. Other government officials pointed out that the goals of consumer and environmental groups were consistent with national policies and that attempts to undermine them would be counterproductive. The threat to public interest law was real because most of the groups thrived on large individual donations and gifts from foundations which would lose their own tax-exempt status if they continued to offer support.

Pressure against class actions came also from U.S. Supreme Court Chief Justice Warren Burger. He made it known publicly that he was concerned that class actions, rather than reducing the number of individual claims as expected, were themselves crowding the docket. Privately the Chief Justice lobbied against legislation that might promote class actions, for example, a Nader-supported bill to create a consumer protection agency. Nixon also opposed the consumer protection bill which died that session and which has not been passed in the seven subsequent years.

But forces at work in the federal circuit courts were countermanding the efforts of the Chief Justice. On October 19, 1972, for example, a federal judge in California ordered the California Highway Commission to halt construction of an Alameda County freeway. He also ordered the state commission to pay the bills of the public interest lawyers who whipped the state in court, setting a precedent that made it worthwhile for other lawyers to sue if they had good cases but were concerned about the costs of litigation. Public Advocates, Inc., of San Francisco had filed the suit on behalf of five thousand Mexican Americans who were to be relocated by the highway project, claiming that the environmental impact of the project and its effect on his clients had not been properly evaluated. U.S. District Court Judge Robert Peckham wrote, in his opinion, that firms like Public Advocates function as "private attorneys general" because they act on behalf of large numbers of people to enforce Congressional policies and, therefore, their fees should be covered by the violators.

Business panicked at the decision, realizing that the lawyer's fee was one of the few remaining obstacles to public interest law suits. Corporate lawyers became nostalgic about the days before class action. "There was a time, and it was not so very long ago," began an Eleanore Carruth article in the April 1973 issue of *Fortune* magazine, "when the legal departments of many sizable corporations led relatively low-pressure lives . . . That was, of course, before the great legal explosion—before class-action suits became a kind of popular sport, before consumerism, environmentalism and other forms of Naderism, before Americans in general became so litigious." The article went on to say that between 1966 and 1972 there was a one hundred per cent increase in the number of law suits filed in federal courts in matters that most often involve corporations.

About the time that article appeared, several attorneys who had worked under the administration of California Governor Ronald Reagan figured that consumer advocacy could be a double-edged sword and established the pro-industry Pacific Legal Foundation. They argued that the public's real interest lay in discouraging government regulation because of the stifling effect of regulation on the economy. The Foundation met with considerable success in the courts, winning decisions, for example, that reversed an Environmental Protection Agency attempt to restrict vehicle traffic in five states and that permitted the timber industry to use the pesticide DDT to save trees in the Northwest. The Foundation also won a court case allowing the Concorde supersonic transport to land at

Dulles International Airport near Washington, D.C., and another case which allowed a government contractor to proceed with construction of a plant where work was to be done on the controversial nuclear-powered, missile-launching Trident submarine.

Also in 1973, the series of landmark social decisions which had issued from the Supreme Court since the 1950s came to a seeming halt. The last to break new ground in a social policy was a January 1973 decision which struck down restrictive abortion laws in the states. Many decisions, thereafter, actually restricted the role of the federal courts in helping to resolve broad social and ethical issues, including those raised through class actions.

In December of 1973, the high court dealt a particularly hard blow to large groups of people seeking financial relief from damages caused by pollution. The case involved a Vermont landowner, H. Keith Zahn, who alleged that pollution from an International Paper Company plant on the New York side of Lake Champlain caused $40 million in damages to his property and the property of two hundred neighbors. For such actions to be brought in federal court, multiple state jurisdictions must be involved—New York and Vermont, in this case—and the sum in dispute must exceed $10,000. Federal courts had long interpreted the rule to mean that at least one of the plaintiffs had to meet the $10,000 minimum on his own before the case could be heard. Zahn, himself, claimed more than the minimum and so did other plaintiffs, but not all of them. When the Zahn case reached the Supreme Court, however, the justices ruled six to three that every plaintiff must meet the $10,000 minimum. The case was dismissed, leaving Zahn and the others with large claims to decide if they wanted to go to the expense of a new trial, each on his own behalf. The three dissenting justices noted that the new restrictions on federal class actions could force people to file their mutual complaints in state courts and could lead to more individual suits in federal courts that could just as well be resolved in a single class action.

Then, in May of 1974, the Supreme Court also put a damper on class action suits in which monetary damages are sought by a large number of consumers who have lost relatively small amounts of money when federal laws are allegedly broken. The case involved Morton Eisen, a New Yorker who alleged on behalf of some six million buyers of odd lot stocks—one hundred shares or fewer—that two brokers were monopolizing the market and charging excessive fees. The court held that Eisen would have to notify all his fellow plaintiffs individually so that those planning separate actions could opt out of the class action.

Public interest lawyers speculated that the ruling would discourage many class actions, even those in which the plaintiffs' case is good, because of the expense and practical difficulties of notification. Following the 1973 and 1974 restrictions on federal class actions, the number of such cases did begin to decline in federal courts. But the number filed in state courts has shown a corresponding increase.[11] The upswing in state class actions has dashed the hopes of corporate lawyers that the tough rulings from the top might be felt throughout the judicial system. Corporations that do business in many states face the possibility of having to defend multiple cases stemming from a single, widespread complaint. Some state judges have been quite restrictive about the cases they will hear, but many have not, and state legislatures are now revising old class action statutes to give their judges some guidelines for determining which cases to hear and which to throw out.

Federal Judge Howard T. Markey, chief judge of the U.S. Court of Customs and Patent Appeals, speculates that the day is not far off when the federal court system will be too burdened with criminal cases to handle any but the most essential civil actions. If that day should arrive, the influence of the federal courts over social policy in technical fields, such as medicine and environmental protection, will be severely restricted. The kinds of issues that are now raised in class action lawsuits would have to settled through legislative or administrative rather than judicial decisions, or would have to be resolved without resort to the traditional public institutions. Some non-traditional approaches to resolving public policy disputes over technical developments will be discussed later.

Federal Courts and the SST. The public controversy over the environmental effects of the Concorde supersonic transport plane reached the federal courts as a procedural dispute over bureaucratic authority, not as a substantive dispute over environmental damage. The judges, therefore, did not need to know a thing about perceived noise levels or ozone depletion to be able to render their judgments.

On February 4, 1976, Secretary of Transportation William T. Coleman, Jr., ruled that the British-French SST would be allowed to operate out of two U.S. airports on a sixteen-month trial basis while the FAA monitored the noise it produced. The Environmental Defense Fund sued to have the ruling overturned so that the test flights would be banned from Dulles International Aiport, which is owned and operated by the Department of Transportation, but the ruling was upheld in federal district court and landings began there in May of that year. The Port Authority of New York and New Jersey, however, under pressure from citizens and politicians opposed to Concorde landings at Kennedy International Airport, banned the plane from operating out of New York, thus foreclosing its most lucrative route.

On May 11, 1977, Judge Milton Pollack ruled that the Port Authority's resolution was unconstitutional because it violated the supremacy clause of the Constitution which establishes the authority of the federal government over state and local governments in certain matters. One of these matters, Pollack ruled, is landing rights at airports. Local citizens, opposed to landings of the Concorde at Kennedy because of the noise it would make, were amazed to find how little power the Port Authority had when it came to blows with the Department of Transportation.

When the Port Authority appealed the ruling, the Justice Department filed a brief basically admitting that the executive branch has never exercised full authority over aviation but has shared it with state and local authorities which have a right to set noise limits for airplanes landing at airports under their jurisdiction. Justice said, however, that the Port Authority had discriminated against the Concorde by refusing to allow its owners to demonstrate that it can meet the noise standards that other aircraft meet. The case, by then a source of tension between the U.S. and its European allies who were losing money on Concorde operations, was returned to Judge Pollack who ruled on August 17, 1977, that the Port Authority was, in fact, discriminating against the Concorde.

The Port Authority lost an appeal of Pollack's order and took the case to the Supreme Court. The high court promptly ruled that the order should be carried out, that the Authority had the right to set noise standards but had unfairly shut out the Concorde while doing so.

It is interesting to note that the public issues and the legal issues in the dispute over Concorde landings in New York were quite different. The public issue was noise and the legal issues were jurisdiction and unequal treatment. The noise issue was not argued in the courts. While the legal maneuvers were taking place in New York, the FAA was monitoring the Concorde at Dulles and found that the plane made about the same amount of noise while landing as did a subsonic jet, but about twice the amount on takeoff. Because the Port Authority was not enforcing uniform noise regulations for subsonic jets, it was in a poor position to start enforcing noise limits on the Concorde. Concorde pilots did not give the authorities an opportunity to try: On its first takeoff from New York, October 20, 1977, the Concorde created less racket than Port Authority standards allow and even less than stricter federal standards allow for subsonic jets.

Federal Courts and Nuclear Power. The federal courts have become progressively more strict in their interpretation of the responsibility of nuclear regulators to protect the public from the environmental and radiological hazards of nuclear power. The consistency of these rulings suggests that federal regulators continue to follow an historic pattern of promoting nuclear energy first and considering its risks second.

The first major ruling came on July 23, 1971, when the U.S. Court of Appeals for the District of Columbia said that, under the National Environmental Protection Act, the Atomic Energy Commission must "consider environmental issues just as they consider other matters within their mandate." The environmental law had gone into effect on January 1, 1970, but the AEC had exempted dozens of plants from it by saying that the licensing boards would not have to consider environmental issues if construction permit applications had been filed by March 4, 1971. Environmental groups sued to halt the Baltimore Gas & Electric Company from building a 1,600 megawatt plant at Calvert Cliffs, Maryland, on the Chesapeake Bay, and the suit eventually resulted in the court of appeal's opinion.

Soon after the court ruling, newly appointed AEC Chairman James R. Schlesinger revised the agency's rules for evaluating environmental effects of plants, and warned the nuclear industry that past practices were changing. "The move toward greater self-reliance for the industry had a certain historic inevitability," Schlesinger told nuclear industry executives. "One result," he said, "will be that you should not expect the AEC to fight the industry's political, social, and commercial battles."[12]

Federal courts, however, are still finding that the federal government is protecting the nuclear power industry to the point that the rights of other citizens are possibly being violated. In a precedent-setting opinion which is still to be reviewed by the Supreme Court, Federal District Judge James B. McMillan of Western North Carolina ruled in March of 1977 that the Price-Anderson Act, which limits the liability of nuclear plant operators to

$560 million, is unconstitutional. The ruling, which now applies only to nuclear plants in North Carolina, was the result of efforts by the Carolina Environmental Study Group, Inc., mainly residents of suburban Charlotte, to fight the Duke Power Company's plans to build a plant on a nearby lake.

If the ruling stands, insurance companies will likely not be willing to indemnify nuclear plant operators against the billions of dollars of claims that could conceivably be filed as the result of a major accident at a power plant. Either the utilities will have to demonstrate that their plants are not capable of inflicting such damage or the federal government will have to guarantee greatly extended coverage for nuclear plants.

Senator Mike Gravel (D-Alaska) has suggested repeal of the 1957 Price-Anderson Act as a method for making sure nuclear plants are built and operated as safely as proponents of nuclear power say they can be. Opposition to this idea in the Congress, however, is overwhelming because the politicians fear that the economics of insuring nuclear plants will discourage utilities from building them, rather than simply encourage the utilities to build safer ones.

The Supreme Court, however, has indicated in a recent ruling that it will not uphold the tough opinions coming from lower courts, if the courts are treading on ground over which the NRC has clear jurisdiction. The high court reversed the opinion of the U.S. Court of Appeals of the District of Columbia—the same court that wrote the Calvert Cliffs opinion—in the matter of the Vermont Yankee nuclear power plant. The appeals court ruled in July of 1976 that the environmental protection laws require the Nuclear Regulatory Commission (NRC) to make a detailed analysis of the environmental effects of nuclear waste disposal during the license review of each plant as long as no review has been done for all plants. The NRC had been exempting these "generic," or common, problems from the safety review of individual plants. The Natural Resources Defense Council, Inc., argued that these problems should not be exempted from review just because all plants share them. The former chairman of the Natural Resources Defense Council, Gus Speth, is now chairman of the President's Council on Environmental Quality and that body has even suggested that licensing of plants halt until a satisfactory solution has been found to the generic safety and waste disposal problems. The Supreme Court ruling means that the safe disposal of increasing quantities of spent fuel will not have to be assured before more plants are licensed, unless the NRC so rules.

Federal Courts and Biological Research. The one federal court ruling that could greatly affect the future of recombinant DNA research will most likely have the effect of stimulating industrial applications of the research technique. This was an October 6, 1977, opinion by the U.S. Court of Customs and Patent Appeals that a company can patent living organisms which it develops. The specific ruling was that the Upjohn Company, a pharmaceutical manufacturer, could patent *streptomyces vellosus*, a microbe which Upjohn developed in order to produce an antibiotic called lincomycin. Should it stand, the opinion could obviously be applied to the issuance of patents on organisms which are developed by recombinant DNA techniques, and not just patents on techniques for producing those organisms. With that kind of protection, industry may be more willing to spend money for developing new biological products. Before the court's action, the only forms of life which could be patented were seeds and agricultural plants which were governed by the federal Plant Patent Act of 1930.

The question of liability for the hazards of recombinant DNA research has not been considered by the Congress or the courts because insurance firms are generally continuing to cover scientists involved in it. Dennis Pillsbury of the Insurance Information Institute, however, told the Associated Press in early 1978 that private companies are concerned about the safety of the research and that the federal government may eventually be forced to provide insurance or limit liability as they do for the operators of nuclear power plants.

- ## SCIENCE AND THE POLITICAL PROCESS: SOME NEW APPROACHES

When a machine fails to function smoothly, the mechanic looks for the source of the problem. The way he diagnoses the trouble and the remedy he proposes depend on his training, experience and even his creativity. So it is when the people responsible for or interested in the mechanics of government notice that the political machinery is not functioning the way they think it should. Many people feel that the machinery of government is not coping with rapid technological change. But they disagree on the diagnosis and the cure. The following is a brief discussion of several remedies that various people have proposed to improve the way public decisions are made when complex scientific or technical matters are involved.

Finding the Facts: The "Science Court"

Ever since his frustrating experiences as an advisor to the Air Force when the Apollo program was being conceived, Arthur Kantrowitz has believed that the major problem for decision makers is that the scientific facts relevant to a decision become clouded if the issue is controversial. Kantrowitz has advocated, therefore, that the government set up a procedure for isolating the scientific information that a decision maker needs, from all other views, opinions or information that might bear on the decision.

The proposed procedure is similar to the FDA's Public Board of Inquiry and could be used by any public agency, even the Congress or the courts. The concept was initially known as "an institution for scientific judgment," but it is known more commonly now as the "science court." The "court" would have no legal standing. The only thing court-like about it would be the use of adversarial procedures, allowing scientists to confront each other's facts as lawyers do to establish the facts in a legal proceeding.

Three scientist-judges would be responsible for encouraging the parties to set out the facts upon which they agree. In disputed areas, the judges would point out what factual conclusions the scientific evidence suggests or state that the evidence is inconclusive. With the adjudicated scientific information thus in hand, the decision maker could weigh it, along with all the other social, political and economic factors, in making a decision.

In 1976, the science court idea got a tremendous boost when an advisory committee appointed by President Ford recommended that the procedure be tried on several controversial issues pending before regulatory agencies.[13] Hungry for any method promising to bring greater rationality to their jobs, regulatory officials backed the idea. So did some research scientists, notably nuclear physicist Hans Bethe, who said at the time that the debate over the safety of nuclear power plants, for example, was so colored by value judgments on both sides that some method was needed to "narrow the limits of disagreement" among scientists.

For almost every proponent of the science court concept, however, there was a skeptic.[14] Public interest scientists were especially concerned that the authority public officials might ascribe to the pronouncements of a science court would mean that social and moral values would exert less force on the decision maker, even if the social or moral implications of the decision were great. Claire Nader, who heads the Commission for the Advancement of Public Interest Organizations, in Washington, D.C., summed up the opposition this way: "Policy, like nuclear energy policy, that is developed almost exclusively on the basis of technical advice, is automatically biased toward a technical solution. Good technical advice," she said, "may result in the best technical solution to a problem, but the best technical solution may not be the best of all possible solutions. If you believe nuclear power has irreversible, adverse consequences," she said, "you don't start by asking the technical question 'how can it be made safe,' you ask 'does society really need it' and, if the answer is yes, then you weigh the risks against the need."[15]

As the pros and cons of the science court approach were being debated, its proponents informally discussed the idea with officials at the National Science Foundation to see if the agency would fund an experiment to test whether the concept could be put to good use. The NSF, according to an attorney there, considered the idea one among many to be explored by a committee the agency planned to establish on science and the law. Because of a Presidential cutback on spending for advisory committees, that committee was not formed, but the NSF is still willing to consider funding a science court experiment, provided the experiment is designed, like other NSF-funded research projects, to measure specific results. So far, no one has submitted for NSF consideration such a research proposal on the science court.

In 1977, the state of Minnesota expressed an interest in using the science court procedure to settle a dispute over a state-approved plan to build a powerline across 180 miles of Minnesota farm land. The Ford Foundation provided funds to help the state set up the procedure, but as of April 1978 the parties to the dispute have not agreed on the procedure. It is not clear what effect the findings of a science court would have, anyway, because the State Supreme Court has already upheld state approval of the powerline.

Arbitrating Environmental Disputes: RESOLVE

Another new approach to settling disputes involving science and technology is based on the view that controversies are difficult to settle, not because the facts are obscure, but because existing government mechanisms rarely allow conflicting parties to reach a compromise. The Congress, regulatory agencies, and even the federal courts cannot handle all the controversies. Those that are handled are often settled with a yes or no decision which carries serious consequences for the losing party.

To meet this problem, some people have turned to mediation and arbitration, the traditional methods for resolving labor disputes. These methods have worked particularly well for resolving environmental disputes. Private companies whose sole business is to settle environmental disputes to the satisfaction of all interested parties have sprung up in several states.

On January 12, 1978, representatives of some of the country's largest environmental groups met with industry representatives and agreed to promote mediation as an alternative to court suits or federal regulatory proceedings. The conference was sponsored by the Alantic Richfield Company, the Sierra Club, and the Aspen Institute. With $200,000 in seed money from Atlantic Richfield, the participants established a new national organization called RESOLVE to promote the idea of environmental mediation.[16]

Though it is a practical tool that has gained considerable acceptance in the past few years, advocates acknowledge that direct mediation between industry and public groups will not be appropriate for settling every safety or environmental dispute. When opponents of a particular technical development object to it on principle, as do the opponents of the plutonium breeder and opponents of recombinant DNA, there may be little or no room for mediation.

Determining Social Values: The Hastings Center *et al.*

Some people who feel that the advance of science and technology has exceeded the capacity of our political system to cope, do not believe the solution lies only in providing decision makers with undisputed scientific facts or in providing contending parties with new opportunities to resolve issues on their own. These people believe that social values must play a greater part in decision making if technical developments are to be used in socially desirable ways. They believe that the use of technology should be governed— encouraged or controlled—by national policies which reflect as accurately as possible the values and the ethical principles upon which society can agree. The current political problem, from this point of view, is that society lacks the necessary methods, first, for reaching agreement on its values and principles and, second, for incorporating these into national policies. The proposed solutions to this problem include a whole array of methods for ensuring that human ethics and social values play a greater part in the formulation of public policies on food and nutrition, medicine and health, energy, transportation, and other fields characterized by rapid technological advance.

Technology assessment and environmental impact assessment are probably the most formal of these methods. Both were institutionalized during the period when disenchantment with technological advance reached its peak in the late 1960s and early 1970s. Both methods acknowledge that technical projects, undertaken by the government with particular social benefits in mind, can have adverse effects and that the government has a responsibility to anticipate the bad consequences before plunging into these projects.

Less formal methods for incorporating social and ethical values into statements of public policy are also being vigorously pursued. One good example is the program of the Institute of Society, Ethics and the Life Sciences: The Hastings Center. The Institute is a non-profit research and educational organization, established in 1969, "to examine the ethical, legal and social implications of advances in the life sciences." Supported by public memberships and private grants, the Institute publishes reports on the ethical aspects of public policies. It also holds workshops to encourage discussion among the clergy, doctors, teachers, scientists, and government officials on subjects like euthanasia, medical treatment of genetic deficiencies, and control of human behavior.

The theory behind the Institute and many organizations like it is that increased public awareness and broad public discussion of the social implications of scientific developments can lead to policies which take human values into account. The collective efforts of these organizations have increased public awareness and discussion. Whether these efforts will lead to the formulation of acceptable public policies for governing the use of recombinant DNA techniques or nuclear power is still far from certain.

• EPILOGUE

Americans are in the process of rethinking the concept of human progress, of redefining it. The general search began for this redefinition when, sometime around 1970, it became overwhelmingly clear that technological advance did not always lead to improvement in the human condition, national affairs, or even the quality of an individual's life. There were early signals of the drawbacks of technology and foresighted people pointed them out; but there was none so dramatic, nor so lasting in the public consciousness, as the nuclear arms race precipitated by the use of the atom bomb.

In the thirty years since the nuclear arms race began in earnest, the popular view of technology has changed so much that now it is conventional to believe that every technical application affects someone adversely. But it is still a popular view that technical applications hold great potential for improving life because they have been responsible for a remarkable improvement in the material standard of living of most Americans over the past quarter century.

So we are torn. We want the benefits of technology without its drawbacks and we are searching for ways to achieve that. Public involvement in technology-related decisions has become important as a method of insuring that no one's interests are ignored when technical development programs are undertaken. Government institutions have become more attentive and responsive to citizens on issues that used to be the exclusive province of scientist-advisors. The responsiveness is showing up in increased public confidence in government institutions,[17] especially executive branch agencies, with the exception of the NRC. This agency continues to get bad marks in the Gallup poll for the inadequacy of its safety regulations, and continues to get harsh rulings from the federal district courts.

Americans are beginning to develop the notion that technology on a small scale can solve problems, perhaps not as rapidly or as economically as large-scale projects, but with less risk in the event of technical or human failure. Perhaps the most appealing thing about technology on a human scale is that it provides people with a sense of control over their own fate—a feeling that has been lacking in this generation despite material well-being. Small scale and simplicity is what makes solar energy technologies, for example, so attractive and what might make them worth paying a little extra for. The idea of personal energy independence is fast becoming as attractive to many Americans as national energy independence is to their political leaders.

Until Americans *do* redefine human progress and figure out how to measure it, if not by technological advance, there will be some confusion over the value of various technical solutions to social problems. In this state of reevaluation—or, as a mathematician might put it, as we reach this point of inflection on the graph—it would be wise to proceed slowly, foreclosing neither the option to follow our technological impulse a little further nor the option to turn back and follow a totally different path.

Notes and References

I. SCIENCE AND NATIONAL POLICY:
A RETROSPECTIVE VIEW

1. National Academy of Sciences, "The Science Committee: A report by the Committee on the Utilization of Young Scientists and Engineers in Advisory Services to Government," (Washington: NRC/NAS, 1972), introduction.

2. The full text of Einstein's letter and many other source documents from the period are conveniently compiled in Young, Louise B., and Trainor, William, ed., *Science and Public Policy* (Dobbs Ferry, N.Y.: Oceana Publications, Inc., 1971), p. 307.

3. Stimson, Henry L.,"The Decision to Use the Atomic Bomb," *Harper's Magazine,* vol. 194, no. 1161, Feb. 1947, pp. 97-107.

4. Franck had won the Nobel Prize in 1925 for his work on "the laws governing the impact between the electron and atom" and also provided experimental support to Niels Bohr's theory of discrete energy states in atoms. He came to the U.S. in 1935 and began work at the University of Chicago in 1938. For the concluding text of the Franck Report, see Young, *op. cit.,* pp. 325-326.

5. On this point, see especially Tugwell, Rexford, *Off Course* (New York, Washington: Praeger, 1971) p. 181 ff.

6. On the reaction of the bomb project scientists following Hiroshima, see also Gilpin, Robert, *American Scientists and Nuclear Weapons Policy* (Princeton, N.J.: Princeton University Press, 1962) p. 49 ff.

7. The lecture was delivered at the George Westinghouse Centennial Forum, May 16, 1946, and appears in Oppenheimer, J. Robert, *Open Mind* (New York: Simon and Schuster, 1955) under the title "Atomic Explosives."

8. Oppenheimer, "Atomic Energy as a Contemporary Problem," *ibid.*

9. On the divided views of the atomic scientists after the failure of the Baruch Plan, see Gilpin, *op. cit.,* especially p. 35 ff. and p. 64 ff.

10. See *Bulletin of the Atomic Scientists,* vol. 5, no. 10, Oct. 1949, p. 265.

11. The complete General Advisory Committee report and analysis of the H-bomb decision by one of the younger Manhattan Project physicists can be found in York, Herbert, *The Advisors: Oppenheimer, Teller and the Superbomb* (San Francisco: W. H. Freeman, 1976) p. 50 ff. and Appendix, pp. 150-159.

12. See *Bulletin of the Atomic Scientists,* vol. 6, no. 7, July 1950, p. 75.

13. Atomic Energy Commission, "In the matter of J. Robert Oppenheimer," also known as "Findings of the Gray Board" (Washington: Government Printing Office, 1954) especially p. 21.

14. A detailed study of the evolution of the powers of the Joint Committee on Atomic Energy from 1947 through 1962 can be found in Green, Harold P., and Rosenthal, Alan, *Government of the Atom: the integration of powers* (New York: Atherton Press, 1963) chapter I.

15. Muller, Hermann J., "Radiation and Human Mutation," *Scientific American,* vol. 193, November 1955, p. 20.

16. Excerpts from *Our Nuclear Future* are reprinted in Young, *op. cit.,* pp. 364-377.

17. *ibid.,* p. 362.

18. A good history of Russian astronautics, published soon after the launching of the first Soviet satellites is Krieger, F. J., *Behind the Sputniks: A Survey of Soviet Space Science* (Washington: Public Affairs Press, 1958).

19. U.S. Congress, Senate, Committee on Armed Services, Preparedness Investigating Subcommittee, *Hearings, Inquiry into Satellite and Missile Programs,* 85th Congress, 2nd Session (Washington: GPO, 1958) p. 1678.

20. *ibid.,* p. 47 ff.

21. Piel, Gerard, *Science in the Cause of Man* (New York: Alfred Knopf, 1962) p. 72.

22. A more extensive quotation from this speech along with his views on President Kennedy's perception of modern science and technology can be found in an article by Kennedy's science advisor, Wiesner, Jerome B., "John F. Kennedy: A Remembrance," *Science,* vol. 142, Nov. 29, 1963, p. 3596.

23. For the reaction to the Gagarin flight, see U.S. Congress, House, Committee on Science and Astronautics, *Discussion of Soviet man-in-space shot,* April 13, 1961, 87th Congress, 1st Session (Washington: GPO, 1961).

24. Abelson's survey is mentioned on page eight of a book otherwise of note because it argues the views of the minority of scientists who thought the Apollo program would have great scientific value. See Ruzic, Neil P., *The Case for Going to the Moon* (New York: G. P. Putnam's Sons, 1965).

25. Greenfield, Meg, in *The Reporter,* vol. XXIX, no. 5, Sept. 26, 1963, p. 26.

26. Young, *op. cit.,* p. 171.

27. Morgan Guaranty Trust Company, *The Morgan Guaranty Survey,* February 1972, p. 3.

28. According to statistics compiled by the Organization for Economic Cooperation and Development in 1971 and cited by Gilpin, Robert, *Technology, Economic Growth, and International Competitiveness, A Report Prepared for the use of the Subcommittee on Economic Growth of the Joint Economic Committee, Congress of the United States* (Washington: GPO, 1975) p. 15.

29. Wiesner, Jerome B., "Science and Presidential Leadership," a speech delivered Oct. 23, 1964, in Los Angeles to "Scientists, Engineers and Physicians for Johnson and Humphrey," and reprinted in *Where Science and Politics Meet* (New York: McGraw-Hill, 1965) p. 17.

30. Gilpin, *Technology, Economic Growth, and International Competitiveness,* p. 15 and p. 34.

II. THE CASE OF THE U.S. SST:
DISENCHANTMENT WITH TECHNOLOGY

1. Kennedy, John F., Commencement Address, U.S. Air Force Academy, June 5, 1963, in *Public Papers of the Presidents,* speech no. 221.
2. U.S. Congress, House, Committee on Science and Astronautics, Special Investigating Subcommittee, *Supersonic Air Transports, Hearings,* May 17, 18, 19, 20 and 24, 1960, 86th Congress, 2nd Session (Washington: Government Printing Office, 1960) p. 9.
3. Federal Aviation Agency, *United States Development of a Commerical Supersonic Transport Aircraft* (Washington: FAA, 1961) p. 3.
4. Dwiggins, Don, *The SST: Here it comes, ready or not* (Garden City: Doubleday & Co., Inc. 1968) p. 11. This is an excellent account of the development of the U.S. SST through 1967.
5. Stanford Research Institute (project #SU-4266) *Final Report: An Economic Analysis of the Supersonic Transport,* August 1963, pp. II-1 through II-4.
6. U.S. Congress, House, Committee on Science and Astronautics, Special Investigating Subcommittee, *op. cit.,* p. 44.
7. U.S. Congress, Senate, Committee on Commerce, Aviation Subcommittee, *United States Commercial Supersonic Aircraft Development Program, Hearings,* Oct. 16, 17, 21, 22, 23, 25 and 29, 1963, 88th Congress, 1st Session (Washington: GPO, 1963) pp. 202-3.
8. Black, Eugene Robert, "Report on the supersonic transport program," (Washington: FAA, 1963).
9. Stack, John, *et al.* (staff of the Langley Research Center) "The Supersonic Transport—A Technical Summary," Technical Note D-423 (Washington: NASA, June 1960) pp. 1-7.
10. *Congressional Record,* May 10, 1966, p. (House) 9744.
11. Johnson, Lyndon B., Statement by the President upon Authorizing Construction of a Prototype Supersonic Transport Aircraft, April 29, 1967, *Public Papers of the Presidents,* speech no. 197.
12. This 18-page document is designated U.S. Office of Science and Technology, *Supersonic Transport Review Committee, Final Report,* March 30, 1969, and should not be confused with the interagency committee report of April 1, 1969, designated *Report of the SST Ad Hoc Review Committee.*
13. Nixon, Richard M., Remarks Announcing Decision to Continue Development of the Supersonic Transport, Sept. 23, 1969, *Public Papers of the Presidents,* speech no. 369.
14. Federal Aviation Administration, *Summary of Current Economic Studies of the United States Supersonic Transport* (Washington: FAA, September 1969) executive summary, p. 1.
15. *ibid.,* p. 38 ff.
16. *Congressional Record,* Oct. 31, 1969, p. H-32599.
17. *ibid.,* p. H-32600.

18. *ibid.,* p. H-32601.
19. *ibid.,* p. H-32602 through 32603.
20. *ibid.,* p. H-32609.
21. National Academy of Sciences, Committee on the SST—Sonic Boom, Subcommittee on the Physical Effects, *Report on Physical Effects of the Sonic Boom,* (Washington: NAS/NRC, 1968).
22. *Congressional Record,* Oct. 31, 1969, p. H-32609.
23. U.S. Congress, Joint Economic Committee, Subcommittee on Economy in Government, *Economic Analysis and the Efficiency of Government, Hearings, Part 4, Supersonic Transport Development,* May 7, 1970 (Washington: GPO, 1970) p. 907.
24. *ibid.,* p. 904.
25. *ibid.,* p. 907.
26. Brown, Clarence J., from an address given on Sept. 10, 1970, to the Dayton, Ohio, Chapter of Old Crows, reprinted in *Congressional Quarterly,* "Congress and the Supersonic Transport," December 1970, p. 298. This issue of *CQ* also has a legislative history of SST funding which is accurate and easy to follow.
27. *ibid.,* p. 296.
28. *ibid.,* p. 303.
29. *ibid.,* p. 305.
30. See *Aviation Week,* June 1, 1970, p. 26.
31. *Congressional Record,* Sept. 15, 1970, pp. S-31675 through 31678.
32. *ibid.,* p. S-31679.
33. *ibid.,* p. S-31681 and 31682.
34. See *Newsweek,* Dec. 14, 1970, p. 84.
35. See *Aviation Week,* Feb. 15, 1971, p. 30-31.
36. A good recapitulation of the ozone depletion argument can be found in the testimony of Harold Johnson, a chemist at the University of California-Berkeley, in U.S. Congress, Joint Economic Committee, Subcommittee on Priorities and Economy in Government, *The Supersonic Transport, Hearings,* Dec. 27 and 28, 1972 (Washington: GPO, 1972) p. 99 ff.
37. See *Fortune,* January 1971, p. 69-70.
38. U.S. Congress, Joint Economic Committee, Subcommittee on Priorities and Economy in Government, *Hearings,* Dec. 27 and 28, 1972, p. 4 and p. 99.
39. See, for example, National Academy of Sciences, Climatic Impact Committee, *Environmental Impact of Stratospheric Flight, Biological and Climatic Effects of Aircraft Emissions in the Stratosphere* (Washington: NAS/NRC, 1975) and Committee on Impacts of Stratospheric Change, Assembly of Mathematics and Physical Sciences, *Halocarbons, Environmental Effects of CFM* (chloroflouromethane) *Release,* (Washington: NRC, 1976).
40. Public Law 92-484, enacted Oct. 13, 1972.

III. THE CASE OF THE NORTH ANNA NUCLEAR POWER PLANT: PUBLIC RISK AND PUBLIC RELATIONS

1. All correspondence and documents cited, unless otherwise noted, are available in the Nuclear Regulatory Commission's chronological file on North Anna reactor units 1 and 2, identified as file numbers 50-338 and 50-339, in the NRC Public Document Room, 1717 H St., N.W., Washington, D.C., and at the Alderman Library of The University of Virginia, Charlottesville.

2. During an AEC investigation, October 31, 1973, a Stone & Webster geologist admitted under oath that the fault under the dam was on a geologic map all along. That map, indeed, appears in Stone & Webster, *Geologic Report—Dams, Dikes, Canals,* Feb. 6, 1969. The AEC investigation was in preparation for a hearing in March of 1974 during which Vepco had to show cause why construction should be allowed to proceed at the site.

3. Dames and Moore Associates, *Report Foundation Studies for Proposed North Anna Power Station,* May 8, 1969.

4. None of the following story came to light until the investigation for the AEC show cause hearing in March 1974 and some was not produced publicly until November 1977 as the result of research for this book.

5. U.S. Atomic Energy Commission, Region II Division of Compliance, *Report of Inspection* (2/19/70) no. 338/70-1, March 26, 1970.

6. Calver, James L., sworn statement in response to questions of the North Anna Environmental Coalition, March 10, 1974.

7. U.S. Atomic Energy Commission, Directorate of Regulatory Operations, *Investigation Report,* March 25, 1974, pp. 7 and 8.

8. Goodwin, Bruce L., interview with the author, Williamsburg, Va., Oct. 3, 1977.

9. Butler, Walter, interview with the author, Bethesda, Md., Sept. 14, 1977.

10. U.S..Atomic Energy Commission, Region II Division of Compliance, *Report of Inspection* (2/20/70 and 7/20-21/70) nos. 338/70-2 and 338/70-6, March 26, 1970 and Aug. 28, 1970.

11. In his official qualifications to testify as a witness at that hearing, Fischer was listed as co-author of an article, "The relationship between earthquakes and geologic structures in Virginia," published by the American Geophysical Union, April 1969.

12. Nuclear Regulatory Commission, chronological file, North Anna, 50-338, Dec. 14, 1970.

13. Dames and Moore Associates, *Report Environmental Studies for North Anna Power Station Proposed Units 3 and 4,* Aug. 18, 1971.

14. In a second volume of this same *Environmental Supplement,* Vepco lists a Dr. Stephen Clement of the College of William and Mary as one of the geologists interviewed about the suitability of the site for reactor units

3 and 4. Dr. Clement is the geologist who accompanied Drs. Funkhouser and Goodwin to the site on March 23, 1970 and agreed that the chlorite seam in unit 1 was a fault.

15. Dames and Moore Associates, *Report Foundation Investigation North Anna Power Station Proposed Units 3 and 4,* Oct. 1, 1971.

16. Vaughan, Phyllis, conversation with author during operating license hearing, Charlottesville, Va., May 31, 1977.

17. Dietrich, Margaret, conversation with author during operating license hearing, Charlottesville, Va., May 31, 1977.

18. According to Robert L. Ferguson, then the AEC's North Anna project manager, the following is what occurred on May 17, 1973: Baum called for Ferguson who was out sick. The AEC's Al Schwencen called Baum back and got the news about the fault. Schwencen told AEC geologist A. T. Cardone who called Vepco's Clifford Robinson to discuss the fault. Ferguson gave the preceding account during an interview with the author Sept. 14, 1977, in Bethesda, Md.

19. Roper, Paul J., in a May 1973 geologic report to Dames and Moore, designated as exhibit NX-22 at the AEC show cause hearing, p. 6.

20. Robinson's journal, May 30, 1973, produced by North Anna Environmental Coalition through process of legal discovery.

21. Interview with author, Oct. 3, 1977.

22. McGurn, John, informal comments at operating license hearing, Charlottesville, Va., May 31, 1977.

23. Interview with author, Sept. 14, 1977.

24. U.S. Congress, Senate, Committee on Government Operations, Subcommittee on Reports, Accounting and Management, *Information Management by Federal Regulatory Agencies, Hearings, Part 1,* July 22 and 24, 1975, 94th Congress, 1st Session (Washington: Government Printing Office, 1975), p. 90.

25. For more on the politics of Vepco ownership, see *Washington Post,* "Howell Sees Dalton Gifts, Vepco Link," by Megan Rosenfeld and Ken Ringle, Oct. 27, 1977, p. C-1 and C-9.

26. Roper, Paul J., "Geologic Report of the North Anna Nuclear Power Station, Virginia," May 1973, reprinted in Senate Government Operations subcommittee hearings, *Information Management by Federal Regulatory Agencies, Part 1,* July 22 and 24, 1975, p. 127.

27. Martin, R. Torrence, in a report that was submitted by Vepco to the NRC as Amendment 53 to its license application, June 1976.

28. Segovia, Antonio V., associate professor of structural geology, University of Maryland, in a letter to the North Anna Environmental Coalition, May 22, 1977, citing D. P. Krynine and W. R. Judd on the characteristics of halloysite in *Principles of Engineering Geology and Geotechnics,* p. 16.

29. Dames and Moore Associates, *Summary Report on the In-progress Seismic Monitoring Program at the North Anna Site, January 21, 1974 through May 1, 1976;* see especially the map designated as Figure 6 and pp. 24-26.

30. The summary of findings, released publicly on Oct. 1, 1977, was in the form of a memo written May 11, 1977, by Bradford F. Whitman, assistant chief of the Pollution Control Section, U.S. Department of Justice. Justice initially refused to release the memo, but this denial was overturned on appeal by the North Anna Environmental Coalition under the federal Freedom of Information Act.

IV. THE CASE OF THE SACCHARIN STUDIES: PUBLIC PROTECTION AND INDIVIDUAL CHOICE

1. Weinhouse, Sydney, ed., "Nutrition in the Causation of Cancer," *Cancer Research,* vol. 35, no. 11, part 2, November 1975, pp. 3231-3550.

2. National Academy of Sciences, Food Protection Committee, Subcommittee on Review of the GRAS list—phase II, *A comprehensive survey of industry on the use of food chemicals generally recognized as safe (GRAS)* Washington: NAS/NRC, 1972) FDA contract no. FD 70-22.

3. U.S. Congress, *Federal Food, Drug and Cosmetic Act, As amended October 1976* (Washington: Government Printing Office, 1976) pp. 34-35, or U.S. Code, Title 21, Section 348.

4. National Academy of Sciences, "Statement of the Committee on Non-nutritive Sweeteners," Oct. 17, 1969.

5. Release no. P77-12, *HEW News,* March 9, 1977.

6. Release no. P77-14, *HEW News,* April 14, 1977.

7. National Academy of Sciences, Committee on Non-nutritive Sweeteners, *The Safety of Saccharin and Sodium Saccharin in the Human Diet* (Washington: NAS/NRC, 1974). The major findings of this review are reported succinctly by Julius M. Coon, chairman of the committee, in National Academy of Sciences, *Sweeteners: Issues and Uncertainties,* the proceedings of the Fourth Academy Forum, March 25 and 26, 1975.

8. For the details of the Canadian test results and the official rationale for FDA action, see the FDA press release, no. P77-12, *HEW News,* March 9, 1977.

9. For a sample of the congressional mail, see *Washington Post,* "Pending FDA Saccharin Ban a Bitter Dose for Many in U.S.," by Peter Milius, April 4, 1977, p. A-2.

10. Quoted in *Washington Post,* "Sweeteners Linked to Human Cancer," by Lawrence Meyer, June 18, 1977, p. A-1.

11. U.S. Congress, Office of Technology Assessment, *Cancer Testing Technology and Saccharin,* prepublication draft, June 1977; see especially p. 9 and pp. 123-127.

12. Public Law 95-203, the "Saccharin Study and Labeling Act."

13. Turner, James, *The Chemical Feast* (New York: Viking Press, 1970) pp. 100-103.

14. See *Washington Post,* "Wide Errors, Possible Fraud Found in Private Lab Testing," by Bill Richards, Sept. 8, 1977, p. A-11.

15. A good statement of the dilemma that public health advocates face in trying to determine whether regulation should be absolute and based on risks, as under the Delaney clause, or more flexible and based on value, as under a requirement to weigh risks and benefits, can be found in "Saccharin and Cancer," an article by Barry Commoner, printed in the editorial section of *Washington Post,* March 27, 1977, p. C-1.

16. National Academy of Sciences, *How Safe is Safe? The Design of Policy on Drugs and Food Additives,* proceedings of the First Academy Forum, May 15, 1973.

V. THE CASE OF RECOMBINANT DNA:
BRAVING THE NEW WORLD OF BIO-TECHNOLOGY

1. U.S. Congress, Library of Congress, Congressional Research Service, *Genetic Engineering, Human Genetics, and Cell Biology: Evolution of Technical Issues,* DNA Recombinant Molecule Research (Supplemental Report II) prepared for the Subcommittee on Science, Research and Technology, of the Committee on Science and Technology, U.S. House of Representatives, 94th Congress, 2nd Session (Washington: Government Printing Office, December 1976) p. 1.
2. *ibid.,* p. 33.
3. See "DNA—Three Narrow Escapes," *Science,* vol. 195, Feb. 18, 1977, p. 378.
4. Cohen, Stanley N., "The Manipulation of Genes," *Scientific American,* vol. 233, July 1975, p. 32.
5. In addition to Berg, the group included David Baltimore of MIT, Boyer, Cohen, Davis, Hogness, Daniel Nathans of Johns Hopkins, Richard Roblin of Harvard Medical School, James D. Watson of Cold Spring Laboratories, Sherman Weissman of Yale and Norton D. Zinder of Rockefeller University.
6. See *Science,* "Letters," vol. 185, July 26, 1974, p. 303.
7. Berg, Paul, *et al.,* "Summary Statement of the Asilomar Conference on Recombinant DNA Molecules," in *Proceedings of The National Academy of Sciences,* vol. 72, no. 6, June 1975, p. 1981, and Berg's comments on National Educational Television program NOVA, "The Gene Engineers," March 22, 1977.
8. *Federal Register,* vol. 41, no. 131, July 7, 1976, pp. 27902-27943.
9. See NIH, Recombinant DNA Molecule Program Advisory Committee, minutes of meeting, Sept. 13-14, 1976, p. 8, and Attachment IV.
10. Hubbard, Ruth, informal remarks, National Academy of Sciences, Academy Forum on Recombinant DNA, March 8, 1977.
11. See NIH Advisory Committee minutes, Sept. 13-14, 1976, pp. 3-4, and Attachment II, p. 4.
12. McKinnon, Richard, comments on National Educational Television program NOVA, "The Gene Engineers," March 22, 1977.
13. Sinsheimer, Robert, conversation with author during Academy Forum, March 8, 1977.
14. Beckwith, John, prepared remarks at Academy Forum, March 9, 1977.
15. Chargaff, Erwin, prepared remarks at Academy Forum, March 8, 1977.
16. Ptashne, Mark, "The Defense Doesn't Rest," a reply to George Wald's "The Case Against Genetic Engineering," both in *The Sciences,* September/October, 1976.
17. *Boston Globe,* "Moratorium sought on genetic research," by Richard A. Knox, July 8, 1976.
18. *Boston Globe,* "Layman is center of scientific controversy," by Richard A. Knox, Jan. 9, 1977.

19. *Boston Globe,* "Cambridge ban is extended on genetic studies," Sept. 29, 1976.
20. Cambridge Experimentation Review Board, *Guidelines for the Use of Recombinant DNA Molecule Technology in the City of Cambridge,* Jan. 5, 1977; see especially pp. 1-4.
21. The Harvard *Crimson,* Jan. 18, 1977, p. 1.
22. Zimmerman, Burke K., *et al.,* "Petition of Environmental Defense Fund, Inc., and Natural Resources Defense Council, Inc., to the Secretary of Health, Education and Welfare to hold Hearings and Promulgate Regulations under the Public Health Service Act Governing Recombinant DNA Activities," cover letter dated Nov. 11, 1976, p. 13.
23. *ibid.,* p. 20.
24. Federal Interagency Committee on Recombinant DNA Research, *Interim Report,* March 15, 1977, Appendix III, p. 2.
25. Ancker-Johnson, Betsy, testimony before the House Committee on Interstate and Foreign Commerce, Subcommittee on Health, March 16, 1977.
26. The proposed revisions to the NIH guidelines appear in National Institutes of Health, *Recombinant DNA Technical Bulletin Supplement,* vol. 1, no. 1, fall 1977.

VI. SCIENCE AND HUMAN PROGRESS: SUMMARY AND PROSPECTUS

1. Juenger was a precursor of the American environmental movement. Technology, he warned in his 1946 book *The Failure of Technology,* promotes the waste of resources and spoils the natural environment. Carson in *Silent Spring* discussed the hazards of pesticide use long before it became a popular issue. *The Education of Henry Adams,* written at the turn of the century, describes the author's anxiety about the dynamo-powered society America was about to become. Huxley's *Brave New World,* written in 1932, tells of the authoritarian state he foresaw in which all human needs would be provided by science but at the price of human individuality.

2. U.S. Congress, Office of Technology Assessment, *Automated Guideway Transit, An assessment of PRT and other new systems,* June 1975.

3. Shapley, Willis H., *Research and Development in the Federal Budget: FY 1977* (Washington: American Association for the Advancement of Science, 1977) pp. 79-81.

4. Tressel, George, interview with author, Washington, D.C., April 22, 1977.

5. National Science Foundation, "Science and Society: Program Report," vol. 1, no. 4, June 1977, p. 14 ff.

6. *ibid.,* pp. 33-34.

7. The figures are from Energy Research and Development Administration, "History of Funding—FY 1971 thru FY 1977," Dec. 15, 1976, identified as ACBu—BO—039-76.

8. See *Federal Register,* vol. 41, no. 125, pp. 26636-26642.

9. Springer, Jeff, FDA attorney, telephone interview, Feb. 2, 1978.

10. Gordon, Virginia, NIH budget analyst, telephone conservation with author, December 1977.

11. See *Business Week,* "Class actions shift to the state courts," Jan. 24, 1977, pp. 53-54.

12. See *Science,* vol. 173, pp. 1112-1113, Sept. 17, 1971, and vol. 174, p. 478, Sept. 24, 1971.

13. Task Force of the Presidential Advisory Group on Anticipated Advances in Science and Technology, "The Science Court Experiment: An Interim Report," in *Science,* vol. 193, Aug. 20, 1976, pp. 653-656.

14. See, for example, Callen, Earl, letter to the editor, *Science,* vol. 193, Sept. 10, 1976, and Nelkin, Dorothy, "Thoughts on the Proposed Science Court," Harvard University *Newsletter on Science, Technology and Human Values,* January 1977.

15. Nader, Claire, telephone conversation with author, October 1976.

16. *Washington Post,* "Mediation Studied as Way to Resolve Environmental Disputes," by Margaret Hornblower, Jan. 13, 1978, p. A-7.

17. See, for example, *Washington Post,* "Confidence in Institutions Up Strongly," by William Claiborne, Jan. 5, 1978, p. A-1.

Index

A

Abbott, Ira H., 52
Abbott Laboratories, 118, 122
Abelson, Philip H., 42
Acheson, Dean, 13, 20
Adams, Sherman, 33
Adams, Henry, 170
Advisory Committee on Reactor Safe-
    guards (ACRS), 91, 93, 94, 103, 107,
    108
Agriculture, Department of, 3, 114, 119
Air France, 51, 65
Alamogordo, N.M., 7, 11
Allen, June, 97, 104
Alvarez, Luis, 18
American Association for the
    Advancement of Science (AAAS),
    42, 180
American Cancer Society, 115
American Chemical Society, 5
American Medical Association, 124
American Rocket Society, 35
Ancker-Johnson, Betsy, 160-61
Apollo Program, 41-46
Appropriations Committee, House, 68, 76
Appropriations Committee, Senate,
    78-79, 175
Armed Services Committee, Senate, 35, 51
Armstrong, Neil, 43, 46
Asilomar conference (International
    Conference on Recombinant DNA
    Molecules), 142-44
aspartame, 122, 127, 191
Aspen Institute, 204
Associated Press, 158, 160, 201
Astronautics and Space Exploration,
    House Select Committee on,
    36, 38-40
Atlantic Richfield Company, 204
atom bomb
    genetic effects of, 23
    government funding of, 6
    Nazi development of, 5, 8
    secrecy of, 12, 14, 16
    Soviet explosion of, 18
    use in war, 7-11
Atomic Bomb Casualty Commission, 23
Atomic Energy Commission (AEC)
    and federal courts, 199

    and North Anna power plant, 84-103,
        110-12
    and nuclear weapons, 17-21, 24
    and Oppenheimer security hearings,
        20-21
    origins of, 179
Atomic Energy, Joint Committee on
    21, 31, 102
atomic fission, 5, 84, 149, 153, 185-86
atomic fusion, 17, 185
Atomic Safety and Licensing Board
    (ASLB), 92-93, 100-101, 103, 109-10
Avco Everett Research Laboratories, Inc.,
    44
aviation subcommittee (Senate
    Committee on Commerce), 54, 56
Aviation Week, 77

B

Baker, Newton D., 5
Baker, Ray Stannard, 3
Baltimore, David, 156, 158
Baltimore Gas & Electric Company, 199
Baruch, Bernard M., 14
Baruch Plan, 14-16
Baum, E. Ashby, 99
Beckwith, Jon, 150, 156, 158
Berg, Paul, 141-46, 153
Berkner, L. V., 46
Bethe, Hans, 16-18, 30, 202
Biometric Testing, Inc., 128
Black, Eugene R., 54-55, 57, 66
Black report, 54-55
Blume and Associates, 95
BOAC, 51, 65
Boeing Company, 59, 61, 64-67, 69-70,
    74-75, 79-80
Boland, Edward P., 76
Bond, J. D., 93
Boston Area Recombinant DNA Group,
    147
Boston Globe, 158
Boxley, Bertha, 86
Boyer, Herbert W., 140, 141
Bravo nuclear test, 23
breeder reactor
    ERDA and, 176, 185
    energy supply and, 189-90
    legislation on, 171

opposition to, 204
R&D funding, 186
Briedis, John, 88, 97-98, 103
Brooks, Overton, 51
Brown, Clarence J., 76
Buchner, Eduard, 136
Bulletin of the Atomic Scientists, 14,
  45-46
Bumpers, Dale, 161
Bureau of the Budget, 33-34
Burger, Warren, 194
Burt, Robert A., 153
Bush, Vannevar, 6, 8, 12, 35
Bushnell, David, 2
Butler, Walter, 89, 93-95, 99, 111
Butylated hydroxytoluene (BHT),
  126-27, 131

C

Califano, Joseph, 162
Calorie Control Council, 122
Calver, James L., 88, 101
Calvert Cliffs power plant, 199-200
Cambridge Experimentation Review
  Board (CERB), 157-58
cancer
  and diet, 115
  and food additives, 117-20, 122-25,
    128-30, 132
  and genetic research, 141-42
  and low-level radiation, 29-30
  war on, 192
Cancer Research, 115
"Cancer-testing Technology and
  Saccharin," 176
Carbon, Max W., 107
carbon-14, 28
Cardone, A.T., 100-101
Carolina Environmental Study Group,
  Inc., 200
Carruth, Eleanore, 195
Carson, Rachel, 169, 179
Carter, Jimmy
  and dietary goals for U.S., 116
  and energy supply, 186
  and medical research funds, 192
  and saccharin legislation, 125
Case, Clifford P., 176

Case, Edson, 89, 100
Center for Science in the Public Interest
  (CSPI), 116
cesium-137, 28
Chang, Annie C.Y., 140-41
Chargaff, Erwin, 150-51
Charlie, of the MTA, 154
Chesterton, G.K., 167
Chemical Feast, The, 126
Ciba-Geigy, 191
citizen participation
  and FDA, 191
  and NSF, 182-83
  and OTA, 174
  in science policy decisions, 206
Citizens' League Against the Sonic Boom
  (CLASB), 72, 74
Clem, David, 159, 162
Coalition Against the SST, 74, 77-78
Cohen, Stanley N., 140-41
Coleman, William T., Jr., 197
Commission for the Advancement of
  Public Interest Organizations, 202
Commerce, Senate Committee on. *See*
  aviation subcommittee.
Commoner, Barry, 29
Compton, Arthur, 6, 8
Compton, Karl T., 8
Comunale, Francis, 157
Conant, James B., 6, 8, 17
Concorde
  competition with, 51-52, 54, 56-57,
    59-62
  landing rights of, 197-99
  noise limitations of, 77
  operating costs of, 64, 66
Congress, the United States
  and class actions, 193-95
  and food protection laws, 114-16, 118-19,
    121, 123-25, 128-30, 132
  and genetic research, 161-64
  and nuclear power, 104-5, 200
  and science policy, 166, 171-78,
    182-87, 191-92, 203
  and the SST program, 50-51, 53, 62-65,
    67-70, 73-82
  and the space program, 33-38, 40-41,
    43, 45-46, 48
Congressional Record, 78, 81
Coufal, Frederick J., 107

Council on Environmental Quality (CEQ), 79, 200
courts, federal
   and biological research, 163, 201
   class actions in, 193-97
   and the Concorde, 197-99
   on North Anna power plant, 104
   and nuclear power, 199-200
   and sonic boom claims, 71-72
   U.S. Court of Customs and Patent Appeals, 163, 197, 201
   U.S. Supreme Court, 121, 194, 196, 198-200
courts, state
   class actions in, 193, 196
   Supreme Court of California, 193
   Supreme Court of Minnesota, 203
Curtiss, Roy, III, 146-47
Curtis-Wright, 60
cyclamate, 118-20, 122, 131

D

Daddario, Emilio Q., 175
Dames and Moore Associates, 87, 94, 96, 98, 101-2, 106
Davis, Ronald W., 142
Defense, U.S. Department of
   and space program, 33, 36-38, 39, 42
   and SST program, 51, 63
Delaney amendment (Food, Drug, and Cosmetic Act), 118-19, 122-23, 125, 128-29, 132-33
deoxyribonucleic acid (DNA), 137. *See* recombinant DNA research.
Dietrich, Margaret, 96-97
Doolittle, James H., 34
Dowling, John E., 157
DuBridge, Lee A., 17, 70, 73
Duke Power Company, 200
Dulles, John Foster, 32, 34
Dunn, Gerald R., 154
Dunning, John, 6

E

Economics, Joint Committee on, 74-76, 81
Edison, Thomas Alva, 4
Einstein, Albert, 5

Eisen, Morton, 196
Eisenhower, Dwight D.
   on "military-industrial complex", 41
   and nuclear weapons, 21, 24, 31, 40
   R&D spending under, 46
   and space program, 33-34, 36-39
Ellwood, Brian, 98
Emporia Gazette, 3
Energy, U.S. Department of, 100, 179, 184-87
Energy Reorganization Act, 185
Energy Research and Development Administration (ERDA), 176, 179, 185
Engleman, Herbert L., 88-90, 103
Environmental Defense Fund (EDF)
   and Concorde, 197
   and genetic research, 159-60, 164
   and SST program, 77
Environmental Policy Act. *See* National Environmental Policy Act (NEPA).
Environmental Protection Agency (EPA)
   chemical testing by, 128
   and class actions, 195
   origins, 179, 194
enzymes, 138
Escherichia coli (E. coli), 137-38, 140-43 146-47, 153, 156
Evans, Ward, 21
executive branch agencies, 178-193. *See also* listing of specific agencies.
Explorer I, 33

F

fallout. *See* genes, effect of low-level radiation
Farrell, Thomas F., 7
Federal Aviation Administration (FAA)
   and Concorde noise limitation, 198
   and SST program, 50, 52, 55-68, 70-75, 79, 81
Federal Power Commission (FPC), 91
Federation of American Societies for Experimental Biology, 126
Ferguson, Robert L., 99-102, 104
Fermi, Enrico, 6, 8, 17, 19
Fischer, Joseph, 87, 94
fission. *See* atomic fission.

Flagyl, 127
Flavor and Extract Manufacturers
    Association, 116
food additives
    benefits vs. risks of, 130-33
    saccharin, 117, 119-25, 133
    safety of, 114, 116-19, 126-33
    use of, 115-17, 127, 130
Food and Drug Administration (FDA)
    attitude of 117, 126-27
    and industry, 114-15, 127-28
    origins of, 179
    public attitude toward, 127-29, 131-32
    Public Board of Inquiry and, 190-91, 202
    responsibilities of, 114, 116-19
    and saccharin regulation, 117, 119-25,
        171, 176, 191
Ford Foundation, 203
Ford, Gerald R.
    and energy supply, 168
    and SST program, 80
    and "science court," 202
Fortune, 80, 126, 195
Foster, Richard, 107
Franck, James, 8-9, 11
Frederickson, Donald S., 144-45, 148
Freedom of Information Act, 69, 102
Friedman, Milton, 78
Friends of the Earth, 74, 77
Fuchs, Klaus, 20
Fulbright, J. William, 53, 78
Funkhouser, John, 88-89, 101
fusion. *See* atomic fusion.

G

GRAS list (Generally Recognized As Safe),
    116-18, 126
Gagarin, Yuri, 42
Gallup poll, 206
Gardner, John, 168
Gardner, Trevor, 44
Garwin, Richard L., 67-68, 74-76, 81
Garwin committee. *See* Supersonic
    Transport Review Committee.
General Advisory Committee (GAC), 17-21
General Electric, 60-63, 80, 159
genes
    alteration of human, 139-40, 148-54

    effects of low-level radiation on, 23-31
    and evolution, 25
    Mendelian studies of, 136
    recombination of, 136-164
Goddard, James, 32
Goodwin, Bruce, 89, 102
Gorback, Sherwood, 163
Gori, Gio B., 115
Government Accounting Office (GAO),
    186
Graham, Saundra, 156, 159
Gravel, Mike, 200

H

Halaby, Najeeb E., 56, 59-60, 63
Hammarskjold, Dag, 27
Handler, Philip, 163
Hastings Center (Institute of Society,
    Ethics and the Life Sciences),
    204-5
Hatfield, Mark O., 79
Hauser, Fred, 100
Hayes, Daniel J., 157
health subcommittee (House Committee
    on Interstate Commerce)
    and genetic research, 161-63
    and saccharin legislation, 123-25
health subcommittee (Senate Committee
    on Human Resources)
    and G. D. Searle Company, 128
    and genetic research, 161-63
    and saccharin legislation, 123-25, 176
Heller, Walter, 78
Helling, Robert B., 140
Henderson, Hazel, 177
Henry, Robert J., 87-88
Hogness, David S., 142
Hollander, Rachelle, 183
Holton, Linwood, 92
Hubbard, Ruth, 147
humanistic movement, 169
Humphrey, Hubert, 33
Huxley, Aldous, 170
hydrogen bomb
    GAC and, 18-19
    genetic effects of, 26-31
    promoters of, 16-23
    secrecy of, 20-22

I

Industrial Biotest Laboratory, 128
Institute of Society, Ethics and the
    Life Sciences. *See* Hastings Center.
Insurance Information Institute, 201
Interim Committee, 8-10
Internal Revenue Service (IRS), 194
International Atomic Development
    Authority, 13-14, 22
International Atomic Energy Agency
    (IAEA), 22
International Conference on Recombinant
    DNA Molecules. *See* Asilomar
    conference.
"An Introduction to Outer Space" (report
    of the Purcell committee), 34, 39

J

Jackson, Henry "Scoop," 33, 67, 77
Johnson, Louis, 20
Johnson, Lyndon B.
    on Great Society, 47-48
    and SST program, 51, 54, 61, 66-67
    and space program, 33, 35, 37-39, 42
Juenger, Frederich, 169
Jungle, The, 3
Justice, United States Department of
    and Concorde, 198
    and food and drug industry, 127
    and North Anna power plant, 109-10

K

Kantrowitz, Arthur, 43-45, 202
Kartalia, David, 93, 101
Kefauver, Estes, 33
Kennedy, Donald, 119, 122-24, 130-31
Kennedy, Edward M.
    and citizen participation programs, 173,
        181-82
    and genetic research, 161-63, 173
    and saccharin legislation, 123, 125
Kennedy, John F.
    and Apollo program, 42-45
    R&D spending under, 46
    and SST program, 50-54, 56, 61, 67
    and scientists, 21, 41

Kennedy, Robert F., 67
Killian, James, 31, 34
King, Jonathan, 156, 158
Knox, Richard, 158

L

Lapp, Ralph, 25
Latimer, William, 18
Latter, Albert, 27, 29-30
Lawrence, E. O., 6, 8, 18
Lawson, Tom, 3
Lederberg, Joshua, 149
Lee, Ezra, 2
Life Magazine, 28
Lilienthal, David, 13, 17, 20
Lilienthal Committee, 13-14
lithium deuteride, 23
Livermore, Shaw, 153
Lockheed, 59, 61-62
Lucky Dragon, 24
Lundberg, Bo, 57, 73
Lunik II, 39
Lysenko, Trofim D., 169

M

MacGregor, Clark, 65
Magnuson, Warren G., 67, 79
Magruder, William M., 74, 78-79
Maguire, Andrew, 124
Manhattan Disrict Project, 5-11
Mansfield, Mike, 33
Marine Hospital Service, 4
Markey, Howard T., 197
Marshall, George C., 6
Martin, James G., 122-23, 125, 133
Mathews, David, 159
Mayer, Jean, 126
Maxwell, Jewell C., 64, 66, 70
McCarthy, Joseph, 20
McCormack, John, 36-37
McElroy, Neil H., 36
McGovern, George, 115-16
McGurn, John, 104, 108
McKee, William F., 63-64
McKinnon, Richard, 148
McMahon, Brian, 18
McMillian, James B., 199
McNamara, Robert S., 42, 61, 63

Mead, Margaret, 29
Mendel, Gregor, 136
Meselson, Matthew, 156
Metcalf, Lee, 105
Metzenbaum, Howard, 161
Miller, William, 122
Mondale, Walter F., 181
monosodium glutamate, 117
Monroney, A. S. "Mike," 67, 71, 80
Morrill Act, 3
Morris, Peter, 85-86, 89-90
Mosher, Charles, 175
muckrakers, 3
Muller, Hermann J., 25-27
Muskie, Edmund, 79

N

Nader, Claire, 202-3
Nader, Ralph, 168, 194-95
Nassikas, John N., 91
National Academy of Sciences
  and food additives, 116-21, 125,
    129, 132
  and genetic research, 141-42, 161,
    163, 173
  origins of, 4
  and SST program, 61, 70, 72-73
  on science advisory process, 2
  and space program, 35, 41, 43
National Advisory Committee on
    Astronautics (NACA), 34
National Aeronautic Association, 80
National Aeronautics and Space Act, 39
National Aeronautics and Space
    Administration (NASA)
  and Apollo program, 43-45
  origins of, 38-39
  R&D spending by, 40
  and SST program, 50, 55-59, 61, 70, 71
National Aeronautics and Space
    Council, 38
National Cancer Institute (NCI)
  and dietary cancers, 115
  chemical testing by, 123
  and genetic research, 142, 152
  origin of, 4, 179
national energy plan, 186-87
National Environmental Policy Act
  and nuclear power, 199

and SST program, 77
National Institutes of Health
  and citizen participation, 193
  and genetic research, 139, 144-49,
    153-55, 157-60, 162-64, 192-93
  origin of, 4, 179
  R&D spending by, 192
National Science Board, 180, 182
National Science Foundation
  citizen participation programs, 180-83
  origin of, 179
  R&D spending by, 180
  and "science court," 203
National Space Establishment (NSE), 35
Natural Resources Defense Council
  and class actions, 194
  and genetic research, 159
  and nuclear waste disposal, 200
Neidhardt, Frederick, 152
Nelson, Gaylord, 118
Neuschel's lineament, 100, 106
Newsweek, 79
New York Times, 181
Nixon, Richard M.
  and class actions, 194
  and consumer protection, 194
  and energy supply, 91, 168
  and food protection, 116, 126
  and SST program, 67-70, 73-75, 80
  and space program, 34
  and war on cancer, 192
Non-nuclear Energy Research and
    Development Act, 185
North American, 59
North Anna Environmental Coalition
    (NAEC), 97, 101-11
North Anna power plant, 84-112
nuclear power industry
  future of, 84, 110-12, 184-90
  insurance for, 96, 111, 199-200
  origins of, 21-22, 84
Nuclear Regulatory Commission (NRC)
  attitude of, 108, 110-11, 187-88
  and federal courts, 104, 200
  and North Anna power plant, 90,
    103-112
  origin of, 84, 179, 185
  public attitude toward, 111, 171,
    187-90, 206
nuclear weapons, 12-20, 23, 25, 27, 29-31

See also atomic bomb, hydrogen bomb.
Nutrition and Human Needs, Senate
Select Committee on, 115

O

Office of Compliance (AEC), 88-89
Office of Science and Technology
(White House), 67
Office of Technology Assessment (U.S.
Congress), 82, 123, 168, 173-78
oil embargo, 168, 184
Oklahoma City Sonic Boom Study, 71-73
O'Leary, John, 100
Olney, John W., 127
Operation Bongo. *See* Oklahoma City
Sonic Boom Study.
Operation Castle, 23
Operation Heat Rise, 71
Oppenheimer, J. Robert, 8, 12-15, 17-21
Orlebeke, Charles J., 92
Ottinger, Richard L.
and genetic research, 161
and saccharin legislation, 124-25.
Our Nuclear Future, 27

P

Pacific Legal Foundation, 195
Pan American World Airways, 51, 56
Pasteur, Louis, 136
Pastuszak, Robert, 97-98
Pauling, Linus, 15, 27-29
Peckham, Robert, 195
Peterson, Russell W., 174-75
Pharmaceutical Manufacturers Associa-
tion, 161-62
phenformin, 191
Philadelphia Inquirer, 121
Pillsbury, Dennis, 201
Plant Patent Act, 201
plasmid, 137-38, 141, 143, 147
plutonium
and breeder reactors, 171, 176, 185-86,
189-90, 204
and nuclear weapons, 7, 17
Pollack, Milton, 198
Port Authority of New York and
New Jersey, 198-99
Power, Sarah, 152

Pratt & Whitney, 60-63
Preliminary Safety Analysis Report
(PSAR), 86, 89
President's Science Advisory Committee
(PSAC), 33, 42
Press, Frank, 164
Price, Harold L., 86, 91, 93
Price-Anderson Act, 199-200
Proxmire, William, 65, 74, 78-81
Ptashne, Mark, 156
Public Advocates, Inc., 195
Public Board of Inquiry (FDA), 190-92,
202
Public Health Service, 4, 92, 94
Pucinski, Roman C., 71
Purcell, Edward, 34, 39
Pure Food and Drug Act, 3

Q

Quarles, Donald, 37
Quesada, Elwood R., 53, 55, 57-58

R

Rabi, I. I., 17, 19
Rabinowich, Eugene, 14
Rand Corporation, 52
Ragone, Stanley, 90-92, 98-99
Rayburn, Sam, 33
Recombinant DNA Advisory Committee
(NIH), 144-47
Recombinant DNA Molecules, Committee
on (NAS, Berg committee), 142
recombinant DNA research
benefits of, 138-40, 149
definition of, 138
ethics of, 148-51, 156, 178, 204-5
federal regulation of, 144-47, 159-64
at Harvard and MIT, 154-59
patents and insurance, 201
risks of, 140-44
at Stanford University, 140-44
at University of Michigan, 151-54
Recombinant DNA Research Guidelines
(NIH), 144-47, 154, 158, 164
Recombinant DNA Research, Interagency
Committee on, 159-60
Reagan, Ronald, 195
regulation, federal
food, 3, 126-30, 132-33

genetic research, 144-47, 159, 164
health, 167, 190-91
nuclear power, 187-90
Remsen, Ira, 120
research and development funds
and change in national goals, 47
DOD, 40
DOE, 185-86
for Manhattan Project, 6
NIH, 192
NSF, 180-81
for SST program, 63-69, 74, 76-77, 79-80
for space program, 43-46
before World War II, 2-4
RESOLVE, 203-4
ribonucleic acid, 137, 148
Reuss, Henry, 69
Robbins, Frederick C., 177
Robinson, Clifford, 98-101
Rodgers, William H., Jr., 103
Rogers, Mollie, 85
Rogers, Paul
and genetic research, 161-63
and saccharin legislation, 123, 125
Roosevelt, Franklin D., 5-7, 10-11
Roosevelt, Theodore, 3, 119
Roper, Paul J., 100, 103, 105
Rosenblad, Lyndon, 97
Ruckelshaus, William, 194
Rutherford, Ernest, 5

S

SST Ad Hoc Interagency Review
Committee ("interagency com-
mittee"), 69-70
saccharin, 4, 117, 119-25, 129, 131, 133
saprolite, 105-6
Satterfield, David E., 86, 88
Schlesinger, James R., 199
Schmidt, Alexander M., 190
Schriever, Bernard A., 36, 44
Science magazine, 42, 46, 127
Science and Astronautics, House Com-
mittee on, 51-52, 82
Science and Technology, House Com-
mitte on, 183
"science court," 202-3
Scientific American, 25, 141

Scientists' Institute for Public
Information, 29
Seaborg, Glenn, 17, 91
Searle, G. D. and Company, 122, 127-28,
191
Serber, Robert, 18
Sharp, Philip, 158
Sherwin-Williams Corporation, 122
Shurcliff, William A., 72-73
Sierra Club, 74, 77-78, 204
Sinclair, Upton, 3
Sinsheimer, Robert L., 143, 149, 154
Skolimowski, Henry, 152
Skolnick, Edward, 148
Solarz, Stephen, 161
sonic boom, 57-58, 69-73, 77, 81
Sorenson, Theodore, 50
Space and Aeronautics, Senate
Committee on, 67
Space and Aeronautics, Senate Special
Committee on, 35, 37-38
Spedding, Frank, 6
Spencer, W. C., 98
Speth, Gus, 200
Sputnik I & II, 31-33
Staggers, Harley M., 163
Stalin, Joseph, 169
Stanford Research Institute, 52, 66
Steffens, Lincoln, 3
Stetler, C. Joseph, 162
Stevenson, Adlai E., III, 163
Stever, H. Guyford, 34
Stimson, Henry L., 6-12
Stone & Webster Engineering Corporation,
85, 87-88, 96, 98-99, 105, 107, 109
Stone, Whitney, 105
Strauss, Lewis, 18, 24
streptomyces vellosus, 201
strontium-90, 28-29
Sullivan, James, 157
Sun Ship (Sun Oil Corporation), 106
supersonic transport. *See* Concorde and
Supersonic Transport Program.
Supersonic Transport Evaluation Group, 60
Supersonic Transport, Presidential
Advisory Committee on the
(McNamara committee), 61
Supersonic Transport Program
appropriations for, 63-69, 74, 76-77, 79-80
design phases of, 55-57, 59-63

economic studies for, 51-55, 64, 68-70
origin of, 50-51
Supersonic Transport Review Committee
(Garwin committee), 68, 70, 74-75
Swift, Jonathan, 169
Swiger, William F., 88, 98-99
Symington, Stuart, 33, 67

T

Tarbell, Ida, 3
Taylor, Dwight, 88
technology
benefit/risk assessment, 130, 174, 205
drawbacks of, 22, 168, 206
public attitudes toward, 166-70, 177-78
value of, 54, 169, 177
Teitz, Joyce, 78
Teller, Edward, 17-18, 20-21, 27, 29, 35
Train, Russell, 76
Trans World Airlines, 56
Transportation, United States
Department of
and Concorde, 197
and SST program, 63, 68, 77
and urban mass transit, 175
Tressel, George, 180-81
Truman, Harry S., 8-10, 12-13, 17, 20
Tsiolkovski, K. E., 32
Turner, James, 126-27, 129

U

United States Court of Customs and Patent
Appeals. *See* courts, federal.
United States Supreme Court. *See*
courts, federal.
Ulam, Stanislaw, 21
Union of Concerned Scientists, 110
United Nations, 27, 35, 39
"United States Development of a
Commercial Supersonic Transport
Aircraft" (FAA), 58
uranium-235, 7
uranium-238, 24
Urey, Harold, 6, 18
Upjohn Company, 201

V

Vanguard program, 33
Vaughan, Phyllis and J. B., 96-97, 108
Velluci, Alfred E., 155-56, 159
Vermont Yankee power plant, 200
Vietnam, war in, 2, 47, 64, 82, 168
Virginia Division of Mineral Resources
(VDMR), 88, 94
Virginia Electric and Power Company
(Vepco), 84-110, 112
virus, 137-38, 141-46
Volpe, John A., 67
Von Braun, Werner, 31, 33

W

Wald, George, 151, 155-56
Wallace, Henry A., 6, 10
Warren, William, 97
Washington Post, 102, 127, 161
Weaver, Warren, 45
Webb, James E., 42
Weiner, Charles, 182
Wessel, R. P., 98
Westinghouse Electric Corporation,
85, 109
White, William Allen, 3
Wiesner, Jerome B., 42, 45-47, 53-54,
57, 177
Wiley, Harvey, 3, 119
Willard, Hal, 102
Wilson, James, 3
Wilson, Woodrow, 4, 41
Winn, Larry, 121
Wisconsin Alumni Research Foundation,
120-21
Wise, Donald U., 99
Wright, Susan, 152

Y

Yankelovich, Daniel, 126
Yates, Sidney R., 69, 76-77

Z

Zahn, H. Keith, 196

3 1543 50079 4898

509.73
A513o

782952

DATE DUE

DE 21			

Cressman Library
Cedar Crest College
Allentown, Pa. 18104

DEMCO